THE WAY BACK HOME

DR. SOK NAM KO

A LIFE IN AMERICA

The Sok Nam Ko Educational Exchange Foundation

Amsterdam, New York

2006

Published by the
Sok Nam Ko Educational Exchange Foundation,
P.O. Box 183, Amsterdam, New York 12010.

ISBN-13 : 978-0-9675242-0-7

ISBN-10 : 0-9675242-0-2

Printed in the U.S.A.

Credits: Office Humor Illustrations by Herbert A.W. Kopper.
Design and layout by Dorline Rokjer.
Cover design by Andiron Studio.
Cover illustration by David Butcher

Proceeds from the sale of this book support the
Sok Nam Ko Educational Exchange Foundation.

For Helen Eldred Smith, who knew
before anyone the reason for this book.

Helen E. Smith

CONTENTS

LIST OF ILLUSTRATIONS

CHAPTER ONE

CHAPTER TWO

CHAPTER THREE

CHAPTER FOUR

CHAPTER FIVE

CHAPTER SIX

CHAPTER SEVEN

CHAPTER EIGHT

CHAPTER NINE

APPENDIX A—CURRICULUM VITAE

APPENDIX B—IN MEMORIAM

APPENDIX C—THE FOUNDATION

PREFACE

This book began as an autobiography in January of 1990, when Sok Nam Ko was first interviewed by Helen Smith about his childhood in Korea. Helen, our mother's youngest aunt, had known our father since the 1950's – before our parents married and years before any of us, Sok and Elaine's children, arrived on the scene. A retired college professor with a strong interest in her own family's past, Aunt Helen saw that our father's memories were the only direct connection that we had to his family's history in Korea. Not long after his 55th birthday, she arrived in Amsterdam, N.Y. with a tape recorder and began to ask Dad questions about his early life in Kaesong. Those interviews were transcribed and later became portions of this book.

Aunt Helen and our father planned to continue their interviews, but the project came to an unexpected end with his death on March 16, 1991. In spite of the despair that we all felt, Aunt Helen and Elaine saw clearly that we needed to finish telling his story. No longer able to ask him the questions that we had waited too long to ask, we turned to our friends and relatives for their thoughts and memories.

In response, the stories came flooding back – filled with sorrow, humor and love. A father's autobiography for his children became an anthology of memories from the communities that surrounded him. Those of us who thought we knew him best learned things about Dad that we had never perceived. While the stories highlight how culture and personality sometimes set him apart, more striking and universal is how the differences inevitably paled in significance compared to what drew all of us to him. This book is not great literature. But it does tell how one life touches many, and in that sense it is meaningful.

We are grateful to everyone who provided Helen and Elaine with stories and photographs for this book. We would also like to thank the Harringtons, who made Dad's life in

America possible. And, finally, we would like to thank Aunt Helen and Mom for finding another way to tell our father's story. We love you both.

Andy, Tim, Steve and Suzie Ko
February 6, 2005

CHAPTER I

EARLY LIFE IN KOREA

Heung Bong Baek.

I was born in Kaesong, Korea. It is impossible to say whether it was a happy occasion or an unexpected accident that I came into this world on November 5, 1934.

What I know of my ancestry begins with my grandparents. My paternal grandfather was Hahn Bong Ko and my paternal grandmother was Heung Bong Baek, who was born in 1889. Her last name, Baek, actually means "white" in Korean. My grandfather was one of a set of twin sons; he was the younger of the two.

My grandmother lived until 1975, I believe. Actually she was like a mother to me. Since I was the oldest of seven children, my grandmother took care of me. She was very strong-willed and a business-minded woman; the head of the family really. My grandmother lost her husband when her two children were small. Therefore, she had the responsibility of caring for the two; my father and my aunt. Since my aunt died when she was rather young, my father was actually brought

Jin Myeong Ko.

up as an only son. His name was Jin Myeong Ko. My father probably didn't know his sister very well.

When my father was young, his mother had to work hard sewing for people and in doing a lot of menial jobs. As a result, my grandmother had many experiences which strengthened her. She was the treasurer of the family and our ceremonial matriarch as she served as head of the house. She was so powerful I used to feel sorry for my mother because she was over-shadowed by my grandmother, who took a lot of interest in our family of growing children. In oriental countries, it is traditional for the oldest in a family to automatically take charge and the younger ones have a tendency to follow what the oldest one does.

My father was more or less an isolated figure. His uncle was a so-called landlord and by Korean standards the family was considered well-to-do. My father was a business man and worked for his uncle. My father traveled all over the country, managing farm producers—rice crops and whatever. I knew my father very little, because most of the time he was traveling all over the country and was very seldom home.

My father was alive until 1950. During the war I was told that he had become a political prisoner of North Korea when the North invaded South Korea. We assume that he was either killed or died somewhere in captivity. We have not known his whereabouts since 1950.

The history of my maternal grandparents is somewhat complicated. My grandfather's name was Kim. He lost his first wife early in their marriage.

Sahm Ohk Kim
60th Birthday Celebration
Kaesong 1975.

His first wife was my grandmother. He was a farmer. I remember my maternal grandfather very well. Our family often went to see him. Since my maternal grandmother died when my mother was young, I never knew her.

My mother's name was Sahm Ohk Kim which is a common surname in Korea. She was the third of five siblings. There were four girls and one boy in the family. My mother was the third girl and her name, Sahm, means third. Ohk means a valuable stone—like jade.

My only uncle died as a young man soon after World War II. His only son is living in the United States now. He lives in Maryland and has three children: one son and two daughters.

My mother's family lived in the country approximately 20 miles from Kaesong. Kaesong was originally in South Korea, but after the War, in 1953, that part of South Korea became North Korea. As a result, all my brothers and sisters and their families live in North Korea and became North Koreans.

None of my mother's family ever lived with our family. That usually never happens in Korea, as long as the father's side exists. Tradition dictates that a family follows through on the father's side and not the mother's side.

Korean marriages at that time were pre-arranged. My father's family was a landlord and business family while my mother's side was a farming family. Their marriage was arranged by the match-makers, I assume. My mother was two years younger than my father. They set up housekeeping in Kaesong.

My mother died on March 29, 1985. In her later years I was told that she was drafted into the working class and became a laborer in a cloth factory. I don't know whether she was there by choice or because she had had experience in her family along the lines of weaving cloth. She had expertise somewhat and I was told that she received a model worker's award because she was a good worker.

The first time I had an opportunity to visit North Korea was in September 1985, just six months after my mother's death. We had the sad situation of not seeing her, but of visiting her tomb instead. She was 70 years old when she died. I feel that my mother's life was somewhat desperate and sad, in a way, because the Korean way of living is so different from the American way of living.

Particularly after my father's death, supporting our family was in the hands of my strong-willed grand-mother. She served as the boss of the family, expecting my mother to serve somewhat like a maid and to do the housekeeping chores connected with caring for our family of seven boys and girls. Her hands were full and, to my observation, her life was not really pleasant.

I was the oldest one in our family of four boys and three girls. In Korea children are systematically named. Sometimes all the boys' first names are the same or sometimes the middle names will be the same. In our family all first names of the boys are the same so everybody is a Sok. Similarly, all the middle names of the girls are the same. Their middle names are Ju.

The second child was my sister, Young Ju Ko, just two years younger than I. She was the closest one to me as far as my life was concerned. I was absent from Korean life for 34 years (since 1952). When I left home, my other brothers and sisters were quite young. When I visited Korea in 1985, I learned that my sister, Young Ju, was killed in 1952 during the Korean War of bombing by United States forces.

The third child in our family was my brother, Sok Dong Ko. He was born in 1938. He is very political and a very good volleyball player. He is an Athletic Director in North Korea.

My brother, Sok Koon Ko, born in 1941, is the fourth child in our family. He is an internist: a medical doctor. He is in charge of a 500-bed hospital in North Korea. He is a Technical Director of the hospital. There are two directors in the hospital: 1) the Technical Director, who is in charge of the medical administration of the hospital and 2) the Political Director who takes charge of the political administration aspects of the hospital. We found out that the administration of the hospital is Communist Party-assigned, and the Political Director has more power in its control. So, even though my brother should be No. 1, he has become the No. 2 man at the hospital.

The fifth child in our family is my brother, Sok Won Ko, who was born in 1944. He is a planning manager of a paper company.

The sixth child was my sister, Hee Ju Ko, who was born in 1946. She died shortly after birth with pneumonia.

The seventh and youngest member of our family was Eun Ju Ko, who was born in 1948. She was only a baby when I left home so I did not know her very well. Today she is a wife and mother; also, a banker in charge of the savings program in the city of Kaesong.

So, if we were to add them all, there were seven children born to my father and mother and there are only five left. All were married and live in North Korea (all except me). All have four children except

L to R: Sok Won Ko, Sok Dong Ko, Sahm Ohk Kim Ko, Eun Ju Ko, Sok Koon Ko.

my youngest brother who has three girls. Four seems to be a special number in our family, except for my youngest brother who has three girls. That's a family joke.

Aunts, Uncles and Cousins

The older twin brother of my paternal grandfather had four daughters. These four girls would be my father's cousins. Since my father was raised as an only child, I have no aunts or uncles on his side.

The Ko family records were documented for centuries and were supposed to come to me, because I am the oldest son of my generation. Efforts have been made by my brother to locate these family records. But, as of this date, the records have not been found.

On my mother's side, there is an uncle. I also have uncles by marriage, because my mother had three sisters and they all married and had children. So I have several first cousins on my mother's side.

Hometown and Early Life

The city where I was born, Kaesong, now has a population of about 100,000. It is a relatively large city, but not very well developed. It is more or less a commercial or business city. It is very congested, because the large population is living in a relatively small area. I can remember when I was a young kid; we had no cars or public transportation. Our best transportation was our legs or bicycles. When I was 14 or 15 years old, I had my own bicycle. That was our family transportation.

My father was traveling most of the time on family business. When I was 12 or 13 years old, I was expected to help take care of the family. I was buying and selling cloth for our family factory. Weaving cloth was done in our house by hired people. My grandmother was like a business agent and I was like a house treasurer. I handled the money of the family when I was very young — age 12 or 13. Occasionally I would find out the price of thread, would take a handful of money and go down to the market to buy the thread. At that time the Korean economy was very inflated. It took a bag full of money to buy the weaving thread needed by my grandmother, who would process it and then have the hired hands weave the cloth. We would take the cloth to a wholesale dealer or to the country farming area where the cloth was sold to the people. This is how our family made a living.

The home where I was born was located right in the middle of Kaesong. As our family grew, our family moved out of the center of the city to the outskirts into a slightly larger home. By the time I was in high school, our family was way out of town in a larger home with more rooms. Relatively speaking, we had more comforts than the average family.

Sok Nam Ko, age 15.

Schooling

My education began at about age four with learning Chinese characters needed in studying Confucianism. My ancestors were Confucian scholars and my father taught me the way he learned from his father.

My formal education began in a Japanese school, when I was six years old. I attended the Mahn Weol Public School in Kaesong for a period of six years (1940-1946) in grade school. I then changed to the Kaesong Commercial Middle-High School for four years (1946-1950).

The school was attended by those with academic ability as well as those with socio-economic status. I had the opportunity to attend the best schools in our hometown. We had to take examinations to get into the schools. Based upon test scores, you have an opportunity to pick out the school you wish to attend— even if you have to walk 10 or 15 miles to get there! I would get up very early in the morning, eat breakfast, pack a lunch of rice and vegetables into a little

Mahn Weol Public School, Kaesong.

aluminum can, then travel to school 6 or 7 miles or more away. When I changed to the middle school I didn't have to travel so far; maybe 4 or 5 miles.

Korean schools traditionally segregated boys from girls. Students wore the same type of uniform. Subjects were very similar to what American boys and girls take: science, English, economics, music, art, math, history, but also Korean and Chinese. Scores on examinations determined what school you would attend. Once enrolled in a school you had no choices, but had to take all the subjects offered by the school. There was no such thing as electives.

Children attended classes from 8 a.m. to 4 p.m. during the week and a half day on Saturday. Each school that I went to had 50 to 60 students in each class. A number was assigned to each student. Attendance was taken by calling numbers.

When I was in grade school the educational system was controlled by the Japanese imperial

Classmates at Kaesong Commercial Middle-High School, Kaesong, Korea.

government. Then in 1945, when I went to the junior high, after the Japanese left Korea, we followed the Korean style of education. The language in which classes were taught changed, but the educational system was similar. Schools were rigid and very like the military. Corporal punishment was nothing unusual. If you did something wrong you'd be severely punished. The schools were more harsh than the average American schools.

One of my favorite teachers was a Japanese named Osaka. He was a very friendly fellow and was very good to me. He was a music specialist and very talented in music. He was my homeroom teacher.

In junior high, I remember a very loud and aggressive teacher. He had eyes that bulged. I didn't know it at that time, but he had some kind of thyroid problem. Now we are able to diagnose such things. He wore glasses. I was told somewhat later that he became a Communist sympathizer, so I never saw him in later years.

Soccer Team — Sok Nam Ko, Front Center.

As a young lad in Korea, I especially enjoyed riding my bicycle. When I was in junior high school, I also liked to swim, and I played second base on our school baseball team. In soccer, I played wing. I was on the first team in my first year of high school. I did a lot of Japanese judo and Korean "taekwondo" which is the skill of kicking and a sort of character building through fighting and martial arts.

The War broke out in June 1950, when I was in my second year at the Kaesong Commercial school. I was15 years old. At the time when I left Korea, I was about half way through high school.

Getting Ready to Make a Change in my Life

The Korean War started on June 25, 1950 and continued for three years until 1953. In 1945 an arbitrary line had been drawn at the 38th parallel by Dean Atcheson, a U.S. diplomat, and a Soviet representative. After that date, both halves of Korea became armed: the North by the Soviet Union and the South by

Sok Nam Ko, Oct 25, 1951, *working for the U.S. Army.*

the United States. After the Korean War ended, instead of the 38th parallel, the D.M.Z. (Demilitarized Zone) became the border between North Korea and South Korea. The cease-fire was signed in 1953 and the northwestern part of South Korea became part of North Korea. The south gave up a lot of land on the west side of Korea. The line was shifted and follows the natural boundaries now. The 38th parallel was not a natural boundary. South Korea gained mountainous territory in the east and lost fertile lands of the west. My hometown became part of North Korea.

In 1950, when the North Koreans and Chinese penetrated down into the South the second time, I was forced to leave my hometown. My age was approximately 15 and too young for a soldier in war. But they were drafting boys for the war. Mostly, the young lads were drafted into labor forces to carry war materials or digging ditches for their trenches. I decided to go to the South with the American soldiers. We were thinking we would go back right away, but it didn't happen that way. I last saw my family in December 1950, when the Chinese entered the Korean War and pushed through the area.

In 1952, I was still with the United States Army. The name of the unit was the 8th Army, 17th Field Artillery. They operated 80-inch howitzers and were divided into five batteries. I happened to work in a so-called service battery. I started out in B Battery and later transferred to the service battery, where I worked as a houseboy and a part-time interpreter.

This is where I met George Harrington, who was a Captain. He came to Korea from the United States. Eventually he was promoted to Major. He became interested in me and after tutoring me in English and algebra, he decided to sponsor me for study in the United States.

When I volunteered my services for the U.S. Army in Korea as a civilian worker, I had plans. First, to learn English and, secondly, to obtain a chance to come to the U.S. to continue my education. Two years later, in 1952, my dream came true when Captain Harrington, a lawyer and teacher, asked me if I would like to come to the United States and continue my studying. I accepted his offer and, therefore, I left Korea. I came to the U.S under the sponsorship of Attorney and Mrs. George Harrington of Castleton, Vermont in 1952, arriving by boat in Seattle.

—Written April 6, 1990
Sok Nam Ko

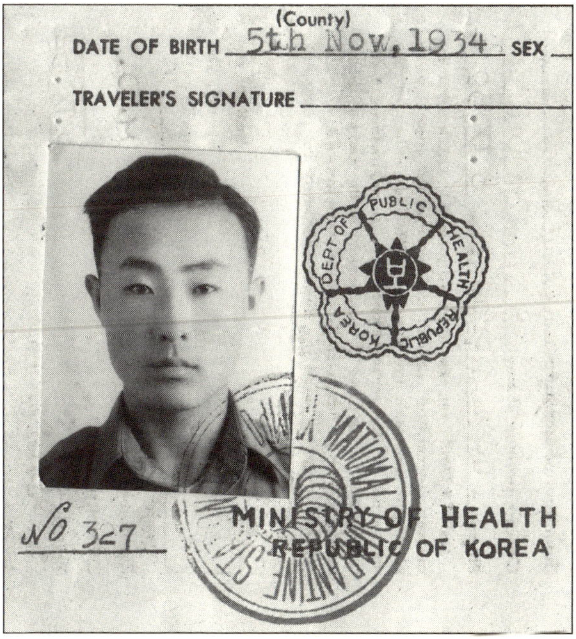
(County)
DATE OF BIRTH 5th Nov, 1934 SEX
TRAVELER'S SIGNATURE
DEPT. OF PUBLIC HEALTH REPUBLIC KOREA
No 327
MINISTRY OF HEALTH
REPUBLIC OF KOREA

Certificate of Health, Republic of Korea.

CHAPTER II

LIFE IN CASTLETON

BEGINNING LIFE IN CASTLETON, VERMONT

I came to this country in 1952, arriving by boat in Seattle. It was cold and wet the day that I arrived in the United States from Korea. I spent the first night here in jail (or some kind of immigration detention center) because my papers were not right and I could not speak English well enough to explain anything.

Fair Haven High School, Fair Haven, Vermont.

During a cross-country bus trip from Seattle I had my first introduction to life in the United States.

On October 20, 1952 , the Harringtons picked me up in Albany, New York, and took me to their home in Castleton, Vermont; a village of about 600 people.

I soon enrolled in Fair Haven High School in Fair Haven, Vermont; a town about five miles from Castleton. It was very difficult for me the first year, but I was able to keep up with my classmates better the next year, which was my senior year. I graduated from high school in 1954.

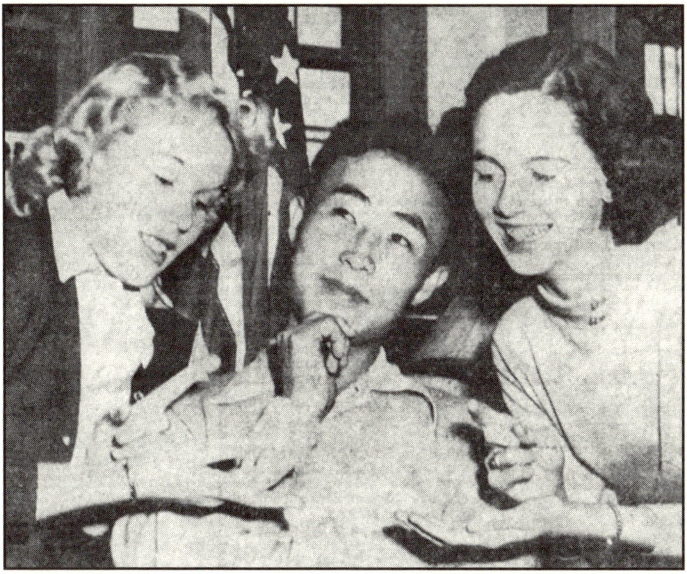

Oct. 29, 1952 *Herald Photo—Merusi.*

LESSON IN ENGLISH—Ko Sok Nam, Korean student enrolled at Fair Haven High School, receives an intensive drill in English from Flora Doane (left) and Judy McGuinness. Flora is the daughter of Mr. & Mrs. Bert Doane. Judy is the daughter of Mr. and Mrs. Edward Owen McGuinness.

During my high school and college days, I was very much interested in sports, such as long distance running, basketball, baseball and soccer. I spent an average of eight to ten hours in sports each week.

—Sok Nam Ko

High School Yearbook

In the June 1954 issue of the Fair Haven High School Yearbook, called "The Slate," the following text accompanied Sok Nam Ko's picture:

> Favorite Quote:
>
> > "Why all this bustle, fret and hurry, Fate will out for all our worry."
>
> Activities: Boys' State 3, Basketball 3, 4; Talent Show 3, 4; Tumbling 3,4; Baseball 4.
>
> Student Popularity poll called "Senior Superlatives":
>
> > Best personality ......First place.....Ko, Sok Nam
> > Most dignified boy.....First place.....Ko, Sok Nam
> > Most courteous boy.....First place.....Ko, Sok Nam
> > Most sincere boy.......First place.....Ko, Sok Nam
> > Most reserved boy......Second place....Ko, Sok Nam
>
> The "Senior Will" item:
>
> > Ko, Sok Nam wishes to leave his fine working habits, his courage and his many abilities to all the Junior Class.
>
> In the section called Senior Review:
>
> > Ko, Sok Nam......Pastime—photography
> > Ambition—To be an M.D.
>
> The Class Gift to Sok Nam Ko was a flag with this note:
>
> > "This flag we give to our pal, Ko,
> > To take with him where 'ere he may go,
> > Though he be here or far away,
> > We'll think of him in every way."

—*The Slate,* Fair Haven High School 1954

Green Mountain

Boys State

Athletic Award

THIS IS TO CERTIFY THAT:

Sok Nan Ko of Castleton

was a member of the Niles basketball team winning the State

Basketball Championship at the 1953 Green Mountain Boys State.

The 1953 Green Mountain Boys State, Inc.

Northfield, Vermont June 21 to June 27, 1953

Athletic Director Boys State Director

Sponsored by

AMERICAN LEGION, DEPARTMENT OF VERMONT

Boys State Athletic Award.

WELL-LIKED BY ALL HIS HIGH SCHOOL CLASSMATES

"I was Mary Bigelow and graduated with Ko from Fair Haven in the class of 1954. I married George Stone who was Ko's roommate during Boys State in 1953. He speaks very fondly of Ko as everyone who knew him did. George, however, graduated from Burr and Burton in 1954.

Ko was a very considerate classmate and well liked by all his fellow students. He was voted for several spots in our Senior Yearbook and he deserved all of them."

—George and Mary Bigelow Stone

High School Graduation, 1954.

Cultural Diversity Unknown in a Small Vermont Town

I do remember Ko's arrival at Fair Haven High School and, in recalling that time, I realize how very provincial we were in our little town. Most of us, I'm sure, had never known anyone whose roots were Oriental; cultural diversity was virtually unknown in a small Vermont town in the 50s! Before long, however, we knew he was a very special person and quickly came to love and respect him.

—Evelyn and Gil Billings

A Welcome to Ko Sok Nam

Ko Sok Nam is a student at Fair Haven High. Born in Kaesong, Korea, this young man was able to come to the States for furtherance of his education through a loyalty and protracted effort of Atty. George W. Harrington who, in quest of this objective, consummated exhaustive negotiations with officials of the U.S. State Department, governmental counselors stationed on the Korean Peninsula and officials of our Vermont Administration. The task was complex and wrapped with much red tape. Conferences, reports, affidavits — it required months to gain admission into the United States for this boy but through diligence and perseverance Mr. Harrington succeeded, Ko is here, charmingly happy and radiant with gratitude to his friend and benefactor.

Ingratiatingly personable, this Korean lad, whose father and mother are captives of the Communists, is creating a mild sensation among students at FHHS. First, because of his impeccable manners and, second, because education, in the opinion of Ko, is the most valuable asset a young man can acquire — a possession which cannot be snatched by an invading enemy. Before hostilities opened in Korea, Ko was the devoted son of a well-known and highly respected family. In the Town of Kaesong his father served as a prominent official of the municipal government and was engaged in retail trade — a successful and respected merchant.

Ko speaks Korean, Japanese and English but his knowledge of the English language is quite limited and he is experiencing considerable difficulty in slang words from proper diction. This problem can prove embarrassing and has, to Ko, on a number of occasions; but he is a smart boy, quick at rebuttal and not unsensitive to humor. His age: Says Ko, "By GI mathematics I am 18; by Korean tabulation I am 20." The distinction: The age of a Korean baby dates from pregnancy and, for the convenience of eliminating fractional periods, a child at birth is one year old. At the beginning of the next calendar year he becomes two years old. By this method of figuring, a baby born during December of 1952 will be two years old on January 1 of 1953.

At FHHS Ko is registered as a special student although, according to Korean educational standards, he has the equivalent of three years in secondary education. On completion of his courses at the local High School Mr. Harrington's protege will enter Castleton State, UVM or Middlebury College.

To FHHS this student from Korea brings not only a passion for education and a delightful code of Oriental etiquette — he also brings an amazing matured sense of fidelity. He is too diplomatic to offend but never evades honesty by resorting to deception.

The other day Mr. Harrington, in a mood for self-expression, sought release through the channels of music. He performed — a vocal solo. On completing the composition the Attorney said: "Ko, how do you like my singing?"

Ko: No response.

Harrington: "Come, speak up. How do you like my music?"

Ko: No response.

Harrington: "I thought you were my friend."

Ko: "I am. One does not lie to one's friend."

The Rutland Herald — *October 1952.*

Threatened with Deportation and Steps Leading to Citizenship

On January 28, 1955, I went to Canada to play in a game as a member of the Castleton Teachers College basketball team. When I tried to return home from the game in Canada, I was charged with illegal entry into the United States, because I did not possess the necessary immigration documents. I was ordered deported by the office in charge of the immigration service in St. Albans, because I allegedly re-entered this country illegally.

Now, before leaving for Canada I had written to the Immigration and Naturalization Service and had been told that it would be all right to go to Canada if the Consulate General in Montreal would give his permission for me to return to the United States. Therefore, on January 29, the day following the game,

JV Basketball Team, Castleton Teachers College. Kneeling: Llewellyn Adams, Coach Taddonio, Bertram Cooledge. Standing: Sok Nam Ko, Raymond Gonzales, Thomas Pfenning, Gary Quinn, Hugh Perkins, Ronald Nagy, John Kelley.

I went to the Consulate General in Montreal, and, for a $10 fee, was given another visa to re-enter the United States as a student.

Following this, Attorney George Harrington and I had to go to Washington, D.C. where we appeared before the Board of Immigration Appeals to plead against my possible deportation. Attorney Harrington maintained that I went to Canada for a basketball game and had no intention of re-entering the States illegally.

The Board of Immigration Appeals recorded, at my hearing held in November 1955, that I was asked what my intentions were at the time of my last entry. I replied, "I'd like to stay here. I'd like to apply for citizenship. My home country is North Korea and I am not able to go back."

My former hometown, Kaesong, Korea, which was in the northern part of South Korea at the time I resided there, became a part of North Korea when the armistice was signed and was now Communist territory. The Immigration and Naturalization Service (INS) had ruled that because I had no home of my own in the world to return to, excepting the one behind the Iron Curtain, I re-entered the United States with the intention of making this my permanent home. This was not permissible in my case, because I originally entered this country on a non-immigrant visa to study here.

The Board ruled that the findings of the INS were inconsistent. First, it was found that the INS could not deny that I was a displaced person because I could still return to South Korea, and later claim that I was not entitled to a student status because I did not have a home to which I could return.

An opinion of the Attorney General of the United States on March 27, 1956 declared that I must choose one of the two paths. I could not continue to assert that I was a bona fide student, while an attempt was being made to secure a private bill granting me U.S. citizenship. I could abandon my claim to student status and rely on George's efforts to secure passage of the private bill, or I could continue to assert my non-immigrant student status and have the private bill withdrawn.

Herald Photo — Merusi.

"Sok Nam Ko, Korean student at Castleton Teachers College, saved *from* deportation by Congressman Prouty."

The Appeals Board ordered that the record must be reopened and remanded to the INS for reconsideration in accordance with the opinion.

Tuesday, April 17, 1956, was the date which was set for a hearing in St. Albans on the reopening of my case.

Much publicity centered around my request for adjustment of status under the Refugee Relief Act of 1953. Little did I realize that this action could place me in danger of immediate deportation.

When Congressman Winston L. Prouty wrote to General J.M. Swing, Commissioner of the INS seeking his intercession in the case, Swing replied, "One of the requisites for admittance and maintenance of status of a student is that the alien has a residence in a foreign country which he has no intention of abandoning. The filing of an application for adjustment of status to that of a permanent resident by Mr. Ko terminated his nonimmigrant status in the United States."

Winston Prouty then informed the Immigration Service that he intended to file a private bill on my behalf when Congress reconvened in January.

J.S. Hershner, officer in charge of the St. Albans Immigration Office, informed Congressman Prouty that since he intended to introduce legislation in the next session of Congress on my behalf, any deportation order issued would be stayed until disposition of the legislation.

This would mean that if the bill passed I could become a permanent resident.

As planned, Winston L. Prouty introduced bill HR9027 to Congress. The bill was referred to the Subcommittee on Immigration and Naturalization of the

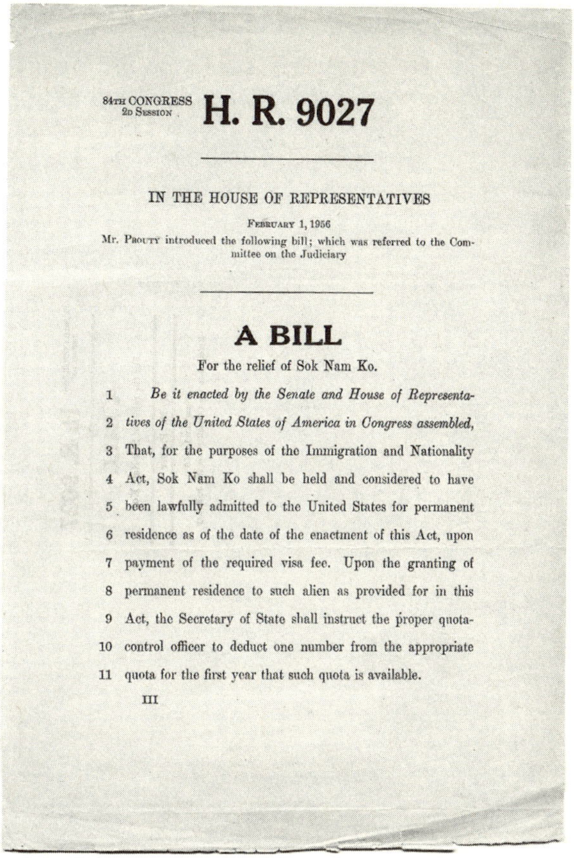
84TH CONGRESS
2D SESSION

H. R. 9027

IN THE HOUSE OF REPRESENTATIVES

FEBRUARY 1, 1956

Mr. PROUTY introduced the following bill; which was referred to the Committee on the Judiciary

A BILL

For the relief of Sok Nam Ko.

Be it enacted by the Senate and House of Representatives of the United States of America in Congress assembled, That, for the purposes of the Immigration and Nationality Act, Sok Nam Ko shall be held and considered to have been lawfully admitted to the United States for permanent residence as of the date of the enactment of this Act, upon payment of the required visa fee. Upon the granting of permanent residence to such alien as provided for in this Act, the Secretary of State shall instruct the proper quota-control officer to deduct one number from the appropriate quota for the first year that such quota is available.

III

Committee on the Judiciary. The sub-committee was headed by Rep. Francis E. Walter of Pennsylvania.

Rep. Prouty's bill read:

In July, the House passed the joint resolution granting me permanent residence in the United States. "My" bill was later incorporated with 19 other alien relief cases under House joint resolution 682, which was favorably reported by the Judiciary Committee and passed by voice vote in the House. On July 11 Attorney George Harrington received a telephone call from Congressman Winston L. Prouty saying that his bill "for the relief of Sok Nam Ko" had been approved by the house Judiciary Committee.

Congressman Prouty said that the measure would probably come up in the House the next week

and he felt confident that it would pass. Even though the bill would not receive Senate action before Congress adjourned, deportation action against me could not be resumed while the legislation was in Congress.

That summer, I was working as a swimming instructor and lifeguard at a camp outside of Albany, New York. When college reopened in the fall, I would be a junior at Castleton Teachers College.

With the approval of the committee the bill would in all probability be voted on by the House of Representatives about March 5, 1956, at the first call of the calendar. It must thereafter be approved by the Senate Judiciary Committee and the full Senate. During the last session of Congress, the bill had passed the House but no action had been taken in the Senate.

—Sok Nam Ko

Note: The bill was passed by the Senate according to the *Congressional Record*—July 17, 1956

THE UNITED STATES OF AMERICA

ORIGINAL
TO BE GIVEN TO
THE PERSON NATURALIZED

No. 8032819

CERTIFICATE OF NATURALIZATION

Petition No. 15098

Personal description of holder as of date of naturalization: Date of birth November 5, 1934 sex male complexion medium color of eyes brown color of hair black height 5 feet 7 inches weight 145 pounds visible distinctive marks scar on left little finger
Marital status married former nationality Korea

I certify that the description above given is true, and that the photograph affixed hereto is a likeness of me.

Sok Nam Ko
(Complete and true signature of holder)

United States of America) ss:
District of Vermont)

Be it known, that at a term of the District Court of the United States held pursuant to law at Rutland, Vermont on November 7, 1962 the Court having found that SOK NAM KO then residing at 24½ Brookes Avenue, Burlington, Vermont, intends to reside permanently in the United States (when so required by the Naturalization Laws of the United States), had in all other respects complied with the applicable provisions of such naturalization laws, and was entitled to be admitted to citizenship, thereupon ordered that such person be and (s)he was admitted as a citizen of the United States of America.

In testimony whereof the seal of the court is hereunto affixed this 7th day of November in the year of our Lord nineteen hundred and sixty-two and of our Independence the one hundred and eighty-seventh.

It is a violation of the U.S. Code (and punishable as such) to copy, print, photograph, or otherwise illegally use this certificate.

Clerk of the U. S. District Court

By Deputy Clerk.

DEPARTMENT OF JUSTICE

Certificate of Naturalization, 1962.

My recollection of exactly when I knew that Ko was coming to Castleton is a bit unsure. My husband, George, was serving in the Korean War as a Captain in the Army. While there he became much interested in a teenager named Ko Sok Nam. (I should mention here that in Korea the family name comes first and when he first came that is how his papers were made out. Here in Castleton we called him Ko. Sometime later he Americanized his name and became Sok Nam Ko.)

George wrote that he would be bringing Ko to America. He asked me to send some textbooks to Korea so that he could tutor him in English and math. Ko had been out of school for a couple of years and George wanted to help him get ready for entering school in Fair Haven, Vermont.

Not long after George arrived home, Ko began the long journey to the States and entered our country through Seattle. Ko at one time made the statement that his first night in the United States was spent in jail. There must have been

The Harrington Home on South Street, Castleton, Vermont.

Captain George Harrington.

something wrong with his student visa and he could not speak English well enough to explain anything. Without doubt, Ko was held in a Detention Center (and not a jail) until the way could be cleared for him to continue across the continent. George was contacted and matters must have been cleared over the phone.

George, in an effort to assure Ko's safe bus trip across the country, arranged for a Travelers' Aid Society to keep track of Ko each time he had to make a transfer. This plan didn't work out very well because Traveler's Aid never found him. Someone had made homosexual advances toward Ko, so he hid at each station and appeared just in time to get on the bus. Finally, someone from Traveler's Aid phoned our house in an attempt to let us know that they had not found him. When the message came in, George and I had already left for Albany to meet Ko there. Dotty, my sister, contacted the New York State Police to stop us from making the trip all the way to Albany, but the police never found us. So we arrived at the bus station as planned.

Lo and behold, Ko was there! He got off the bus wearing his shiny blue suit and carrying his little satchel. This suit meant a lot to him. The servicemen in Korea had taken up a collection to buy him a suit. His satchel, which was a little like an athletic bag, a camera, his suit and whatever other clothes he was wearing were his entire worldly possessions!

Not being able to speak English, it must have been a bit difficult to handle bus changes across the continent. He probably had an itinerary with places and times indicated. By matching the names of places and telling time, he was able to make all the necessary bus transfers from Seattle to Albany. Doing this and hiding so many times must have been quite a challenge.

Ko never said much about his trip across the continent. He did mention what he had to eat—eggs, eggs and more eggs! No matter what he ordered, he always seemed to get eggs in some form.

George had made arrangements for Ko to enter Fair Haven High School; a school about six miles from our home. On Ko's first day, George took him to school. Prior to his arrival, Principal Siegl had invited several boys into his office to prepare them for the new student. They were urged to welcome Ko and help him to become acquainted with the school. Teddy

Rice was one of the boys, but I don't know whether or not Ed Pritchard was one of them. Because Ko arrived here about October 20th (1952), school had been in session for awhile. I believe Ko was enrolled as a special student. He obviously had different needs than the rest of the student body. It appeared that Ko adjusted very quickly to Fair Haven High School, perhaps mainly through his involvement in sports.

Ko playing his harmonica.

At that time the Lions Club was preparing to put on a Minstrel Show. Ko participated by playing a harmonica and in singing "Arirang (Ah-De-Dong)". He wasn't proud of the Korean National Anthem. He was very upset that Korea had been divided into North Korea and South Korea. When people asked him what he thought of Syngman Rhee, (President of South Korea), he would say, "What do you think of Harry Truman?" He never gave a direct answer to the question.

When Ko first came to our home he had what eventually became known as Gram's room. (Gram was George's grandmother, Sarah Roberts.) Within a month after Ko came, Gram came to live with us and Ko gave up his room. His bed and bureau were put out into the hall. A screen covered with green fabric was put around his make-shift room. For some reason Ko took the mattress off his bed and he slept on the springs for awhile! Ko's dresser was very handy for Butch (another guest in our home later) to snitch Ko's underwear. This invasion of the dresser caused considerable friction between Ko and Butch!

During Ko's early years with us, our family owned a small convenience store which served the neighborhood. To help out, Ko clerked in the store during his out-of-school hours. The store sold meats, sodas and everything that one would expect to find in such a store. Ko was the stock boy, the meat cutter and he did whatever had to be done to run the store. While working he became acquainted with the people in the area. Having to wait on customers necessitated communicating with English-speaking people. He learned a lot of English words waiting on customers.

Even though Ko wasn't very fluent in handling our language, he was very perceptive. With a suspicion that someone was stealing things from the store, he set a trap. I don't mean a trap trap, but rather a certain way of having the door or a certain position of a window. He knew that the would-be burglar was a local kid; a teen-ager. The "trap" worked. He got finger prints and the kid was caught.

Ko was not only observant at the store but he was very perceptive to different situations elsewhere. Even though he had arrived in mid-October, by Halloween he had sized up many individuals by the tones of their voices, I guess. When children came to the door dressed in their Halloween costumes, he'd say, "You are so-and-so!"

Ko also conveyed a considerable amount of self-confidence, which led him to feel that he could do anything he set out to do. He had come from a good family background; probably a family which was much better off than the one to which he came. It is doubtful that he ever felt inferior.

Our home was always filled with residents and guests. Besides George, Dotty, young George and me, we took in Aunt Clara. Even though she was my father's aunt and my great-aunt, George thought she should come to live with us. Aunt Clara died in 1952 before Ko came.

Then came Ko, followed by Gram within a month. Young George was only nine months old when Ko came. Larry Stone (a foster son) came when young George was two and Butch Holden came after that.

Of course, Uncle Dan (my uncle, Daniel Woodbury) was there all the time, even though he didn't actually live with us. He lived in the apartment in the barn. He would come in and take food out of our refrigerator. When we sold out the store, we brought the stock home. We had all those canned goods in the cellar. Uncle Dan would come in and help himself to a pound of coffee and whatever else he wanted.

Uncle Dan was a rather unique member of the neighborhood. He used to go out with his cats and they would follow him like the Pied Piper of Hamlin.

One time Uncle Dan wanted to mark off our property and put the pieces of a telephone pole to mark the corners. Bob McClure, our next door neighbor, was angry so after dark after Uncle Dan had gone to bed, Bob sent Ko out to take out the markers. I guess Uncle Dan thought Bob did it. At any rate, that was the end of that project.

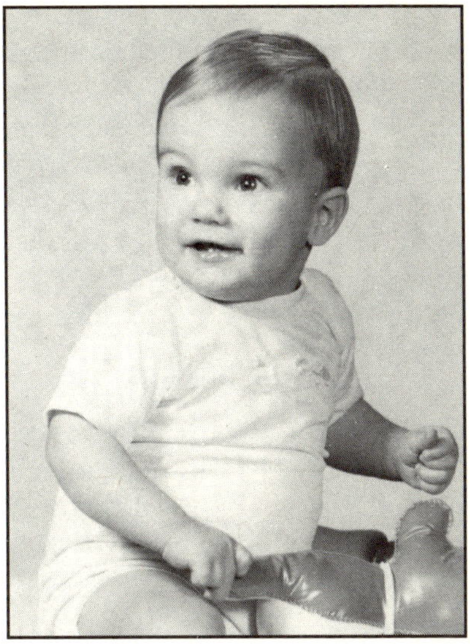

George White Harrington.

Our house was always a crazy place. Folks were coming and going so much of the time. Sometimes there were people there whom we didn't know; coming and going! This was somewhat like Elaine's home today except that our house was smaller! I guess Ko got used to our "open house" atmosphere.

One very funny incident occurred while Ko was living at our house. He had a dark room in the cellar. He had chemicals in gallon jugs; small-necked jugs but he didn't have any stoppers. So he took condoms and filled them with cotton to serve as stoppers. The idea worked, but they ballooned out.

Coming from a different culture, Ko brought with him some mannerisms which are not evident in our country. One thing in particular which I noticed was that he bowed to everybody whom he met. Elaine says that he did that to his dying day to other Koreans. He was *very* polite and especially showed respect to his elders.

Ko's ideas about women were a little different from our American ideas. In his culture, women are secondary to men. He thought it was terrible if anyone came into our house and saw me (or any other woman) lying on the sofa watching television.

After Ko became quite well acquainted with our household, he began to show some independence by cooking some of his own foods. He made soup every night and would often eat out of the saucepan he had cooked it in and watch television. I can remember those hot peppers in a jar. He saved the juice from the pickles and cut up some onions to put in the jar; thus making hot onions. Kimchee soup smelled awful cooking. When Ko discovered that we had a full freezer downstairs, he would go down to get a steak now and then. Finally, George put a lock on the freezer!

Besides doing a fair amount of studying, Ko stayed up hours and hours watching sports, especially wrestling. He and Gram enjoyed immensely seeing Argentine Rocca who wrestled in his bare feet. Ko would laugh so hard that he would practically fall off the couch. George took Ko to a wrestling match in Albany where he came to the realization that a lot is faked. From that point on, his interest in wrestling waned.

At one point Ko asked if we could have a rabbit. Even though I said, "No," we got one rabbit anyway. Then we got two rabbits. We probably had fifty rabbits at the end. I think Ko built the first hutch. Then we had the Taggart Brothers build us more hutches. They were quite fancy ones having two floors; an upstairs and a downstairs. At first the rabbits were behind our store but later moved to the lot beside our home.

Eventually, some of the rabbits ended in rabbit stew. Gram vowed she would never eat rabbit, but Ko didn't mind. He really liked rabbit. I used to buy packages of chicken wings and put them in with the frying rabbit. Gram would see the chicken and think she was eating chicken!

Besides rabbits, we had our frustrations with horses. There were three of them. They were my Uncle Frank Woodbury's horses. George took them on a retainer for Uncle Frank. Elaine remembers hearing Ko sputter about having to build a corral. It was very big and it was the back part of the lot next to us. Ko was supposed to help take care of the horses. Yet Uncle Dan seemed to think that it was *his* responsibility to care for the horses. He used to walk a horse with a rope on it up and down the street like you would a dog. Sometimes one of the horses would get away. People would call up and tell us the horse was way down Main Street and someone had to go after it. I was afraid of the horse, so Ko would have to go after it. Another time the horse got out and chased one of

Elaine's girl friends who was walking down the road. The horse had to be retrieved that time, too. But one time the horses took off and went over into West Rutland. Every night after school for awhile, they'd gather up a bunch of kids. I'd make a lunch and the bunch would go out to try to find the horses. Somebody may have stolen the horses, who knows?

Ko became quite adept at handling horses. So much so, it was believed that he saved some children's lives one time. The O'Neils lived across the street and they owned a pony. Mary O'Neil told me about the time that she and her brother were in a cart being pulled by their pony. The pony ran away and Ko chased it up South Street and stopped it. Of course, the children and everyone else were scared and praised Ko for saving the children's lives.

Ko and Attorney George Harrington.

Besides building a corral for the horses, Ko spent a considerable amount of time building some wooden bars on which he used to work out. He even went into the woods to get some saplings for his project. He built the bars in the yard next to ours; on the lot which we later sold and a house now stands. Ko used to spend a lot of time on his bars. He enjoyed gymnastics.

When college was mentioned, Ko did *not* want to go to Castleton Teachers' College. George said, "I think you *will* go to Castleton, because I can't afford to send you anywhere else." George also told him that he wouldn't make it out of that high school into a big college, mainly, because his English was still not good enough. In a very large college he would have been discouraged. So, even though Ko did not want to attend Castleton, as time went on, things worked out and he was glad that he did go there.

Both Elaine and I agree that Ko did not work very hard in college. He depended upon Elaine and me to do some of his papers even though he was capable of working much harder. He always had a job of some kind to earn money. He tutored kids in math; a tutoring job which George had taken and then turned over to Ko. Then, of course, he played many sports and had a good time. Elaine says that he really didn't begin to study hard until he began at the University of Vermont.

Sometime during his years in sports he tried both skating and skiing. He used to go skating with Uncle Dan. That was about all they had in common. We had a skating rink next door where the rabbits used to be. Ko apparently wasn't too steady on his skates. He actually wrapped a pillow around his back sides to serve as a padding in case he fell down.

His attempts at skiing were not too spectacular either. He shoveled snow for neighbors, the Breckwidells, and they gave him a pair of skiis and some ski boots. He went skiing, came down a hill too fast and in some way broke a ski. That was the end of his skiing.

Funny things happened sometimes, like the time that Ko went to a sports event and wasn't quite prepared for what took place. When he took his sweats off, much to his surprise and everybody else's, Ko hadn't put on a suit underneath. I thought it was at a basketball game, but Elaine and Ed think it was at a track meet. Wherever it took place, it was a surprise!

Ko and Ed Pritchard were very good friends all during high school and college. They did many things together. They participated in baseball, basketball and track. They even took ballroom dancing lessons for a short time from the same teacher who gave young George and Larry tap dancing lessons.

Other friends of Ko were Bill Whitworth and Teddy Rice. Both of them are dead now.

Ko kept busy every summer during his college years at one job or another. One year he worked at a summer camp in the Albany area, perhaps during his second year in college. He was a Waterfront Director at Shawnee Institute in Wallingford, Vermont. He was a Waterfront Director at a 4-H camp one summer, too. It was at one of these camps where he met Noel Potter. Ko also worked at Staso Milling Company here in Castleton.

After four years of college at Castleton, Ko graduated in 1958. I can remember his Graduation very well. It was outside where the Chapel now stands *and* it was an extremely cold day.

Of course, Ko's special young friend was young George. Ko was like a big brother to him. He used to take young George fishing and hunting. Even though they really got along quite well together, occasionally Ko took it upon himself to exert a little Korean authority. Ko told about the time he took George fishing and George didn't want to do something Ko wanted him to do. So Ko said, "You can walk home then!" George ended up walking the whole length of South Street.

One time in Burlington when George was just a little boy, Ko gave him half a dollar bill and said, "If you'll go downstreet and find your way home, I'll give you the other half." I guess George managed to do it.

When going hunting, Ko would put a whistle around George's neck so that if they got separated, he could blow the whistle.

George's father used to do the same kind of things. He would take young George to the Legislature and turn him loose at six years old. The legislators would be in a closed session with the doors locked. Young George couldn't get in so he'd be out wandering the corridors waiting for his father to come out.

Elaine said that Ko did the same kind of thing to his own son, Stephen, while at a Dental Convention. He left Stephen all alone somewhere and expected the child to stay seated and wait for his father to return.

In transferring his authority from young George to his own children, Ko didn't change his procedures at all. That's one way you can think of Ko, he was consistent. You could depend upon what he might do and think.

Ko had a very close relationship with big George. I don't know but he kind of considered him as a father figure, even though there wasn't that much difference in their ages. He respected big George and depended upon him to guide him through different situations. I don't think Ko ever tried to tell big George what to do. Big George was Ko's only stability. The position of the male in the Korean culture always overpowered that of a woman. George's death in 1960, just two weeks after Elaine and Ko were married, was a terrible blow to Ko. By that time Ko and Elaine had returned from their honeymoon and Ko had gone into the service at Fort Drum.

I don't remember just when the following event happened but it does represent Ko's way of not planning for

Betty Harrington Zahnleiter.

details. It probably occurred in the second summer after George died. We set out for Maine on the Labor Day weekend for a fishing trip. We went out on the boat not knowing that we were supposed to take our own lunch with us. When it came lunch time we sat there with nothing to eat while the other fishermen reached down underneath and picked up their lunches. There was a candy machine on the boat so we bought candy bars and ate them. We were gone all day with practically nothing to eat. It was a dirty old boat but we caught lots of fish. Our fingers were all cut from hauling in the salt water fish. When we returned ashore, we had no reservations for the night. We should have made reservations before we went out on the boat. Ko just didn't think. If he did inquire anywhere he probably thought the prices were too high. Actually, in the end we did find a little housekeeping cottage which wasn't too bad a place. It could have been anything. By the time we got there we didn't care.

Elaine said that the Ko children can tell you that experiences like this one were repeated over and over again while they were growing up. The settings might be different, but the stories are similar. Ko was consistent. That's one thing, he was always consistent!

These memories which I now cherish so much will always serve as a reminder of my good fortune to have had such a fine young man come to my home and become a part of my life almost forty years ago. Throughout these years, our relationship grew to a point when he even called me on Mother's Day to wish me a nice day. What warm memories I now have!

—Betty Harrington Zahnleiter
Sok Nam Ko's Sponsor Mother

Settling In

I have a letter painstakingly written to me by Ko in 1952. He was preparing to come to the United States. At that time I was a member of the Harrington household living on South Street in Castleton. My sister, Betty, wife of George Harrington, was co-sponsor of Ko. I was seventeen and a junior in high school. The letter seemed an attempt for contact between teenagers. We would be attending the same school and I think Ko was thinking ahead. He arrived eight months later, concluding a trip by boat and by bus.

As Ko talked to me about his trip across the continent, he mentioned the lack of menu choices that he had in restaurants along the way. Once he told me that whatever he pointed to on the menu, they gave him eggs. Since he couldn't read English very well, he could have been pointing to anything. I don't think the gap was all that noticeable, because he was very clever about it. People learning English often understand more than they can verbalize.

Ko's adjustment to the family, school and community went smoothly. Our household was crowded; we ranged in age from an elderly uncle to my nephew of less than a year.

Letter written to Dorothy White Knapp by Sok Nam Ko while still in Korea.

20 Feb 1952

Dear Dotty,

How do you, Tow days ago I receved your lette and was very glad to hear from you, Please excuse me for not writing sooner, as I don't understand English very good, so I needed a little time to answer you, Korea is a little country the population is about 80000000 people, right now North and South Korea are fighting, but a great number of boys and girls still manage to school, My home is in Kaesong, which right now is in the hands of the Reds, Kaesong has 20 grade, 10 Jr High and 10 Sr High schools, and 1 college, I don't know how thing are in Kaesong right now,

I am very glad to hear that you are very happy and that you like to dance, We have a very peculiar dance here, some of the boys and girls can dance same as they do in the states, when I get to com to the states I will need your help in a lot of things, If there is any thing that you need or that I could send you, pleas let me know, Capt Harrington is a good capt, he must be a good Brother-in-law, He has help a lot of the Koreans over here, Since Capt Harrington left, SU Btry miss him very much, sometime he visit SU Batry and I get to talk to him, I am looking forward to the day when I will be able to the states, Pleas send me your pictore, I am sending one of mine hope you like it, Pleas write me when ever you can

as always

Ko Sok Nam

Herald Photo – Merusi. Sok Nam Ko, refugee, puts finishing touches on life-sized elephant of the GOP, which he created at Castleton. The seven-foot elephant will be conveyed through the county on a truck in a move to rally Republican strength. Ko, a Castleton Teachers College student, makes his home with Atty. and Mrs. Harrington of Castleton. The elephant will be shown at the Rutland County GOP rally and banquet to be held tonight in Castleton. Sen. Aiken will be the principal speaker.

There were hitches, but remarkably little real contention. We numbered nine or ten at times. Our new family member was the first Asian any of us had known. He studied, played sports, ate our food and seemed to accept our ideas about manners, dress and social behavior. Later, I learned that this acceptance was not entirely whole-hearted, and as he became increasingly independent he saved some and threw away others of our conduct that did not fit his code of behavior. His intelligence was obvious. His experiences were beyond the ken of the rest of our household and his schoolmates. However, equally obvious was an astute upbringing and a willingness to work hard for success.

Ko made friends at school, particularly among his teammates, but he did not lose sight of the goal he had set for himself. He was popular with both sexes, but I think he found our social interaction faintly shocking.

Dorothy White Knapp.

At that time our family was operating a small variety store in town. A sort of Mom and Pop operation. Working in this store was a ready-made language lab for Ko and not incidentally, a help to the family. Ko quickly learned family connections and habits. He had an uncanny ability to identify people within families and to pick up on family quirks; things we knew, but had forgotten we knew, about the townfolk.

Castleton benefitted from Ko's adaptation to our way of life. He participated in the Lions Club Minstrel Show—a yearly event, built a papier-mache elephant (life-sized) for the Republican Party rally, which traveled the state, and worked with the Little League. He quickly ceased to be an exotic and became a contributing member of the community. This caring attitude, particularly as concerns young people, has always been apparent. Education seemed to be his driving force.

High school finished, Ko began classes at Castleton State. His English needed polishing and while I don't think teaching (which was Castleton's major offering at that time) was his aim, it was a means. On to UVM, Howard University with a National Science Foundation Grant, Dental School, marriage and a family—all someone else's story.

Since 1952, Sok Nam Ko and now his family have been a part of our family. I know that I and my family were important to him and I feel the loss of a brother. Those two or three years in the mid-50's were crowded for all of us. We were all preparing for life, but Ko seemed to know better how to go about it. It is shocking how short that life was for him; his accomplishments, however, are obvious.

—Dotty White Knapp
Betty Harrington Zahnleiter's sister

George's Memories

George White Harrington and Ko.

What I would like to do is to start off with the early history of what I remember about Ko. Right now, I am nearly 40 years old. When I was about 9 months old, Ko came to live in our home. So I was literally starting out in life at the time when Ko was restarting his life. Obviously, I don't remember any incidents when I was a baby, so my story will begin with memories of events when I was about 3 or 4 years old.

One of the first things I remember was living in a home that seemed like there were lots of doors opening and shutting all the time. This was true because there were many people living in the Harrington home. Our house wasn't a very big home but everyone seemed to have a place to call his own. Ko's spot was in the upstairs hall. There was just enough room for his bed, a bureau and a little table-like stand. Around his bed was a folding screen to provide a small amount of privacy.

At this time there was another guy in our home named Larry Holden; more commonly known as Butch. He was the American teenage version of what Ko did *not* want to become. Butch and Ko were constantly at each other, either to get my father's attention or just because the chemistry wasn't right between them. Butch was constantly helping himself to Ko's things without asking permission. This greatly annoyed Ko!

One of the first incidents I *literally* remember involved my foster brother, also named Larry, who was 2 years older than I. At the time of this event, Larry was probably 6 and I was 4. We had gotten these boxing gloves for Christmas. I can remember this guy, Butch Holden, taking my brother, Larry, and giving him tips on how to fight with those boxing gloves. Ko took me aside and gave me tips on how to fight. At a given point, someone in the room said, "O.K. Go!" Now I was no match for Larry. He would bang me up and hit me very hard. Ko would say to me, "Toughen up! You've got to be tough. You're not going to be tough unless you get in there and fight!" While I did not realize it at that time, this incident foretold the relationship I would have with Ko for many years to come. Many incidents were aimed at toughening me up, making me independent and able to take care of myself. However, at this age of 4, I became very upset because I just *couldn't* beat Larry. The two years age difference certainly gave Larry the edge.

Ko working as a lifeguard.

Another method which Ko used in order to "toughen" me up was to tease me a lot. Ko felt that I was being spoiled by my mother and Dotty. They *always* protected me. Ko was trying to prepare me for life when my mother and Dotty wouldn't be around to take my part in a situation.

Another thing Ko did was to take me wherever he went, whether it was to the store or a ball game. I was his shadow. I remember going so many places with him. I don't know why my mother let me go, but I guess she totally trusted Ko and knew he would take good care of me.

One of the first traumatic events in my life was when I left my family to go to camp with Ko. Now, he knew that I was likely to become homesick so, again to toughen me up, he took me to camp with him. He was sometimes a director of water-front activities or sometimes a life guard. I don't remember just what I did at camp, but I was there one or two weeks at a time. I was probably 5 or 6 years old.

While I was at camp, Ko was always trying to show me off. He would say to the campers, "Look at this kid. Let me have him sing the Korean National Anthem!" He'd wind me up and I'd sing the song. Or he'd say, "Let me see if he can count in Korean." Again, he would wind me up and I'd count in Korean. As a little kid, he liked to have me do this type of thing.

When I was a child, I used to be able to sing. One time they had this broadcast from camp. My part was to sing the song, "You'll Never Walk Alone" on the radio from this camp. Ko made me do that. Again, he was trying to give me confidence and "toughen me up."

Ko often made me do things that I may not have wanted to do–like eat rice. I found a note I had written on my father's stationery in his scrapbook which read, "My Mommy says I don't *have* to eat rice!" Ko must have had his way, because eventually I learned to eat rice and he was proud of that fact.

Later when Ko was living in Burlington, he was teaching at South Burlington Junior High and working on his master's program at U.V.M. This was before Ko was married. I remember going to Burlington to stay several days with him. I was about 6 years old and would go to visit his classroom. Ko delighted in having me tell his students when they were wrong. He'd prime me on what to say and what to do. He'd try to shame his students by saying, "Hey, this little kid knows the answer, why don't you know it?" This was one of the ways he used to get his students to work a little harder.

Besides teaching and working on his master's program, Ko was in the Army Reserve. One weekend per month he had to participate in some way in this program. One time when I was visiting Ko, he took me with him to a place in downtown Burlington. It was a Sunday morning and there was no one in this building. It was quiet there and I became bored. Because Ko had a lot of paper work to do, he devised a plan to occupy my time. He said, "Georgie, see this dollar! I'll give you this dollar if you go outside, go down the street and spend an hour or so away from this office. Learn the streets, find out where you go. Make sure you pay attention so that you can come back!" He ripped the dollar in half, gave me half of it and said, "When you come back, I'll give you the other half."

Now, in those days, a dollar was a lot of money, so I was anxious to get that other half. I left the office and walked down the long flight of stairs. When I got outside the building, I looked up and down the street. I headed down the hill and walked as far as I could right to the shores of Lake Champlain. I went around a couple of blocks and then headed back up the hill. After walking around another couple of blocks, I looked at my watch which was my prized possession. I knew I couldn't go back to Ko until at least an hour had gone by. So, I kept track on my watch to make sure that I used up my hour. I very carefully made it back, went upstairs, knocked on the door and went inside the room where Ko was. As promised, he gave me the other half of the dollar, thinking, of course, that this was contributing to toughening me up. He was getting me used to life outside of Castleton, Vermont. I appreciated that.

Back home, life with the rabbits is a popular family story. I remember that Ko was raising these rabbits out in the lot next to our home. I saw him time after time going out to their pens, getting water and feeding the rabbits, cleaning the pens and taking full responsibility for their care.

Besides rabbits, our family had some horses. Because our home is in a town and on about three acres of land, in order to keep horses we had to build a corral and provide a stable for them in the barn. I can remember going out with Ko in *very cold* weather and digging post holes and putting posts in so we could string wire for a fence to contain the horses.

I can remember Ko cooking a lot at our house on his own; making all kinds of soup and other dishes made with vegetables. He was capable in the kitchen and certainly would never starve as long as there were ingredients available.

Our family had a number of different vehicles. I can remember him driving a truck we had and, of course, wherever he went, if possible, I went with him.

Our family used to have a camp at a lake. I can remember one summer going with Ko and my father to this camp. It seemed like it took us forever to get there, but it really wasn't very far. My father always had his "ear to the ground" trying to find someone who might remind Ko of his own roots. About this time my father had located another Korean boy. I think his name was Jimmy Pak. My father invited Jimmy to visit us for a couple of weeks. Even though Jimmy was much younger than Ko, they got together and talked a great deal.

My father and Ko were together a lot. My father was the kind of person to have 29 balls in the air trying to juggle them all at once. He relied upon Ko, Butch and Larry and whoever else was around to keep all the balls in the air. Ko worked *very* hard for my father. The thing I *do* remember is that Ko always discharged his duties to the umpteenth degree. He did what he was told, while Butch Holden did not. That created much tension. Ko was *always* doing his part. Yet Butch was getting away with many things; as we say, "getting away with murder." That was not fair. Ko knew it wasn't fair. Years later Ko used to tell me stories about things that Butch did. His behavior really upset Ko.

By this time (about 1959) I was beginning to see Elaine quite often. She used to come to our home. During her last year of college she lived at Rev. and Mrs. Johnson's home. Ko and Elaine introduced me to the Johnson family. They had a family of four boys; all of whom were older than I. With Elaine living in the Johnson home, I had free reign of the place. With the active family interested in so many things, I can remember all those bicycle parts and radio parts being ready for various projects. I also took piano lessons from Mrs. Johnson. The Johnson home was a nice place to visit.

It was in August 1960 that Ko and Elaine were married in Rev. Johnson's church in Castleton. It was a big event for this small town. I can remember practicing for the ceremony because I was one of the ring bearers.

Soon after the wedding my father died, and Ko and Elaine moved to Burlington. I can remember going to their Brooke's Avenue apartment with my Mom and Dotty.

It was there that Ko was talking about how dumb his students were. He asked me how to spell the word "mechan ical." I spelled it correctly. Ko was really bugged because his students couldn't spell words like "mechanical."

Eventually they moved from Brooke's Avenue to Mary Street. It seemed to me like the coolest house I had ever seen. It had nooks and crannies and dormers. I spent a week here and a week there at their home in Burlington.

At this point, Ko was trying to interest me in becoming a doctor. He was in medical school and had all these things around—like test tubes—hoping to get me all psyched to be a doctor.

One of the official holidays of this part of the country is deer hunting time in November. It seemed that everybody went deer hunting. Ko was no exception. Each November he would drive down to Castleton, so as to participate in this yearly adventure.

One year Elaine's father joined our hunting expedition. That made three of us. We went up to the Pritchard's land on the North Road, on what they called the 40 Acres. We went to the chosen spot and we hunted and we hunted *and* we hunted. Nothing happened. Toward the end of the day, around 4 o'clock, there was a sighting of some deer. We all ran to the open field. Ko shot off a couple of rounds and missed. Then he said, "Quick, Georgie, give me your gun!" I gave him *my* gun because I had bullets in it. Ko shot a couple of times and missed again. About that time Ed O'Neill came aboard and said, "What's all the shooting about?"

"Well," we said, "we saw this deer and we almost got him!" And then we heard this shout. In all this melee we had forgotten grandpa—forgotten Elaine's father who had shot a deer. This was kind of ironic because he wasn't the hunting type like Ko was. Mr. Hogaboom *got* the deer. I expect this sort of bothered Ko because he missed the deer.

It was getting late and dark and it was very cold. I don't think Mr. Hogaboom knew how to gut the deer.* The men had to pull the deer out of a thicket. Of course, the deer was very heavy and hard to handle. I got relegated to carry the guns. I was probably 9 or 10 years old and all those guns, ammunition and knives were heavy for me to carry. This whole event was a lot of fun. At least, I thought it was. It was Ko who wasn't very happy.

For some reason I was always tagging along with Ko and, now that he and Elaine were married, I began following them to no matter what state. I was *always* around!

Upon leaving Burlington, they moved to Philadelphia where Ko attended dental school and Elaine taught school. Andy was little and Timmy was born while they lived in Philly. Ko worked really hard in school and every summer he worked

---

*Editor's note: Ruthford Hogaboom, Elaine's father, actually was a very experienced outdoorsman who had hunted and trapped since his childhood on a farm in northern Vermont. But he was also playfully mischievous. Pretending that he did not know how to field dress a deer that he had shot, so he could watch another person do it for him, would have amused Grandpa Hogaboom.

to make money. Elaine worked very hard, too, teaching and taking care of the family and apartment. Both Ko and Elaine struggled *hard* to make their plans work. I used to visit them from time to time.

One summer, in order to earn some money, Ko and his family moved to Minerva, New York in the Adirondack Region. They lived in a *very, very* tiny little trailer while Ko worked for the construction company that was building the Northway. What I remember is his taking me to work with him; just like I'd gone to work and school with him a number of times. This time, however, it was all night work. Ko's job was to drive a water truck. The construction crew cleared the land by cutting the trees and piling the brush up to be burned. As the fires burned, it was Ko's job to watch the piles burn and be ready with his water truck if it was ever needed. We sat all night long watching these fires. We would move from one area to another; just he and I, watching all night long. I thought this was pretty cool! If my mother only knew that I was sitting up all night long! I remember thinking that!

While living in Minerva, on weekends Ko and his family would occasionally visit our home in Castleton. Andy and Timmy were little. We'd play ball in the backyard. Ko was always trying to get Andy to play ball when he really didn't want to play. I always sympathized with Andy because I remembered times when I didn't want to do things Ko asked me to do.

In early June 1966, when Ko was attending dental school from which he eventually graduated, I spent a couple of weeks in the Ko home. At this time I was getting ready to go to Arizona to work for my grandfather for the summer. I had gotten a ride down to Philadelphia with Ed Pritchard. In a couple of weeks Ed was going to take me to Arizona and drop me off at my grandmother's (who was his aunt) and then he was going to go to California to attend summer school at Berkeley. This plan meant I would stay a couple of weeks in Philadelphia with the Kos.

It was a great two weeks. I had just finished 8th grade and was really interested in lots of things. Ko took me to a couple of ball games to see the Phillies. It was actually a doubleheader. He took me around the city to see all the historical sights, like Independence Hall and the Liberty Bell. I really appreciated that.

To earn a little on the side, Ko was substitute teaching in a junior high. Of course, I had to follow him to school. Before going to school, he tried to prepare me for this school, which was very different from what I was used to in Vermont. He remarked, "Now, Georgie, you know that this isn't like Vermont. This is inner city. There are lots of blacks (Negro was the word used at that time) and so you be careful what you say. It's a tough school!"

So, once again, I went to school all primed to meet this new experience. When every class came into Ko's classroom, he made me stand up, introduce myself and tell everybody where I was from and what I was doing. This was really embarrassing. These were my peers, but they were city kids and I was a country kid. It was *very* embarrassing, but Ko felt that he was making me strong by insisting that I do this.

I can remember one specific instance when I was introducing myself and I said I was from Castleton, Vermont. Ko stopped me and said, "Does anybody know where Vermont is?"

One girl stuck her hand up and said, "Isn't that part of Canada?" Ko, exasperated by the lack of knowledge of these kids, said, "*No*, it's part of the United States." Then turning to me he said, "George, do you believe that these kids don't know where Vermont is?" I'll *never* forget that! I was really embarrassed. As for Ko, he was trying to shame the students and he wanted to make them more serious about school.

As time moved on, I went to high school and Ko and his family moved to Weymouth, Massachusetts. Here Ko began his post-graduate work in oral surgery at Tufts University in Boston. This was a great deal for me. The Boston area is a great place to go—especially for anyone who enjoys history and politics like I do. I'd take a bus from Castleton down to Weymouth or would travel down by car. I can remember going to Weymouth a lot.

Ko kept saying, "Bring somebody down to visit us!" I told this to my neighbor, David O'Neill, who grew up with Ko in our town. He was about the same age as I was. David knew Ko from the earliest time he could really remember. At this point, I was about a junior in high school. David and I went down to Weymouth in August 1968. I remember the day because it was the day that the Soviet Union invaded Czechoslovakia. Ko took

David and me into the city of Boston. We were to spend the day there while he was doing his work at Tufts. I can remember being in the bus station and waiting and waiting and waiting. Ko was supposed to pick us up. He was late, but told us not to worry. I guess he wanted me to have the same bus station experience as he had when crossing the country—and we did.

In 1969, I was a senior in high school; still living in Vermont but looking for a way to get out of a small town. I was turned on by the city. I had visited Ko, Elaine and their family many times and had discussed what I should do after high school. Ko was convinced that: a) I should become a doctor and b) I should go to the best school available.

Harvard happens to be one of the best schools available in the Boston area. So, Ko scheduled an interview for me with a Harvard Admissions Officer. He took me to the interview, which turned out *not* to be a good one. The Admissions Officer told me that, basically, with my high school record of having a B- in one subject in math one semester that I would probably not be accepted at Harvard. Ko was very upset because he thought that I was bright enough and felt I deserved a chance. Perhaps Ko was reliving his own experience of rejection years before this.

At this time, Ko was working at the V.A. Hospital in Boston. He decided it would be a nice idea for me to spend a day at the hospital with him. Now, I had been to work with him many times during my life, so this idea was no big deal for me. So we went to the hospital. There was going to be an operation that day, and Ko happened to be doing that portion of his residency in anesthesiology. His job during the operation was to administer the anesthetic to the patient. He got me all dressed up in operating room garb, because he wanted me to observe the operation. He showed me on the door what the schedule for the operation was going to be. The guy's name (who was going to be operated on for a very serious cancer problem) was Harrington! This really psyched me out! However, by now I was in the operating room and Ko was doing his thing. I was watching and soon realized that this was not a happy day for me. I started to get light-headed. "Oh, no, oh, no!" I thought. The next thing I knew (which was about 30 minutes later) I was waking up on a stretcher in the hall. The operation was still going on, but there was a nurse standing over me saying, "You fainted!"

I was saying, "Where's Ko? "The nurse said, "He's still in the operating room."

By the time I got my senses back, Ko had come out and the operation was done. He said that he was sorry for what had happened, but that it happens all the time. He didn't want it to bother me; it probably was because I didn't have enough to eat for breakfast and my stomach wasn't full. Meanwhile, I was trying to tell him, "No, I don't like this. It isn't for me."

Again, trying to encourage me, Ko said, "Nah, everybody goes through this. Don't worry about it. You have to stay here, because I've got more work to do today. Why don't you either stick around *or* you can go back home!" Now going back home meant about two rides on the Boston T and about three buses to get back to Weymouth. But I tell you, I wasn't going to stick around that hospital any longer and I found my way home.

I *think* this incident began to alert Ko to the fact that, even though it was his dream, I would never become a member of the medical profession.

Instead, I chose another university in the city of Boston; Boston University. It is a good school, but very expensive. We figured out a way between Ko, Elaine and my Mom for me to be able to afford that school through scholarships and being able to live with the Kos in Weymouth. So from September 1970 to May 1971, I lived in the Ko home and attended college at Boston University.

There are not enough tapes in the whole city of Amsterdam to record all the things I experienced while living with the Kos. But I'll hit some of the highlights of that time in my life.

One of the enjoyable parts now was that I could engage Ko in intellectual conversations. It was fun to be able to challenge some of the ideas he was throwing at me in regards to politics and history. I realized at this point that in a lot of the positions he would take he was only acting as devil's advocate. He was trying to push me to see how much I really believed in the opinion I was stating. He felt that too many people had opinions that were not substantiated. He always tried to force a person to say what he really, *really* believed.

For the first couple of months that I was at Boston University, we had an opportunity to have *many* discussions, because we spent a lot of time together. Where we spent our time was in a little black Plymouth Valiant driving from Weymouth to the V.A. Hospital in Boston every morning and coming back every evening. It took about an hour to make the trip to the hospital. Ko would drop me off at the hospital and I would wind my way over to Boston University. At the end of my day, I returned to the hospital. In case our schedules did not coincide, I would take public transportation to Weymouth. We had a lot of good times as we commuted to Boston each day.

As was always the case, the Ko home was an extremely busy household. Elaine was teaching and Ko was going to school each day. Then Ko always had some kind of a project going. He constantly schemed about ways to better himself.

Since he was already licensed to practice dentistry, he did some moonlighting in the nearby town and had some dental patients. This was a low budget operation and he didn't hire an assistant except for me. At least once a week, we would go to this office and I would be his dental assistant for the pay of a dollar an hour! It was a little bit "nervousing" in the beginning but once we got the procedures learned, I had a good time. Again, we had a chance to talk. When a patient would leave the office, Ko really liked to talk about that patient and tell me all the things I shouldn't be doing. He would mention how these people were ruining their teeth and all this kind of stuff.

It was while I was living with the Kos that Elaine helped me to buy my first car. It was a 1967 black Volkswagen and I dearly loved that car! Actually, Elaine loaned me $1000 because I had the money coming but I couldn't get it there in time to pick up this car. So she loaned me $1000 for a week. That was great!

The Ko house was not very large, so my living quarters were in the basement. Actually, this sounds worse than it was. The room was nice and I had a private bathroom so nobody bothered me. I could do what I wanted. They didn't even tell me to turn the music down very often. I had a good time.

Little Stephen was born in December of the year that I was there. A lot of the time I was there, Ko wasn't because he was so busy. I really got close to Elaine and the children. Occasionally, visitors would come and we'd all go to see something of interest in the area. The Kos were very hospitable and felt obligated to give visitors a good time and show folks the unique things in the area. We spent a lot of time going back and forth to Cape Cod. We visited Scituate, Cohasset and Plymouth a number of times. We went out on Ko's boat deep-sea fishing. We went to a parade honoring the 350th

Anniversary of the Landing of the Pilgrims at Plymouth. There was a big parade and Teddy Kennedy was there. We thought that was all pretty cool!

The Kos would include me in going to many receptions of different kinds. At these parties we would meet dignitaries. I remember meeting the other senator from Massachusetts, Senator Brooks, at one of these receptions.

At this time, I was madly in love (and still am) with Susan Nelson. She was back in Vermont still in high school because she is two years younger than I. From time to time on weekends, I would go back to Vermont to see my girlfriend. When spring rolled around, I convinced her that she really must get acquainted with the Ko family. So in the spring of 1971 I brought her down to Weymouth and she spent some time getting to know Ko, Elaine and the children. As I recall, Ko and Elaine took us out to dinner. It was a nice affair.

It so happened that Ko had some unfinished business with me and that was with my teeth. I still had a couple of wisdom teeth left which Ko said I should have taken out. I *really* didn't want them to be taken out but this time Ko had a captive audience. He could have Susan serve as assistant when he operated on me. We went down to his office and he started cutting. He got one tooth half out. It was really badly impacted and there was a considerable amount of blood! Susan was getting sick! She was trying to play the role of the assistant and he was running into complications. An hour and a half later he got the tooth out. I said, "This is enough for me. We're not going to do the other tooth right now!"

Ko said, "I think you're right. We can do it at another time." Well, that other time never came. I've still got that tooth! I'm never going to go through that. It wasn't his fault. Now that I think of it, it was quite a way to introduce my future wife to this clan!

Ko used to also push Susan during conversations to find out where she stood on various issues. She really enjoyed it because she likes intellectual stimuli and they would really go at it. Coming not from the closed Vermont scene, Susan was more international. Ko liked that. So they hit it off very well.

That pretty much wraps up my Weymouth stay. Ko really didn't get on me for either studying or not studying. I appreciated the fact that he really left me alone to do my thing. He let me hang on my own.

I lasted only a year at Boston University. It was also the Ko's family last year in Weymouth. Ko had finished his work in oral surgery at Tufts and was going to start his own practice in Framingham, which was about 50 miles west of Boston. The family moved to Holliston. So it wouldn't have worked out very well for me to continue at Boston University. I put in my transfer to Brigham Young University and moved west.

At that point we parted company on a day by day basis with the Kos, because now I was living out west. I finished my studies out there. The summer that we came back, we stopped to call on the Kos who, within that time, had moved from Holliston to Amsterdam.

My story is picked up four years later, after I finished my undergraduate work and moved back to Vermont for a couple of years. I then became reacquainted with the Ko family, which had now added Suzie to their family. I was now married and had a child.

I remember a Thanksgiving at my Mom's house when Ko and Elaine and their family came for the holiday. We have a nice picture of Elaine and Ko holding our son, Nate. Ko took a shine to my children. I think this was because they were my children and he could see me all over in Nathan. Here was a timid little kid and Uncle Ko pushing to get this kid to toughen up a little bit.

When our son, Matthew, came along, Ko took a real shine to Matthew. He is a very quiet kind of kid, a big guy, the athletic kind. Ko nicknamed him the Incredible Hulk or just plain Hulk. To this day the children refer to Matt as Hulk because of that.

Our families have stayed very much in touch and end up spending some holidays together. Ko is remembered for giving unique little gifts to the children like commemorative silver coins. He loved pulling a $20 bill out of his pocket and giving it to Nathan. Ko was always trying to make our load lighter.

However, these were busy times! We didn't have the quality times that we used to have when we were captive in one another's homes. When we did get together we talked way into the night. Every time we would go to Amsterdam as a family to visit, it was let's go out to dinner or let's order pizza. We were always doing something and we really appreciated that. My kids always loved to visit the Kos because something was always going on.

Nathan Harrington, Ko and Elaine.

Ko helped me to buy a house. When all is said and done, Ko was more like a father to me, because I had lost my father early in life. Ko took care of me and watched over me as a father would. So when it came time to buy a house or there were financial problems, he was there to help out. Ko wanted to be close. Those were tough times; a recession. I didn't have a good job, even though I had an undergraduate degree. Ko gave me every benefit of the doubt during that time period. I've been very indebted to Ko *all* through my life.

It is true that my father helped Ko. So he, in turn, has always helped me. He was highly motivated and had his head screwed on right. He had goals and knew how to accomplish them. He knew how to set goals and worked hard to attain them.

There was a period of time when my family and I lived in France. I convinced Ko that he and Elaine should visit us in France. They spent about 10 days with us and we enjoyed every minute of our time together.

One incident which happened over there illustrates how determined Ko was. He refused to give up no matter how trivial the task was. When he was in France, I wanted to take him to Avignon, to tour the Pope's Palace and to see other historical places over there. It was about 100 miles or so from where we were living, so it wasn't hard to get there. So, I made arrangements to go.

Now Ko had also been very involved in the Rotary Student Exchange Program here in the States. There was an Amsterdam student or a Montgomery County student who was somewhere near Marseille. Well, Marseille is a city of a million or so people and there are a lot of places *somewhere* near Marseille.

When we got to Avignon, Ko said, "George, you gotta find the telephone number of this person." He had the address but didn't have the telephone number. He wanted to call the girl.

Ko and George White Harrington in France.

I said, "Ko, it's O.K. But we don't need to do that now." This was about 9:30 at night!

"No, no. I promised I would call," he continued.

"But you don't have the phone number," I responded.

"But you can find the phone number, " said Ko.

I added, "But, Ko, we're in a foreign land. This is France. It's not just like calling up directory assistance like we can do in the States."

Ko explained, "You can find a phone number. Go down to the hotel clerk." At that time we were staying in a hotel.

Finally, I said, "O.K." I went down to the hotel clerk. There was a system called Mini-Tel and I convinced the clerk in my not-so-good French what I wanted to do. He got out his Mini-Tel. We looked up the number of this person. So, I went back up to the room and said, "I got the number!"

"Good, call 'em!" said Ko.

"Me? It's *your* call!" I remarked.

"No, *you* call. You speak French. I don't speak French."

By now it was 10 o'clock so I said, "Ko, it's 10 o'clock!

"No, she'll *really* appreciate it," urged Ko.

So, I made the phone call. I got somebody on the line. Now it's hard to speak in a different language on the telephone. When I was trying to ask for this student, I was getting this long-winded answer that the student didn't live there any more. She had moved on to another location. I said, "O.K. may I have the phone number?" After I got what I thought was the phone number for the next location, I hung up the phone.

Ko said, "What did she say? What did she say?"

I answered, "She's not there. She's moved on." You would have thought that would have settled it but it didn't.

"Then call the other number," remarked Ko.

I said, "But, Ko, it's late. It's 10:30. We can make this call in the morning!"

"No, no," he insisted. I couldn't argue with him. I knew he wanted very much to make this call. So I made the second phone call. I woke the people up. They got the girl up. After talking to the girl briefly, I gave her to Ko and he visited quite a long time with her.

To make a long story short, it wasn't the fact that it was 10:30 that made Ko want to do this or not want to do this; he didn't worry about the conventions of the time. He knew that the girl was homesick. He knew that just to be able to talk to somebody from home, no matter what time of day, was worth it. Once again, Ko taught me a lesson. Don't let *anything* get in your way if it's the right thing to do.

Ko was extremely thoughtful of others. Even during his last illness when he was *so* sick in the hospital, he remained concerned about others. He specifically inquired about my mother's health, even when he could barely talk!

The one thing Ko and I had planned on, I was going to go to Korea with him on his next trip. We were working on that, dreaming about a trip that would never happen.

—George White Harrington

A Special Friendship Existed Between Us

Trying to remember incidents which occurred so many years ago is very difficult. It has taken a considerable amount of jogging my memory to recall the details of my early friendship with Ko. A few incidents remain vivid in my memory; yet there are others which have been almost entirely forgotten.

George Harrington had given me prior knowledge about the young Korean boy who would be coming to live in his home in Castleton, Vermont. Knowing this, I was somewhat prepared to meet the new boy from this land so far away. I really can't remember exactly where or when I first met Ko, but I think it was at Fair Haven High School in October 1952. School had already started. Our principal had explained to us that a new student would be entering our school and we were urged to welcome Ko and help him to become acquainted with the school.

When Ko entered Fair Haven High School, I believe he came in sort of as a special student. Obviously, his needs were different than those of the rest of the students. I expect that we may have had a few classes together, but I really only remember being in physics together. We both graduated in 1954.

Adjustments to subject matter must have been difficult for him. Being bright and determined helped him to learn quickly. Math and science were the easier subjects for him. Whereas English and social studies presented problems with vocabulary. He had good ideas, but putting them on paper was a challenge.

Ko and I used to ride the school bus to Fair Haven each day. I suspect that those many trips helped us to get better acquainted.

I remember Ko as a friendly, outgoing lad who had a very limited knowledge of the English language. He had to pick and choose his English words carefully whenever he made an attempt to communicate with anyone.

One thing about Ko which helped him to get acquainted with the boys was his sincere interest in sports. He enjoyed all kinds of sports and participated in most of them. One of his first attempts to participate in a sport was in football. It was a new game to him and he had so much to learn. He was quick and eager. He would have done well as a running back. Many of the players on the team had been playing the game since they were freshmen. The coach, in his eagerness to have a winning team, sometimes played favorites and chose the most experienced players to play the game. George became angry because Ko was not playing more, so he withdrew Ko from the football program. I think Ko would have been patient enough to stay with the game and would not have given up practicing if he had been given the chance to make the decision himself.

Soccer, a game Ko knew something about, was not played much at Fair Haven High. So he didn't have a chance to participate in a game that he knew already.

Ko liked tumbling. I know he participated in gymnastics a lot.

Soon after Ko arrived in Castleton, George Harrington introduced Ko to the family-owned store. During his out-

Ed Pritchard.

The Rutland (VT) Herald, ***1953. Photo – Merusi,***

"Ko Sok Nam 18, of Korea, a special student at Fair Haven is expected to be Coach Bob Juckett's ace-in-the-hole this season. Juckett, who will use the Korean as an offensive back, says the 145-pound youth has speed to burn."

of-school time, Ko worked long hours at the store. I think he felt that George kept him very busy and didn't give him as much play time as he would have liked. After Ko got into college, work at the store lessened until it finally closed sometime during his freshman and sophomore years at college.

One good thing about working in the store was that he got to know a lot of people in the area. This was beneficial because he *had* to communicate with the customers. They, too, got to know him well. There wasn't any feeling that he was an outsider. The people in this community really don't have a lot of prejudices. Ko was unique and well-liked by everybody as far as I know.

One summer I believe he worked at the Staso Company. I don't know just how he got the job but it was probably some of George's doing. Even though the money was good at this point, it was not a safe place to work. People who were there for years had problems with their lungs because of the dust. The company made granules for roofing. They took the slate out of the quarry and crushed it into fine little granules. Then they colored it various colors. There was a lot of dust due to the

Pyramid tumbling group at Fair Haven High School.

crushing process. It was a Chicago-based company, but people liked to work in the Castleton plant because of the money. They said there was no dust on the checks! The money was good and it had to be because of this construction kind of work.

After graduation from high school, Ko had to consider what next? George was the one to decide, so Ko entered the college there in Castleton. I think he was not too happy about this decision, but I think he realized he needed additional language facility. He still needed help in writing and speaking English. I can remember that lots of times he would ask me words and/or the derivation of words.

While in college, between his freshman and sophomore years, the basketball team went to Canada to play a game, and I was told that Ko had a difficult time getting back into the United States. I played J.V. basketball, too, but I wasn't on this particular trip.

The sport which Ko and I enjoyed together was hunting. We didn't have much spare time, because both of us were working during our after school hours. But, I do remember one particular hunting trip while we were in college. It involved Dominic Taddonio. The three of us went to Rice's Hill, which is now cut away, and we were using bow and arrow. Taddonio looked around and said, "Right over there! I can see there are droppings right there!" Now when Ko and I looked, we knew that these were not deer droppings. They were more like rabbit droppings but we did not say anything. We just looked at each other and laughed. Even though Ko and I had been brought up thousands of miles apart, halfway around the world, each of us knew the difference between deer droppings and rabbit droppings!

Other sports in which both Ko and I participated were cross country and track. We used to run pretty much together. Frequently we ran meets; sometimes coming in first and second.

Ko played baseball some in high school and then became more interested in playing on the Town League Team in summers. There were a lot of older adult men who were playing. The teams had names like the Bomoseen Bombers. Ko and I were just high school or freshmen in college, so we were playing with a group a lot older than we were; 30 years old or older! We were often stuck in the outfield, but we didn't mind that. At any rate, we had a chance to play a game once in awhile. Our ball fields were usually in a cow pasture. We had one field at Castleton Corners and one up in Hubbardton. Of course, both of us had jobs which consumed much of our time, so we had to plan carefully in order to have time to play ball.

After baseball games or other sports activities, Ko and I used to go to George and Betty's for a snack of some kind. It was not unusual for us to cook a pound or two of spaghetti with lots of spaghetti sauce. These treats tasted ever so good after a ball game.

Ko was fond of some rather unusual foods like kimchee. I tasted it, but found it to be rather hot. I guess you have to get used to such foods and I wasn't.

From the time Ko began his schooling here in the states, he, of course, had to deal with teachers. He was capable and willing to work at the many subjects which faced him. All he asked was a fair chance to succeed and at the same time he wanted to respect his teachers. At times he was disallusioned. There were times when he lost respect for a specific teacher.

First of all, Ko resented it when anyone was demeaning to him and implied that he could not do something. Bushnell was one of those teachers. He told Ko he should be a restaurant cook. This idea probably came from the point of view that Ko did not have adequate language facility to become a teacher. I didn't do well with Bushnell either. The worst grade I ever got was from him, but he didn't tell me to be a cook. Ko was very irate about Bushnell's attitude toward him.

Then there was Miss Hale who was teaching Asian History. It is ironic that a person so steeped in Asian History should fail the subject!

With Miss Ewald, she and Ko had an argument over the colors of the blood in the veins and arteries, which she said were red and blue. She also said that blood ran only on one side of the arm. Ko quickly lost respect for teachers who gave misinformation.

While at college, Ko made friends with a few guys down at Morrill House. He became acquainted with George Cross and a few other guys. It was like a small fraternity down there where all the men were living together. I was down there once when the boys lifted weights. I think, as far as really close friends were concerned, he was limited. He had a lot of friends but not close ones.

A very special relationship was the one Ko had with George. Of course, at times George and Ko were annoyed with each other. George expected a lot of work out of Ko and at times very unreasonable tasks were imposed upon him. At the same time, I think, Ko appreciated the opportunities the Harringtons had given him, so he probably felt obligated to help where he could. Ko depended upon George and trusted him. He was the main male figure in Ko's life. This was very important to Ko. The only time I ever saw Ko show real emotion was at George's funeral, which took place just two weeks after Ko and Elaine were married in August 1960.

Ko went into the Army Reserve along toward the end of his years in Castleton. I waited until after college before I entered the service. At that point in time, the idea was that if you got into the Reserves it was better than being in the military. They were drafting men at that time. There was a lottery. My number was so far down the list that I wouldn't be called. I don't think Ko's number ever came up either.

After our graduation from Castleton in 1958 we began to be involved in a variety of activities which separated us. I worked for the State Highway Department driving my Dad's truck. Our time in the service separated us. Gradually each went his own way and there just wasn't time to be together. We kept in touch down through the years at special times.

I went to one of Ko's fraternity parties while he was there in Dental School. The music was so loud; unbelievable! I couldn't imagine Ko being president of *that* fraternity.

I also went to Philadelphia to see Ko graduate from Dental School. It was a special day for him and he had every right to be proud of his perseverance in attaining this point in his educational career.

There are many characteristics which can describe Ko's goals in education. His ambition to succeed has been evident as he progressed from college to college. His work ethic was admirable. He believed that a person must work hard to get ahead.

In sports he was very competitive. He tried to win; to be the best in any sports in which he was competing.

He was very argumentative and wanted people to think things through as they presented a viewpoint.

Ko and Ed Pritchard.

Ko was not a person to show worry. There were times in his life when it would have been so easy to worry; times like when he was threatened with deportation. If he worried, he did so to himself.

Lastly, Ko was a very quiet man. In fact, there was a quality of quietness which existed between us. We did so many things together we could sense what the other was thinking. I guess it is one of the tests of friendship. I have lost a *real* friend.

—Edward Pritchard
Sok Nam Ko's Close Friend in Castleton
and a cousin of the Harrington's

Was Sometimes Hard to Understand

In 1952 Capt. George Harrington, my cousin, brought Ko to the United States. I remember George telling me that when he met Ko, he was shining the soldiers' shoes and translating for the U.S. men. George grew attached to Ko. And why not; he was a bright boy who would go places—and he did.

I can still remember the first time he came to our house with George. My cousin introduced him to my mother and father, Beatrice and Edwal Pritchard, of Castleton, Vermont. He also met my brothers and sisters, all 10 of them. I'm sure he probably said, "Wow, look at all these kids!" He said we could call him Ko, since that was easier than saying Sok Nam. Ko always got a big kick out of my mother. She had nicknames for all of us. I can still picture him laughing at her.

On Saturday nights I would babysit for George and Betty Harrington. Ko and I would talk about Korea. It was hard for me to understand some of the things he would say, but we overcame that after he was here for awhile. I tried to make him feel at ease while we were talking. I'm sure it was hard for him to leave his homeland and his family, and come over here to live. That made me so proud of him. Ko was a generous giving person. He always saw the best in everyone. He was a caring person. Ko and I were special friends since the time he came to the United States.

Ko was always looking out for other people. For instance, my sister, Irene, was having an operation on her hip, so they could replace a bone in her jaw. She was uncomfortable staying at the hospital. So Ko invited her to stay with him and his family. They took special care of my sister for a few days. Irene said she just loved it there. They were great to her.

We'll all miss Ko very much, but we still have Elaine, who is a wonderful person, and their children. They will always be in our hearts and in our prayers. God bless you, Ko.

—Wilmah Pritchard Elliott

THE CHURCH BELL RINGER

I think Ko, as he was known to his friends in Castleton, was the first Korean I had ever met. I thought George Harrington was a wonderful person to bring him home, adopt him into the family (not legally but figuratively), and see that he went to church, got an education, and became a contributing citizen. I know that Betty Harrington (George's wife) had a big part in Ko's upbringing, also. Ko was very intelligent, learning our sometimes odd American ways quickly, including the language. He was very polite and an agreeable young man. I remember that he used to be the church bell ringer. I went to his wedding to Elaine, who used to baby-sit for my retarded son. I am glad that I have been privileged to know them both!

—Martha Langdon Towers

An All American Immigrant Success Story

My first recollection of Sok Nam Ko was as a student teacher at Rutland Junior High School in the late 50's. He had been introduced to our family through an international experience that my brother Noel attended at Elfin Lake in Wallingford, Vermont. He would play ping pong with me after school. I was never able to outscore him. Somehow the nickname "Boss" came to be associated with us. It was used commonly thereafter.

Later, as a freshman at the University of Vermont, I recall visiting the Ko's and "Bootsie's" apartment in Burlington. Ko was a 1st year med student and he gave me a tour of the facilities, including the anatomy lab. I remember having a very nice supper and evening with the Kos. This was a break in what was a difficult academic year for both of us.

Ko later entered Temple University Dental School at the same time I was attending Tufts University School of Dental Medicine. I left dental school near the end of my sophomore year, and Ko entered Tufts the following year for graduate work in oral surgery. Our paths never really crossed a lot during the dental school years, but we did compare notes.

Ko and family visited Vermont and I visited Amsterdam on a few occasions. He was now an established professional. He had achieved his life long goal of being a doctor against tremendous adversity. I listened to his experiences involving complicated oral surgery and observed his office setup. He was a wonderful man in a wonderful setting.

Many traits can be associated with Ko. The ones that stand out were his determination and work ethic. He was businesslike, but dedicated and compassionate. He was charitable and treated people of all walks of life with dignity. He was very supportive to family and friends alike. He had a good sense of humor. He was truly the All American Immigrant success story.

Being a many generation Vermont Yankee, I was especially interested and overjoyed to hear Ko was able to visit North Korea and reestablish contact with his family. His roots were important to him and I could empathize with his diligent efforts to search into his past against more than the usual obstacles. I was very moved by his reflections on this adventure.

—David Potter

Castleton Admired His Bravery

Castleton in the 1950's was still a small, close-knit rural community; the kind in which every baby and child under the age of twelve got a wrapped, tagged gift at an annual Christmas party in the town hall. A new Lions Club, made up largely of young veterans of World War II, had underwritten a first in-school dental program for all the children in town, and their big money raiser was a home talent show in the form of that old racist genre, the minstrel show. In Castleton the fun was never cruel. Banter between black-faced clowns was just a format for townspeople making fun of themselves.

Local children loved the shows, and the children in our house always enjoyed it for an extra long time because their father and George Harrington were perennially the chief organizers of the event. Biggest treats were the evenings when the end men and moderator rehearsed in our living room. I think there were eight or nine shows in all, and in the years when Castleton men were in Korea with Vermont units, somebody always saw to it that the show was taped and sent to George, so that soldiers could listen to the jokes and songs even if they couldn't see the pantomimed antics.

When the local units came home, everybody in town heard about the young Korean boy called Ko, who had been completely separated from his family and whom George Harrington had arranged to bring to Castleton. The whole town caught its collective breath thinking about the bravery of setting out alone for a strange place half a world away: our town. Certainly, he was a very real hero in the minds of all the children I knew. I can remember the relief we all felt when the Harringtons had word he had arrived in Seattle, although he still had the long trip across the continent to make.

As it happened, his trip across the country took place during the week that would be climaxed by the minstrel show. George saw an opportunity to introduce him to everybody. "Ko can sing the Korean national anthem as a part of the show," he suggested. To all of us, the courage that would take seemed immense. The children were particularly conscious of the scariness of such a situation. But Ko arrived in the nick of time, and

International Students and Ko.

sing he did. I don't think any of us will ever forget the sight of a thin young man dressed in a white shirt and black trousers standing up in front of a couple hundred strangers and singing a home song half a world away from home and family lost, in all probability, irrevocably.

—Margaret K. Onion

Cherished by a Six-Year-Old

My mother, Mrs. William Onion in Castleton, encouraged me to write you when she and I talked soon after Ko's memorial services. She thought you might like to have a view of Ko's arrival in Castleton from the vantage point of someone who was six years old in 1952.

I remember being fascinated by Ko, who obviously was foreign to my small world; but more than that, I (and I'm sure others my age) felt very protective of Ko for the following reason. As a six-year-old, it was horrifying to me that someone like Ko could lose his family in war and be suddenly transported so far from home. I suppose it was the first time I realized that I, too, could suddenly lose my seemingly permanent family of two parents and two brothers. I think because of this awareness, my peers and I not only admired Ko's courage, but wanted to protect him from any further losses after this one which frightened us so.

When my husband (who is not from Castleton) asked me if anyone ever made fun of Ko for being different, I answered very quickly, without a lot of thought, "Oh, no! The whole town cherished him." And I realized my choice of words to an outsider who didn't know Ko really captured how the school age population (if I can be taken as a representative sample!) of Castleton felt about Ko. We cherished him.

—Carlie E. Banks

Cutting the Necktie

I grew up in Castleton with Ko, from whom I learned so many things. He helped me in playing baseball, because as you know he was fond of many sports.

He also helped me to make decisions. I can remember one time in particular when I needed advice. I had a necktie that was too long. I asked him if he would look at it and make a suggestion. He said very little but he took some shears and cut the tie in half. When I sewed it back together, the tie was the length I wanted. I rarely asked him any advice about my ties after that.

Ko helped me to gain confidence in myself. I always knew he had confidence and that I could learn to take care of myself in whatever came up. That means a lot these days when things are real tough. I will always be grateful that Ko gave me confidence in myself.

—Andy Johnson

"Big Brother" Kept His Promise

In June, 1956, I graduated from high school, and that September I would be entering Castleton Teachers College as a member of the freshman class.

One morning in early July of that year, I received a letter with the name "Sok Nam Ko" neatly written in the return address corner. I had read Ko's story in an article in the local newspaper, but had forgotten about it in the excitement of high school graduation and college preparations until his letter arrived that day. He explained the Big Brother/Big Sister Program at Castleton, and went on to describe the college, its programs, and student life there. He ended by emphasizing the fact that he would gladly answer whatever questions I might have, and that he would try to help me in any way possible to feel more at home when I arrived on campus. Three characteristics of that letter impressed me then, and continue to impress me now, thirty-six years later—the deep kindness and sincerity with which it was written and the clarity with which everything in it was explained and expressed.

I wrote to Ko shortly thereafter, thanking him for writing to me, and asking some questions concerning the college that had been on my mind. He promptly replied with the same clarity of the first letter and answered every question fully and completely.

When I arrived at the college that Sunday in September, feeling somewhat lost and apprehensive, Ko was there to meet me. Shaking my hand warmly, he wanted to know if I had been comfortably settled in the dormitory, assuring me that I would find Morrill House a warm and friendly place to live, and generally putting me at ease without being overly protective or overwhelming me with a flow of words. He was quiet, kind, and reassuring.

Throughout that first year he always went out of his way when we met, to inquire as to my well-being, and to ask how studies and college life were going for me—he truly cared.

Ko's Senior year at Castleton was my Sophomore year, and that spring I had been assigned a leading role in the Castleton Players major dramatic production. Through a lot of hard work, I managed to achieve some success in the part. After the opening night performance, Ko came backstage to congratulate me. Smiling, he shook my hand, telling me how much he had enjoyed the play, and complimenting me on my acting. That compliment and handshake have always meant a lot to me, because Ko did not give compliments lightly. When you received one from him, you knew he thoroughly meant every word.

For those two years I knew him at Castleton, Ko, in his kind way and friendly manner, proved to be a "Big Brother" who kept every promise.

—Don Boardman
Ko's Little Brother at Castleton Teachers College

A Spirited "Me Got It!"

Although I did not know Ko very well when he was a student at Castleton State College, I heard a great deal about him through my parents and others who were associated with the institution at that time. My father, Robert C. White, joined the English Department in 1954. All of the professors of that gentler era liked Ko very much. He impressed them with his zest for life, and his determination. Some of the professors of that time were Charles Wright, Chandler Mosher, and Elizabeth Hale. Dean Florence Black was in her prime.

A friend in Fair Haven recalled a few days ago that when Ko played on the Castleton State College baseball team, he had a tendency to play more than one position at a time! Perhaps he was skillful in shading the hitters as an outfielder, but in any case he chased after many more fly balls than he should have, calling out, "Me got it! Me got it!" He occasionally missed one, but he certainly had spirit.

—Christopher C. White
Math Department, Castleton State College

Hang in There; You'll Get a Second Wind

Trying to go back thirty-six years ago and recall some times when I participated in cross country with Ko makes me wish I could be that slim again, but I can dream, can't I? However, I do remember one of my first conversations with Ko.

When you're running, you have a mind set that tells you this is one tough, sometimes grueling sport! Runners started out at the old Castleton College Field House. (I believe the new pool facilities have replaced this building.) Each individual runner would start there and head out of the village on South Street. Eventually we would turn left going by Staso, trying to somehow pace ourselves. The run was four or five miles if my memory is correct. I can remember slowing down to a walk when we were in the Ellis Orchards. That was the area where most of the runners had a chance to talk. It was here that, for the first time, Ko and I had a conversation which revealed one of his philosophies. Neither one of us were prolific conversationalists, but I believe I had an edge on Ko!

Having never had cross country or track in high school, I wondered if this sport was for me. Ko and I were walking together to rest for a short time before we embarked again on running. I think psychologically he was trying to encourage me by mentioning that a runner often gets a second wind. His idea was, "Hang in there and continue not only for the good of the team but more importantly for yourself."

I went on to be a member of the team and, yes, I did get a second wind in several of the races. We had five meets that year winning three and losing two. Ko and I usually ran nip and tuck just like the picture shows in the '57 Castletone Yearbook. This is a cherished memory from the past.

—John Kelley
Castleton Teachers College

Part of the Package of Good Times

Whenever John and I reminisce, the good times of the past were at Castleton. Ko and Elaine were always "part of the package" of the good times during those years. From the Freshmen year when Elaine and I were roommates and John and Ko were on sports teams together all through school, we shared times that hold good memories. We have always been glad that we had a chance to visit together occasionally since then, too. One particular evening I can remember was when Ko demonstrated his culinary skills. He was especially capable in preparing Korean dishes.

It was wonderful to be able to spend time together at the 30th Reunion from our graduation from Castleton. Reliving past good times and catching up on years since then was a highlight of 1990 for us.

Ko's life has been an inspiration to so many people. He overcame the hardships of his early life and made a good life for himself here in our country. Besides overcoming many obstacles regarding his personal and professional life, he and Elaine had a lasting marriage with commitments to family, young people world-wide and many community projects. There is no question but that he will be greatly missed.

—Cecilia Kelley
Castleton Teachers College

FROM THE "CASTLETONE"

The college yearbook called the "Castletone" listed the accomplishments of each student year by year. When I was a freshman (1954-1955) my list was as follows:

Vice-president of freshman class, Science Club, Basketball, Cross Country, Baseball

As a sophomore (1955-1956) the list included:

Social Recreation Committee, Basketball trip to Montreal, Cross Country, Vice-president of sophomore class

In the 1956-1957 issue when I was a junior, the yearbook read:

Athletic Association Officer, Cross Country, Junior Varsity Basketball

In my senior year (1957-1958) the yearbook included my accomplishments for all four years:

Social Recreation Council 2

Science Club 1,2

Athletic Association Vice-President 3

Cross Country 1,2,3,4 & Co-Captain 2
J.V. Basketball 1,2,3,4
Baseball 1,2,3,4
Ski Club 3
Winter Carnival Co-Chairman 3
Snow Sculptor 2
Class Vice-President 1,2
Class Weekend 1,2,4
Good Citizenship Award 2
Alpha Lambda 1
Governor's Conference 2,3
Orientation Committee 2
Athletic Association Council 2

The yearbook also gave this quote from me: "Strive on, strive on; 'till you reach your goal."

—Sok Nam Ko

Not Afraid of Work

While in Castleton, Ko was involved in a variety of jobs all designed to help out his sponsor family as well as to earn what he could at this young age. He seemed eager to serve others. His first job in the United States was working as a clerk in the general store owned and operated by his sponsors. He worked about three hours during each week day and sixteen to twenty hours on Saturdays and Sundays.

One summer he worked at Staso, a company in Castleton which made slate granules for roofing.

Also while a resident of Castleton, Ko served local schools and Rotary Clubs by being a guest speaker at various functions. Among his many engagements, he spoke about his life in Korea in West Rutland on March 12, 1956 and in Wallingford on September 10, 1956; thus enriching his capabilities as a public speaker. This was the beginning of his contacts with the Rotary!

In 1956, Ko attended the National Aquatic School under the auspices of the American National Red Cross held at Camp

Cross-Country team at Castleton.

Tevya in Brookline, New Hampshire. He completed courses in First Aid, Swimming, Water Safety Instruction, Boating, Canoeing and Camp Waterfront Leadership. During that summer he served as Waterfront Director, swimming instructor and lifeguard at a camp near Albany, New York.

While enrolled as a student at Castleton State College, Ko attended summer school at Columbia in 1957, taking a Language Course entitled, "American English." During this time in New York he earned money by working as a waiter. He was willing to work at most any job which would bring in a little money!

On December 16, 1957, Ko began his military service here in the United States by enlisting in the U.S.A.R., Corp of Engineers. Then about the time of his graduation from Castleton, he was on active duty at Fort Dix, N.J. during 1958-1959.

—Helen Eldred Smith

Army Issue Khakis and Ankle Height GI Shoes

Among my memories is the year that I taught with George Harrington in Plainfield. We were quite opposite in character, but did become close friends. He was a go-getter every day and was a fellow of great potential.

Later, in 1949 when I brought seventeen-year-old Mitsuo Kawamoto to the states for an education, George was very impressed and perhaps this gave him the idea that it might be something he'd like to do.

So while in Korea, George met Sok Nam Ko and offered him a chance to come to the United States to attend school. When young Ko arrived in Castleton, all his worldly possessions were not even enough to fill a duffle bag. As I remember first meeting Ko, he was wearing army issue khakis and ankle height GI shoes.

"Sok Nam Ko of Korea, who came to America after the Korean War, holds his Castleton Teachers College diploma. Ko, sponsored while in the states by Atty. and Mrs. George Harrington of Castleton, will spend six months in the Army."

One weekend I brought him to my sister's home in Plainfield. Although I followed his progress in later years, there was not much actual contact between us. Ko knew that I had indirectly influenced part of his life and always showed his respect and gratitude for that.

We all know that he applied himself diligently. None of us would have fared so well if we had gone to Korea to carve our careers. Having accomplished so much is proof enough as to how well he succeeded in this land so far away from his early home.

—Bob Pierce, Kahgawa, Japan

CHAPTER III

TEACHING AND THEN A CHANGE OF DIRECTION

From 1959 to 1963, I taught junior high school science and math and senior high school general science in South Burlington, Vermont. While living in Burlington, I visited hospitals as many times as I could to observe physicians. In this way I felt I could learn the real meaning of medicine. Even though I had a profession as a teacher established, I wanted the medical profession badly enough so that I gave up teaching and returned to undergraduate college for pre-medicine to satisfy my curiosity in that field. I was eager to accomplish my lifetime ambition and to make myself more useful to the world.

—Sok Nam Ko

In 1958-1959, Ko was on active duty in the army at Fort Dix, N.J. and received his Honorable Discharge U.S.A.R. on December 22, 1963.

Ko attended the University of Vermont in Burlington and graduated with a B.S. degree in 1963. His major was zoology and minor was chemistry. While at UVM, he received a National Science Foundation Grant for Physics in 1960. The following year, he attended Howard University in Washington, D.C. on a National Science Foundation Grant for Biological Science.

SUNDAY, SEPT 20, 1959

SOK NAM KO, a former South Korean and assistant to UN artillery unit in the Korean War, is now a successful American teacher. Mr. Ko teaches the youngsters of the South Burlington Central School math and science. James McClusky Jr., 13 and Eileen Shepard, 12 daughter of Mr. and Mrs. Howard Shepard are in the new teacher's classes. He is a graduate of Castleton State Teachers College. — NEWS Photo — Bob Callahan.

Because acquiring an education is so expensive while attending college at UVM, Ko continued to search for ways to earn money. He served as a baby sitter and lawn boy in one home. For a while he worked as a store clerk in the First National Store in South Burlington. The store was one-half mile from his apartment so the walk added to his work hours at the store.

For a summer or two, he worked as a Camp Director, where he was responsible for a program for approximately twelve girls at a Camp Fire Girls Camp.

While in South Burlington, Ko coached intermural basketball and Little League Baseball. He also served as water-front director and swimming instructor for various Vermont summer camps.

VERMONT SUNDAY NEWS

South Korean Teacher Likes Vermont Post

By HUNTER HOLLOWAY
Daily News Staff Writer

A young South Korean has taken full advantage of the opportunities found in Vermont. The youth, who aided American servicemen during the Korean War, is now a teacher in South Burlington.

Sok Nam Ko, born Nov. 5, 1934 in Kaeseong, Korea, was a civilian employe of a U. S. Army artillery unit when United Nations troops were sent to Korea.

Coming to this country in 1952, he was sponsored by George W. Harrington, an attorney and commander of the American Legion. Ko then attended Fair Haven High School two years and went on to Castleton Teachers College for four years. After graduation, he took several science and math courses at the University of Vermont.

Now, as a fully-qualified teacher, he is teaching the South Burlington youngsters math and science at the Central School on Williston Rd. Mr. Ko has 20 "home room" students and about 80 who attended his classes. He has mastered the English language and has no difficulty expressing himself to his pupils.

Though he has taught before as a substitute teacher, Ko started his first full time reading position Monday. He believes that he has a "good group" of students and is enjoying his work.

Comparing the two systems of education, Korean and American, he said, "The American student has much more choice in his selection of subjects. We, of Korea, have been desperately trying to catch up with the educational standards of the United States."

Ko explained that though physical punishment was permitted in Korean schools, it is not necessary here in Vermont as the students have a thirst for knowledge. He handles his discipline problems by keeping his students after school is out.

Ko is a supporter of the General Douglas MacArthur philosophy concerning the Korean War. "I feel, as most Asiatics, that President Truman made a great mistake when he demanded that General MacArthur pull the UN forces back from North Korea. He violated the basic military strategy by losing the advantage of the attacking force."

And in Laos? "It looks to me as if it will be another Korea. The Communists want all they can get. I hope the U. S. will not stand for this impertinence and violation of personal freedoms."

Ko had to economize when it came to furnishing his home. Since necessity is the Mother of Invention, he became adept at repairing broken down furniture that he sometimes found at a local dump.

Because of his multilingual capabilities, he served as a translator for a chemistry professor at UVM in 1959. Ko could read and translate Japanese and Korean. Therefore, he quite frequently served others as an interpreter.

Besides this variety of jobs, Ko also did work related to home maintenance such as house painting.

During the summer of 1959 Ko worked in the home of the President of WCAX doing whatever jobs were needed.

—Helen E. Smith

"They Sit Real Good Now"

Ko lived in our home for about a year when he was teaching in the South Burlington School System. The arrangement was bed and board in return for doing various odd jobs.

At the time he was teaching there, South Burlington was predominantly a rural community and, since World War II was only recently ended, I wondered how an Asiatic would be received in this very parochial town.

One evening at dinner I asked him what subject he was teaching. It was science and he had been given the section of the slowest learners. So I asked him if he was having any trouble with discipline in the class. He replied, "Well, not now."

To which I said, "Well, you *did* have some trouble then?"

Ko said, "Oh, yes, you know some of them, they think they are big shots. They slouch in their seats and pay no attention."

I responded, "Well, what did you do about that?"

He said, " I tell them, you don't like your seat? Go kneel in corner." Then rather shyly he continued, "They think very easy. After awhile their knees, they hurt. Sit real good now!"

I will never forget this ingenious solution to a discipline problem.

—Stuart Martin
President of WCAX TV
Burlington, VT

Determined and Strong-Willed

Our first recollections of Sok were at the Mary Fletcher Hospital in Burlington, Vermont around 1960. He came to talk to Sanghwan about entering the medical school there.

Sok was a very determined and strong-willed person. Sanghwan says he was typical of the people who came from that part of Korea.

Sok was remarkable in so many ways. He was hard-working, stubborn and when he set a goal he got there. Of course, he had a wonderful helpmate in the name of Elaine.

—*Sanghwan and Inja Lew*
Friends in Burlington

Entering the Field of Dentistry

I was accepted in the freshman class at Temple University in 1964 in Philadelphia, Pennsylvania. It was a most unforgettable day in my life. To me dentistry was a very important and responsible profession. I wanted to believe and see that my being on the earth was not just an unexpected accident but a worthwhile and meaningful event. During my junior year, I found oral surgery to be very exciting and challenging. Many times I volunteered for extra duty to learn more about it. I volunteered for assisting in oral surgery at the Pennsylvania Hospital in Philadelphia for a period of six weeks and decided then to apply for oral surgery at Temple. I graduated from Temple in 1968.

—*Sok Nam Ko*

Peripheral Jobs

During Ko's years in Philadelphia, he had less time for peripheral jobs due to his concentrated dental studies at Temple University. However, he did considerable substitute teaching between the closing of each college year and the end of the high school year. These experiences proved to be very challenging and further convinced him that he didn't care to pursue a career in teaching.

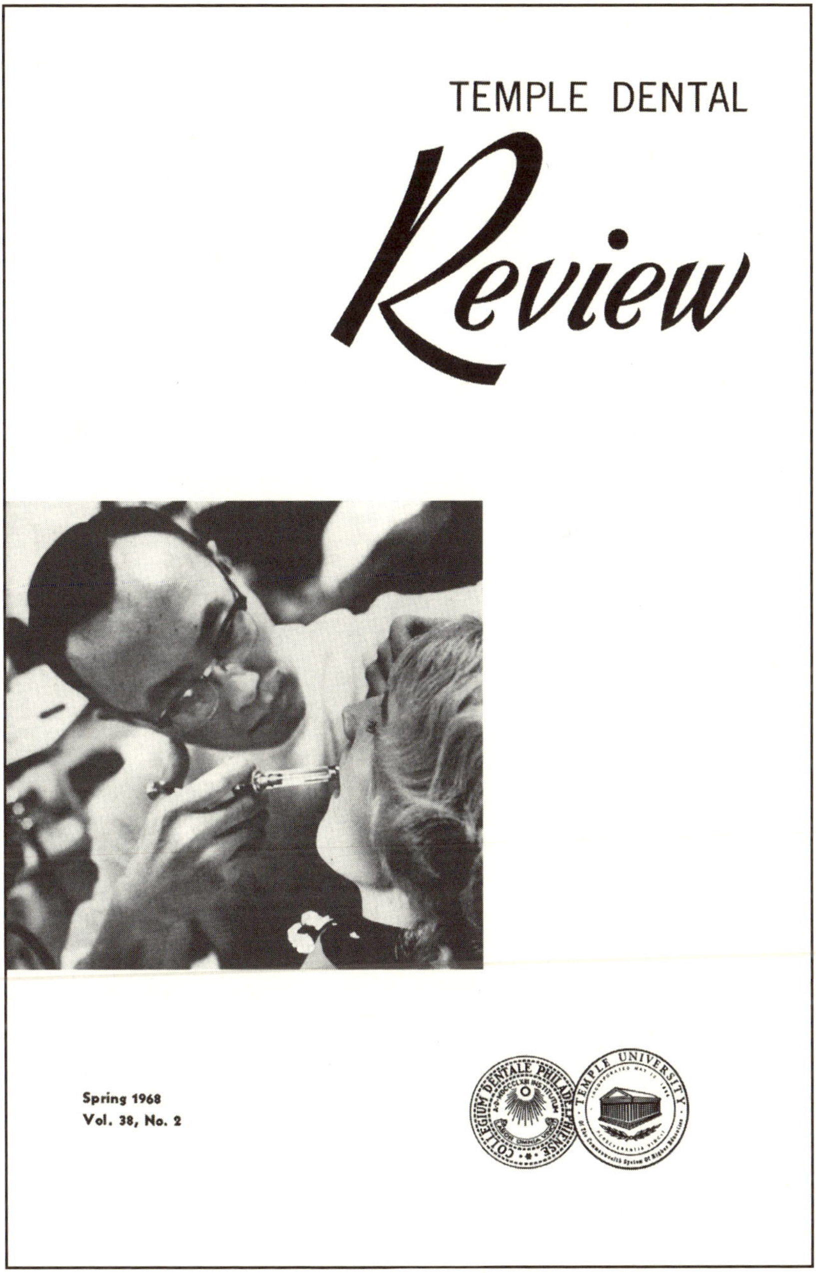

Cover of the Temple Dental Review *Spring 1968.*

Following through on his ability to repair junk-like furniture, like he did in Burlington, he showed his fraternity brothers how adept he was at upholstering the club house furniture. Dexterity with his hands was evident long before he demonstrated such skills in the dental world.

One summer he moved his family up to North Creek, New York and hired out with a company building the Northway. Ko's job was driving a water truck. As the countryside was cleared of trees, brush and other debris, the refuse was burned. Ko's work on the water truck was to control the fires which were set by the day crews as they cleared the land. This construction job was very different from any of his previous summer work, but Ko adapted quickly to this change of pace.

—Helen E. Smith

A Trip Down Memory Lane

Not so very long ago, a gentleman passed through my door; he wanted to say hello to the Dean, who was his teacher many years ago.

I am the Secretary and Assistant to the Dean, but when I greeted the visitor who stood in front of me, my thoughts drifted back to when I was the Secretary to the Chairman, Department of Physiology and the man he came to see that day chaired that department.

Dr. Ko was recognized by me immediately as "sophomore dental student, Sok Nam Ko" and I began to reminisce with him about what I will always feel were special students. I use the word "special" because I remembered how most of the students seemed so committed to and serious about their dental education.

When I told Dr. Ko I remembered him and why, a smile came to his face. I guess we both took a brief walk down "memory lane" as our thoughts drifted back, mine to the many names and faces that passed my way back then; for you see it was before the age of computers and my responsibility was to keep the grade book or sometimes help a student check on a perceived grade discrepancy. His thoughts drifted perhaps to many hours spent in the lab or at home studying for what would eventually be the final achievement—the D.D.S. degree.

Dr. Martin Tansy greeted and also immediately recognized Dr. Ko. He had taught what was considered to be a tough but fair course when Sok was a dental student. However, after most students passed their boards and graduated, they admitted two things; first, the course prepared the student well for boards and secondly, they were proud of their scholastic achievement. Dr. Ko was such a person, I'm sure.

As I said goodbye to Dr. Ko and told him how very proud he and his family should be, I could see that indeed he was.

—*Rosann Souders*
Secretary and Assistant to the Dean
at Temple University

Ko, the Upholsterer

There are two little incidents which I recall that will tell you something about his resolve. One involves a simple incident at the fraternity house (Delta Sigma Delta) when we were trying to make the place presentable. There was an old chair there. It was torn and tattered and looked hopeless to me. Ko bought some type of cloth or fabric and began tacking a new covering on the chair. In what seemed like five minutes, he had this old chair looking like new. I was amazed at his speed and the fact that, when the job was done and looking so good, he merely nodded and went on to his next project. No "plodder" was Sok Nam Ko!

Another thing I remember is his persuasive power. I was renting on Park Avenue next door to the Ko family. I was 26 or 27, married, and had been supporting myself since age 18. I had not lived in New Jersey, my parents' home and the place of my high school graduation, for eight or nine years. I intended to settle in Pennsylvania and therefore applied for PA residence in order to qualify for lower tuition. Ko applied also. Ko was granted residency status. I was not. Upon graduation, Ko immediately moved to Massachusetts. I settled in PA and have been practicing dentistry here for 23 years. Oh well...

Ko was a special guy!

—*Dr. Pete Richter*
Dental school classmate
and neighbor in Philadelphia

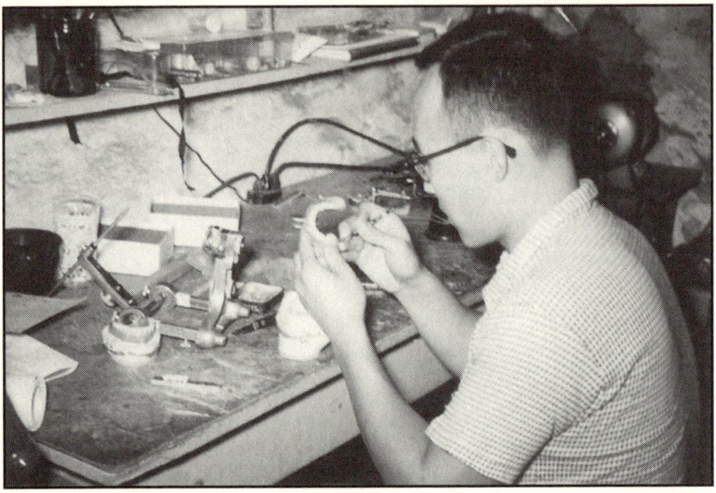

Sok Nam Working during dental school, Philadelphia, November 1966.

Often Doing Things for Others

My years at Temple University are filled with fond memories of Ko. He was a major influence in my life at college. I can well remember studying with him and going over exams in the sciences. He was so kind to help me with lab work. One of his contributions to dentistry was the dexterity of his hands. Not many (if any) of our classmates could match his skilled hands.

Ko was one of the students who made things tolerable in dental school. He worked hard on his own lessons; yet, to the detriment of his own work, he was always willing to help others.

On the lighter side, I can remember playing ping pong with him. Ko was such an excellent player; nobody could beat him.

Then, of course, there were the events related to our personal lives. I can remember baby sitting for Andy and Timmy, who were little pre-schoolers at that time. Their dog, Bootsie, had to have attention sometimes, too.

There were the times when Ko would go to the Philadelphia fish market and bid on lobsters. Then I would enjoy sitting around the family table eating the delicious lobster which had been prepared. More fond memories!

On a more frightening note, Ko had a gasline piped into his basement for use in his dental lab work. With the open flame, it is a wonder he didn't have a major disaster considering how explosive this gas is.

Ko was one of the most interesting people I've ever met. He had a unique personality and was a very pleasant part of my life.

—Tom Gosselin
A close dental school friend at Temple University

Graduation from Temple University, School of Dentistry, 1968.

COMPLETING HIS GRADUATE DEGREE WHILE LIVING IN WEYMOUTH, MASS.

Following my graduation from Temple University in 1968 with a degree of D.D.S., I went to Tufts University School of Dental Medicine and trained at the Boston Veterans Administration Hospital, Boston, Massachusetts. In 1971, I completed my Oral and Maxillofacial Surgery internship and residency.

—Sok Nam Ko

Ko was enrolled at Tufts University School of Dental Medicine, Graduate School of Oral Surgery 1968-1969. At the same time he was doing his internship in Oral Surgery at Boston Veterans Administration Hospital. His residency at the V.A. Hospital was undertaken during 1969-1971. He was a Clinical Instructor in Oral Surgery at Tufts University School of Dental Medicine from 1969-1971.

Saga of Success For Sok Nam Ko

Rutland Daily Herald July 4, 1968

CASTLETON — (Special) — Remember Sok Nam Ko, the pint-sized Korean "displaced person" with a "GI English" speaking vocabulary who in the early 50's surprised everyone by winning a regular berth on the heavyweight varsity football team at Fair Haven Union High School?

Well, he's Dr. Sok Nam Ko now.

He graduated June 14 from Temple University School of Dentistry. In addition to his D.D.S., he received the Gold Foil Society award as the outstanding clinician at the school during 1967-68.

He's the same person who, with the help of U. S. Sen. Winston L. Prouty, R-Vt., successfully survived deportation to his native land.

Dr. Ko was 16 and underweight when he came to Castleton in the fall of 1952 on a student visa for a year with Army Capt. George Harrington, who with Mrs. Harrington "adopted" him as their son.

He had lost his parents in war-torn Korea when Communists destroyed his village. He fled for sanctuary to a U. S. Army camp where Capt. Harrington and others became interested in his welfare and future.

Tutored by Capt. Harrington in Korea, Ko arrived in Castleton able to speak "G.I. English."

DR. SOK NAM KO

He graduated in 1954 from Fair Haven Union High School where, despite his size, he played varsity football and was a candidate for varsity basketball and baseball.

Artistically inclined, he created a life-sized paper-mache elephant for use in a Rutland County GOP political rally.

He next enrolled at Castleton State College, and it was when he accompanied the basketball team to Canada that the question of his legal residence in the United States came to the fore. The issue provided considerable newspaper copy.

When he checked back through customs while returning from the trip, the status of his papers was challenged by Canadian authorities.

Twice Ko went to Washington with Harrington, an attorney, to plea for a renewal of Ko's visa and to make his stay a permanent one.

The battle was eventually won. Later in U. S. District Court in Rutland before Judge Ernest W. Gibson, Ko became a naturalized citizen.

After graduation from Castleton, Ko taught in South Burlington Junior High School and attended the University of Vermont, graduating in 1963 with a bachelor of arts degree in zoology.

Just before the death of Harrington in 1960, Ko married a Castleton State College sweetheart, Miss Elaine Hogaboom of Enosburg Falls. Harrington was best man at the wedding. The Rev. Olof C. Johnson, then pastor of the Castleton Federated hurch, officiated. The Kos have two sons, Andrew, 5, and Timothy, 3.

Dr. Ko has accepted an oral surgery residency at the Boston Veterans Hospital. His first year will be spent at Tufts University School of Dentistry, Department of Oral Surgery.

Mrs. Harrington has remarried. She is now Mrs. William A. Zahnleiter of Castleton.

Between 1969 and 1971 Ko served in the Naval Reserves while at Tufts University School of Dental Medicine. He worked at 1) Chelsea Naval Hospital, Chelsea, MA and 2) U.S. Naval Air Station, South Weymouth, MA. (Complete military record may be found in the Appendix.)

Ko was awarded the rank of Lieutenant Commander on July 1, 1972.

During his years at Tufts University, Ko continued to earn a living in all possible ways, but most of his jobs were now related to his dental career.

Over the years,there were many jobs which contributed to the support of his family and provided funds for his educational expenses. Being involved in this variety of over fifteen different jobs was a demonstration of Ko's ability and willingness to work at most any job that would contribute to accomplishing his goals. Each job served as a stepping-stone to a better life.

—Helen E. Smith

Going to the Navy Yard

Dr. Ko was a happy professional with a pleasant personality, eager to help in things social and professional. The doctor's private practice in Oral and Maxillofacial Surgery was most successful.

We have vivid memories of Sok— his diligence, dedication and ambition to learn!

Our son, Jim, recalls going to the Navy Yard with Sok to select a boat. Sok selected one which needed a heavy trailer. He then decided the boat was too large. To hear Jim tell the story was very humorous!

—Dr. Charles and Betty McCann

Compassion, Caring and Integrity

"Gerry and I always respected Sok for his compassion, caring and integrity. He had an excellent sense of humor, too. We always commended his efforts and aspirations from such humble beginnings. He was a solid citizen! It was a privilege to have worked with him.

—Dr. Salvatore Esposito
Administrator of Dental Unit at Jamaica Plains
Veterans Administration Hospital

L. to R.: Dr. Salvatore Esposito, Dr. Francis Carroll, VA Hospital Administrator, Dr. Dudley White, Dr. Charles McCann.

TWENTY-SIX YEARS IS A LONG TIME!

The first time that I ever saw Sok Nam Ko was shortly after he was chosen to be the second resident at the Veterans Administration Hospital. Dr. Esposito was showing him through the clinic. I remember thinking "great, just what I need, someone else to share what little Dr. McCann left me to do." Dr. Esposito introduced us and Sok gave a little bow.

He returned to the hospital in July and spent the summer before going back to school at Tufts. During the summer we had a lot of time to talk in Mel Prioli's lab. I would eat Mel's Italian sausage and Sok had a cup of noodles. That was the first time that I had ever seen instant soup. It did take him awhile to get me to try that soup.

Sok would spend vacations and Saturday mornings with us at the V. A. Hospital. He was able to see my frustration at assisting and not doing what I felt was enough surgery. At one time I told him that I thought I would quit and reapply to another program. His reply was for us to speak to Dr. Esposito and see if we could resolve the problem and, if we couldn't, we would schedule when Dr. McCann was at Boston City Hospital. Fortunately, the program was due for review by the American Dental Association and Oral Surgery Societies in October. After Sok and I had a private meeting with the reviewer, at which he did most of the talking, the direction of the program changed.

I remember when Sok bid on government surplus boats and ended up with all of the boats, some of which would never float again. He always seemed to be looking for a bargain. I seem to remember that he bought some dental equipment at a surplus sale. It is probably still working in his office.

Our social life was limited, since none of us had any money. But, Mel would come to the rescue and take us fishing on his boat. I do not remember ever catching anything on those trips! Sok loved those trips.

I remember going to the Korean restaurant in Cambridge. It was the only one in the area at that time. (There are now at least two in that area of Cambridge alone.) Sok and Elaine were the only people who knew what we were eating!

When I opened my office in Melrose, Sok asked me to consider joining him in Amsterdam. He offered to take over my loan and buy my equipment (I guess he had a thing for used equipment) if I would consider coming to the Amsterdam area. We even made a trip to look at the area. It is sad that this did not come to pass, because we would have made a good team. But, home has a strong hold on people.

There are times when something or some event reminds me of Sok. I have no sad memories. The only sadness I have is that Gen and I were not able to be there with you and your family when you needed us. However, I know that Sok touched many people and I am sure that you did not lack for friendship and support.

—Dr. Frank McNamara
Senior Resident and friend at Tufts

Captain Ko of the Town River Yacht Club

I met Dr. Sok in the year of 1969 at the Veterans Administration Hospital in Jamaica Plains, Massachusetts. He was a Resident and I was a Senior Dental Technician. It was not very long before a striking friendship began that still remains.

This was also a respected and Doctor-Technician relationship. We worked hand in hand, side by side. Days went into months, months into years with a continuation after. Separation from the V. A. Hospital came as he began his amazing practice in private life and onto my retirement in 1977.

Mel Prioli.

While Dr. Sok was a Resident at the V. A. Hospital, other members of the staff included:

1) Dr. S.J. Esposito, Chief
2) Dr. Charles McCann, Assistant Chief of the Oral Surgery Department (Known to Ko as "Great White Father"—a real athletic sort, really in shape, and with snow white hair)
3) Myself, Carmine M. Prioli, Senior Dental Technician of the Laboratory

I deem it a privilege and an honor in being a part of the memories of Sok's great, humble teachings in every day life. I knew him not only in the Resident and Dental Technician relationship, but also in family get-togethers and in boating and fishing. Besides the times when we fished, we spent many hours in fishermen talk!

I recommended him for membership in the Town River Yacht Club, where we had many good days. He was known as Captain Ko, U.S. Navy. One of our best memories was when he made a few biddings on U.S. Navy surplus boats—Life Boats—26 foot double enders. Sok had bid on all four boats that were up for sale. He, being not one of haste but caution said to himself, "Bid on all four!" So he did and came in with flying colors. Sok, not only got one but all four! Now, he did not only have a boat, he became an Admiral of Doc Ko's Navy. How he made out is his own smart intelligence. Success!

Another one of his strengths was his care of patients. Every one was a challenge. He loved his work. He spent many hours in the Oral Surgery Department of the Operation Rooms at the V.A. Hospital.

Even when he was tired, he could joke. One day after five hours in the O.R. he returned to the clinic just to be approached by a patient who was dressed in a johnny, a bathrobe, V.A. slippers and a fracture splint on his mouth. The patient said, "Hey, Doc! I've been here all day waiting for you!"

Sok replied, "Why, you going some *prace*?" Oh, that man! This really "busted me up."

I, like many of his friends, just loved Sok. If he had any enemies, I would say, "Not him. I loved that guy!"

—Carmine M. Prioli
Senior Dental Technician
Veterans Administration
Hospital

Never Refused to Offer His Help

It was at Tufts University, around the winter of 1969-70, when I first met Ko. I was a lonely bachelor. He invited me to his house in Weymouth, Massachusetts. I had to take a train to get there and he picked me up at the station.

His sweet home was tiny and had a basement because I remember the stairs. It had a kitchen with a booth in the corner. I met his American wife and two playful children: Andrew (1st grade) and Timothy (kindergarten).

I can say that Ko was a man who offered kindly to others. One day he took me on his boat on a fishing trip to the Atlantic Ocean. On the way back he stopped to talk with a family on another boat. They seemed to enjoy staying inside their boat, which I would not like to do at all. There was a young daughter. Ko was talking with them pretty long time by my standards. He liked to chat. I felt he wished me to get the girl, but I was a very reserved person and there was no way that I could move. Ko was considerate.

I left Tufts University for Ontario, Canada in the summer of 1970. When I came back to Tufts University the second time in 1972, Dr. Ko's family had moved to Amsterdam, New York.

In November 1973 I married a Korean girl. Ko was still generous to me and my wife and we were always welcome in his house. He was always busy with his work. I can remember his cooking, making soup by throwing in cabbage and other vegetables.

My wife and I moved to Denver, Colorado in 1975.

Next I had a teaching job at the University of Connecticut, Farmington 1976-78. While there, we had another chance to visit Ko. He used to take me along to the hospital to observe him at work.

One day I pronounced the word "very". Since we don't have "v" sound in Korean, my "v" sound was more like a "b" sound and since we don't have an "r" sound in Korean, my "r" sound was more like "l" sound. Ko kindly pronounced "very" several times. When I was not able to correct my pronunciation, I think he was a little annoyed.

I think he wished me to move to this area. He took me to an old dental office in Johnstown, but I was not interested in going to the country like Amsterdam. My bringing up is not going to the country, instead going to a city.

My wife and I moved back to Denver for 3 years of practice (1978-1981) and then to Saudi Arabia for teaching 5 years (1981-1986). Then we went back to Denver for practice (1986-1991). I sometimes encountered problems regarding oral surgery. For example, a patient kept bleeding after an extraction. I called Dr. Ko for his advice. He was never stingy with his time in helping me. I miss him very much.

—Dr. Han S. Pyo
A friend at Tufts

CHAPTER IV

PROFESSIONAL LIFE IN AMSTERDAM

It is not that I made my mind up overnight and decided to take up the medical profession, but my desire of becoming a doctor has grown since I can remember.

My grandfather was both a farmer and an herb doctor in Korea. I observed him prescribing herbs to many patients when I was young. He checked the patient's pulse, observed the color of his face, tapped the dorsal and ventral portion of the body; then sliced some roots, leaves, and stems of dry plants and gave them to the patient with instructions on how to use them.

My curiosity grew as I grew older and I wondered how he diagnosed and prescribed certain herbs. It was strange and amazing, but we heard that many patients were cured. I questioned him on many occasions about his reasons and methods of diagnoses and prescriptions, but I never received a satisfactory scientific reason or method. His answer was "I just follow what I learned from my father and what the good book prescribes" and then he would show me a thick old book which I didn't know how to read.

—Sok Nam Ko

A Respected and Admired Working Companion as Well as a Dear Friend

When I first met Sok, he was considering coming to Amsterdam to open a dental office. During our visiting he asked many, many questions, trying to be sure that he was making the right decision about establishing a business as an oral surgeon in this area. Among his questions were ones about the operating facilities available and what types of operating procedures were used at our hospitals. I had to admit that I could not answer his many questions, because we had never had an oral surgeon in our city. All that I could tell him was about our dentists who limited their practices to extractions and regular dental work. When patients needed oral surgery, they had to go to Schenectady or Albany. Nobody at our hospitals specialized in setting a broken jaw or broken facial bones.

Sok decided to come to Amsterdam and became the first oral surgeon here. He established an office on Pine Street and eventually moved to 80 Locust Avenue.

As time went on, I became better acquainted with Sok and gradually began working more and more with him. I administered the anesthetic to his patients and assisted him with most of his operations. As a team we understood each other very well and were able to communicate without speaking sometimes.

Sok was a *very hard* worker. It didn't matter who the patients were, he treated everybody the same even if they were on welfare or had no insurance. I admired him for treating patients evenly. It didn't matter who they were, he cared for them.

However, it did upset me when some doctors would send their poor patients to Sok when they knew the patient wouldn't be able to pay a penny. Sok would always take care of the patient. I said, "Sok, I know you want to help everybody but some people are abusing you."

His answer was, "Well, somebody's got to take care of them."

A few times I would get upset with Sok because he was supposed to be at the hospital early in the morning to begin his day of operations. He wouldn't appear and when he did come I would ask, "What happened to you?"

He would say, "I was in the office."

I questioned, "What were you doing in the office at this hour of the morning?

"Well," he said, "Dr. So-and-So's patient was bleeding. The patient called me early this morning and wanted me to help him."

I said, "Was that *your* patient?"

To this he answered, "No."

I added, "You put that patient ahead of your own patients who are waiting here for you. I don't think you should do that."

This is an example of how he tried to serve *everyone* who came to him.

As a hard worker, he put in long days in the operating rooms at St. Mary's and Amsterdam Memorial. During his busy years he would do fourteen or fifteen operations a day. We worked from 7:30 in the morning until 7:30 at night. Sok never seemed to get tired. I found it difficult to keep up with him. Many times I urged him to slow down and not try to do so much!

Sok was a perfectionist and really wanted everything to be just about as perfect as it could be. He loved his work and was happy serving others. It was in his system! He didn't believe in cutting corners, nor did he believe in doing more on the patient than was necessary. His work ethic will be hard to follow as he set a fine example for others.

Sok's dedication to his work was demonstrated through his 24-hours-a-day commitment to his profession. He always responded to a call for help no matter what time of day or when the occasion. He would attend to a patient in the evening, in the middle of the night or early in the morning. Added to this was when he would graciously leave his Thanksgiving Day dinner, family Christmas Day festivities, or other holiday celebrations in order to attend to a patient.

Most of his work consisted of repairing broken jaws, broken cheek bones and occasionally a broken nose. One operation was done to restructure the bones in the face of a patient as a result of a snowmobile accident. The person had run into a barbed-wire fence. Noticing the extent of the damage and the problems involved in repairing the face, Sok remarked, "If I have my way, my boys will never ride around on snowmobiles!"

Another time he had to operate on a woman who was involved in a motorcycle accident in which she was the passenger. All the bones in her face were shattered and

Dr. Emiliano Ilagan.

the reconstruction process seemed impossible. Wanting to be sure that he was doing everything possible for this woman, he consulted with his oral surgery professor, Dr. McCann, in Boston about the case. The doctor came to the hospital and assured Sok he was following the right procedures and made a few suggestions regarding what could be done next.

Sok showed his enjoyment in his work when the events in the operating room were going along smoothly. For one thing he liked to sing. His favorite songs were: "Home on the Range," "Danny Boy," and patriotic songs like, "God Bless America." We harmonized when we knew the lyrics and just hummed along if we didn't. Sok could not pronounce "l's." So the nurses used to make fun of him about this. He understood. He knew they were just teasing him.

The only negative thing about Sok which used to upset me was that he was always late! For him to be on time was rare. He didn't own an alarm clock, nor did he want one. A good many times when I was at the hospital waiting for him to come in for the day, I would have the nurse call Elaine. Her usual answer was, "He's on his way!" This meant he was still at home and probably just barely going down the stairs! Or he might be out in his office working on a patient.

It is commonly known that Sok liked to argue. He and I rarely argued about anything pertaining to our work. If we argued at all it was about politics. He was a die-hard Republican. It wasn't wise to talk against Republicans, because you would create an argument every time. He would argue even if he knew he wasn't right. It didn't matter what the topic was, he had an opinion about it. Even when he didn't have much grounds for his arguments, he used a lot of logic.

While working for so long with Sok, our friendship grew. With the exception of his family, I probably knew him better than anyone else. Our families exchanged visits in our homes and celebrated most holidays together.

The first year he lived here in Amsterdam, we did a lot of fishing. One thing I noticed about Sok was that he had a lot of patience. I don't have patience. When I don't get any bites within an hour, I want to go home. I got bored easily. There wasn't any use in hanging around when the fish weren't biting. I noticed he would stay there for two or three hours without any action and still seem to enjoy himself. That's one thing I noticed about him. He was patient and very persistent.

Over the years, we even traveled to the Atlantic Ocean to go deep-sea fishing a few times; probably three or four times. This was always a bad experience for me. He was good at deep-sea fishing, but every time he threw out the anchor, I would begin to get sick. Because I knew this would surely happen when I went on a boat, the first thing I looked for was the john. My sessions of seasickness amused Sok, but I didn't think they were so funny!

One of my favorite pastimes was to go to the horse races. On occasion I asked Sok to go with me. One time he agreed to go and insisted he wanted to drive. I agreed but warned him we should be there by one o'clock. He was sure that we could get there in plenty of time. Now, what I didn't know was that he was making some other plans. Besides the two of us, he decided to take three boys and to have a picnic during the races. Before going to the race track, he had to stop at the grocery store to buy soft drinks to fill his ice chest and to purchase all sorts of snacks and good things to eat. I discovered that he didn't care as much for the races as I did. It was apparent that he'd rather go on a picnic!

Another time we went to the race track in the evening. While watching the horses in the parade, he said he always picked out a good-looking horse as a possible winner. During a race he disappeared. I wondered where he went, but decided that perhaps he had gone to the men's room. I went looking for him and found that he was right in the middle of a circle standing near a celebrity, Phil Rizzuto, the New York Yankee announcer. Of all things, Sok was having Phil Rizzuto sign an autograph and at the same time was inviting him to be a guest speaker for the Cancer Society! These are some of my memories of going to the track with him. Every time he went with me, he got mixed up with something else besides the races. He wasn't concerned about playing the horses.

The Ilagan Family — Paul, Laurie, Alan, Emil & Gram Mitchell (Laurie's Mom).

All of these fond memories I will always treasure. I have lost a respected and admired working companion and, most of all, a very dear friend!

—Dr. Emiliano Ilagan

A Patient and Compassionate Role Model

I first met Dr. Ko during the summer of 1983. He had heard through my mother that I was in the process of applying to dental schools and was also interested in oral and maxillofacial surgery. Without ever meeting me, he graciously offered me the chance to observe him at work in the office as well as in the hospital setting.

So, early one Monday morning, I nervously set out for 80 Locust Avenue anticipating the man I was about to meet. By the time I had arrived at the office, I had already determined that this Dr. Coe, (for some reason I was thinking Jewish; a stereotype of the profession on my part), would be a rather tall, intense, somewhat abrasive man; the latter two qualities associated with the pressures placed upon him by his speciality. After meeting Kathy at the reception window, I was immediately thrown off kilter when I passed through the door into the operatories and met Dr. Ko, the furthest from my picture of him mentioned above, especially Jewish. As I shook hands with Dr. Ko, I knew that a very enjoyable and informative summer lay ahead. Dr. Ko's low key and relaxed personality can make anyone feel comfortable around him.

We chatted a bit in his cluttered office, getting to know each other. He then handed me one of his smocks, and we ventured to see the first patient. I felt very out of place and I'm sure I looked the part as well. But, Dr. Ko was careful to include me in his observations of the patient so I wouldn't feel further removed than I did. As we finished the morning recall patients, I was feeling a little more at ease. We then moved onto the first surgery of the day; extraction of some 3rd molars, I believe. While the patient was "out," I became better acquainted with Karen, Norma, surgical instruments and blood. Call it beginners luck, but I didn't even get queasy. I was too interested in observing Dr. Ko's gentle but sure technique in retrieving those impacted molars.

As the days rolled along and I became more comfortable with the whole routine, I set into picking up on as much of Dr. Ko's chairside manner and technique as possible. At the same time, I was learning a lot of the dental jargon and becoming familiar with a variety of instruments and supplies.

On the second Thursday, I accompanied Dr. Ko to Amsterdam Memorial Hospital to observe his hospital surgeries. That day it was mostly extractions. However, the Thursdays that followed really caught my interest. I witnessed vestibular deepenings, complete denture implants and most impressive of all, the maxillary and mandibular repositioning surgeries to correct malocclusions caused by skeletal malformations. By the end of the summer, I could think of nothing other than oral surgery.

Probably what impressed me most about Dr. Ko was realized in the years since my summer with him. I have witnessed many of my colleagues' chairside manners. I have seen few who have shown as much patience, compassion and gentle techniques as Dr. Ko's. I always try to keep my patients as happy and comfortable as Dr. Ko seemed to achieve so easily.

My summer in Dr. Ko's office came to a close sooner than I would have hoped, yet not without one of the funnier moments I have experienced—at Dr. Ko's expense. As I recall, Norma, Karen and Dr. Ko were in the process of a 3rd molar extraction case. The patient was "out" due to the NO^2 that Norma was administering. Karen was assisting Dr. Ko and I was forever observing. I found out early in the summer, jokes and good humor were not uncommon while the patient was "under." That day, I had found out that Karen had just recently had a baby and somehow we started on the subject of getting pregnant. Well, as we all know, there is a common but crude saying to describe a woman with child; this being, she's knocked up. I'm not sure whether Dr. Ko wasn't familiar with the saying or just preoccupied with the surgery, but he described Karen's impregnation as, "She's got knocked out." Norma, Karen and myself immediately cracked up at hearing this. As we clued Dr. Ko in, he chuckled and blushed a little as he kept digging for those impacted molars.

Since leaving Dr. Ko's office, I have not been without his assistance and guidance. Thanks to my summer's experience and his written recommendation, my experience with the dental school admission process was very positive and enjoyable. I had been exposed to dentistry first hand and my interviewers, I'm sure, could tell that I was very happy with what I had seen.

Dr. Ko's help had not diminished since my enrolling in dental school. He provided me with various instruments that I needed while in school and supplied me with extracted teeth that I needed for lab projects.

The summer of 1983 was the beginning of my learning experience in the field of dentistry. Dr. Ko made me realize the importance of a firm biological background, a patient and soothing personality and a gentle yet sure technique. I feel that I couldn't have had a better role model than Dr. Ko. I hope that the learning process of 1983 that has since turned into a sincere friendship lasts far into the future. His commitment to his profession along with his upstanding ethics definitely served as a guiding force as I pursued my dental studies. Much of my success at Georgetown I owe to Dr. Ko, trying to achieve the professional standards he lived by.

—Dr. Jon P. Galea
Mentored by Dr. Ko as a pre-dental student

PROFESSIONAL ASSOCIATES

The respect and friendship of members of the medical profession in Amsterdam is often remembered by those who worked with Dr. Ko during his life as an Oral Surgeon. Here are a few of the memories of his professional colleagues.

OUR MEETING AT 149 MARKET STREET

Sok and I met in the waiting room of my office at 149 Market Street. He wanted to know if there was room for an oral surgeon in Amsterdam. I assured him there was and I urged him to come.

He became a good friend, both professionally and personally. He was a tremendous asset to the professional community as well as a provider of oral surgery to his patients. Sok never refused to help a patient. I often wondered about his energy and ability to put in so many hours of work!

—Dr. William Szypula

TRUSTING, HONEST AND A REAL MAN

I first met Sok at a Fulton-Montgomery Counties Dental Society Meeting when he first came to Amsterdam. He was a very trusting and honest person; going out of his way often to see to the welfare of others. He was a real man in my estimation.

Socially, at his various lawn parties, he was a gracious host!

—Dr. W. C. Richardson, Jr.

A SIGNIFICANT LOSS TO THE PROFESSION

Dr. Ko's death is a very significant loss to the profession and to the hundreds of people he served so well, and a tremendous loss to the community of Amsterdam.

I recall very well his move to the area and remember the pleasant meetings we had as the Doctor made plans for his practice in the Montgomery/Fulton Counties.

—Sister Mary Theresa
Former administrator at St. Mary's Hospital

A Hushed Silence in the Emergency Room

As I walked into work yesterday there was a hushed silence in the Emergency Room. Without having to ask, I knew that Dr's fight was over; the caring silence said it all.

Dr. Ko was well respected. Not only is his passing a true loss to his profession, but also to the community. He will be remembered as a gentleman, a model of what human goodness is all about.

—Dr. Anthony Gilstan
St. Mary's Hospital Emergency Room

A Kind, Genial, Loving Man

I worked with Dr. Ko for years on med-surg floors and in the ER at St. Mary's and never did I see Dr. treat anyone, even the most surly patient, with anything but patience and kindness. He was always the gentleman, always helpful and a true charm to work with. He was a kind, genial, loving man who viewed everyone as a human being and gave each person the opportunity to be his best. Because he touched so many lives and made those lives better for that moment, his memory will spur us all on to continue his work and spread human kindness around. I am very proud that I could consider Dr. Ko my friend. I will miss him.

—Dr. Hugh Nowakowski

Tops in His Profession

When Sok came to Amsterdam, I first met him in the Doctors' Room at the Amsterdam Memorial Hospital. I found him to be very intelligent and all-around well educated. He was not only tops in his profession but also an outstanding human being. I always felt it was a privilege of having known him.

—Dr. Max Dreyfuss

A Day Which Stands Out in My Memory

I remember Sok best as I think back two or three years ago to a day when he came bird hunting at our place. It was one of those perfectly clear fall days when everything else seemed perfect as well. After hunting we sat around and had pumpkin pie. Sok, as usual, was in an expansive mood and made that day stand out in my memory as one of such great happiness.

Dr. Ko was widely respected and held in high esteem by both his peers and the hospital staff. We will miss his presence deeply.

—Dr. Russell Cecil
Former President of the Medical Staff
Amsterdam Memorial Hospital

Missed by the Hospital Family and Community

Sok will be sorely missed by the hospital family and the community which he served so devotedly. His memory will be kept alive through his many good works.

—William A. Wilde, Jr.
Board of Trustees
Amsterdam Memorial Hospital

Love of Patients, Profession and Family

I always considered Sok to be a mentor and friend. I learned so much from him during our year together. His love of his family, his profession, and his patients will always be my memory of him. I miss his kindness.

—Dr. Richard Reisman
Friend and former associate

Our Picnic on Boston Commons

Our friendship with Doctor Ko began in early 1972. We were happy to have him on our staff. He was a very capable dentist, well-trained, but above all most concerned about his patients. They came first! As some particular cases presented us with more of a challenge, Doctor Ko was always there to encourage and to help. We would discuss methods and techniques, and when the obstacles had been overcome, he would always have

Amsterdam Memorial Hospital.

a little twinkle in his eye. He always appreciated our efforts.

I always felt very close to Doctor Ko, as our roots could be traced to Vermont. After he had taken care of his patients, our discussion would reach Vermont and all the wonderful things that happen there...like listening to grass grow. Inevitably our visit would turn to the Red Sox and we would agree what should be done to the team that would make them winners! We would always leave our visit with the thought that things would be better next year!! He always had that little chuckle as he left.

I have always felt that I have a "triple whammy" with the Kos. Not only the Doctor was from Vermont, but also his wife and mother-in-law. There has always been a special bond here.

One summer day in the later 1970s, Doctor and Elaine asked Sister Margaret Raphael and me to go to Boston to see the Red Sox. We were delighted, as neither of us had been to a big league park.

Our contingent started out in the early a.m.—two cars. Doctor Ko, Mr. Makarowsky, a couple of the boys and the Sisters were in the station wagon. Mrs. Ko, Mrs. Makarowsky and the rest of the children were in the car. It was also the day of the "Tall Ships" arriving in Boston, so you can imagine the crowds of people we encountered. Mrs. Ko had packed a delicious lunch, which we enjoyed on the Boston Commons. People were taking our pictures. We often wondered what families have us on "home video"! All the fellows and the Sisters went to Fenway Park. The ladies and girls went on a walk to see the Old North Church and other historic sites.

We regrouped about five and drove to a Korean restaurant for supper. Then off to a delightful evening at Harvard to enjoy a stage production—a company of singers from Korea. It was rather late when we left there and proceeded to the turnpike. We were going by Howard Johnson's and Doctor Ko said, "How about a coke?" So, we all went in and sat at the counter. I don't think the waitress knew what was happening. We have had many laughs about this. We arrived home in the wee hours —but had a wonderful time!

We have lost a good friend and the community has lost a great humanitarian. Dr. Ko was most concerned for all, and most generous to all. I am sure his goodness has been rewarded. May his dear soul rest in peace—we miss him.

—Sister Anthony Marie
St. Mary's Hospital
Amsterdam, New York

Always Available to Serve

I can't help but recall the many times Dr. Ko demonstrated to our staff at St. Mary's and the patients under his care that he was always available. He was a true professional in every sense of the word. He was global in caring for patients and was ready to serve regardless of the time of day, day of the week, on call or not on call.

Robert Louis Stevenson once said that a man is a success who has lived well, has filled his niche and accomplished his task, who leaves the world better than he found it, who never lacks appreciation of earth's beauty or fails to express it, who looks for the best in others and gives the best he has. All of these were accomplished by Dr. Ko in a very short space of time.

—Sister Margaret
Head Nurse in the Operating Room
St. Mary's Hospital
Amsterdam, New York

My Letter to Sok Nam Ko

It is now almost 2-1/2 years since the death of my friend and mentor Sok Nam Ko, only now am I capable, willing and ready to write to him. You see, since that moment in time I too ceased to exist emotionally. Only with passing time and months of counseling and the grace of God can I talk to you, my friend, Sok.

Death is a strange phenomenon that I didn't quite understand. At the time of your death I lacked the skills to deal emotionally with your death. I asked God how he could possibly want to take such a wonderful person as you. You were one of the finest people I have ever had the unforgettable pleasure of knowing. Together we shared life. We shared life by talking, listening and communicating our pleasures, troubles and concerns. Each trusting the confidence of the other, each respecting the profession we had chosen and the help and advice that came with years of experience. Sok, you were truly an amazing person, so full of energy that your diverse interests astonished me. How could I or anyone be as successful as you were in your personal life, private endeavors and professional career? You were born to be an example to all that despite seemingly insurmountable obstacles one person alone can make a difference.

I know, Sok, that your life was full of struggles and suffering yet you always kept an optimistic outlook on life and its many challenges. You were always willing to stop and listen and when appropriate you were there to give advice. Thank you for sharing your beliefs and opinions. (And by the way you never ran out of opinions.) But they were good ones, well thought out before you offered them up for discussion. Rarely did Sok Ko have a harsh word to say about any of the people who had mistreated him, yet anyone who mistreated Sok Ko did not truly know him the way that I and many others knew him. To know him was to love him. Sok, you were an extremely generous man. You not only gave of your time, money, and resources but you also shared yourself with others that they might be encouraged or inspired to help themselves or others as you so exemplified. It is with great admiration and pleasure that I had the opportunity to know you and to share life with you. Your constant concern for the well being of others stands as a monument of remembrance to me as I proceed along in my journey of life.

St. Mary's Hospital.

I will always cherish the moments that my conscious mind remembers and can only hope that any unconscious memories will continue to surface.

I especially remember our trip to New York City where I was introduced to Korean cooking. It was there that I first experienced kimchee. I remember our trips in search of new hunting grounds. But they weren't so much trips in search of new hunting places as they were trips into life. I especially remember our trip to Ft. Plain in search of a place to experience the comraderie of hunting. Instead we spent most of our time talking to the Klock family on their farm. Yes, the wife had been a patient of yours and had invited you to hunt on their farm. But you came not to hunt, but to talk, share and experiencc their way of life with them and me. And, oh yes, there must be dinner on the way home even though it was late we still must not waste any of life's precious time to share good food and conversation with each other and in this particular case sharing life with a youngster, my son along for the ride. Your compassion for children was unremitting. It was so reassuring to know that you would take care of me and my family whenever the need arose that we needed dental or surgical care. But tell me, that memory of yours, how did you remember all the people and all their names and what you had done for them and the stories they told you and the relationships between them? Yes, relationships between them, that were so important to you, Sok, as you struggled to find your past relationships in Korea. How difficult that must have been for you, but yet how rewarding it must have felt to have found your biological family after such a long search. Only through your outstanding trait of perseverance were you able to finally meet and share once again with those whom you loved and missed so dearly.

Never did you let go of your culture and identity. Always you will be remembered as one who persevered through your will and convictions.

Sok, you touched many people's lives and always with such gentleness, patience and understanding that I marveled how you made time for everyone. For surely there must have been sacrifices. How could one person accomplish all that you set out to do? I know you had help and thank God for all of those people who guided you along and instilled in you, values, convictions, belief in what's right, fair, in family and in an understanding and love for all people of different ethnic and cultural backgrounds. You lived a very humble man with an insatiable appetite for life. Your dedication to helping less unfortunate people was pursued by you on a daily basis. I will never forget the times that you helped me and my family asking nothing in return. I still can remember those early morning breakfasts during hunting season when it was still dark outside and the kitchen of the Ko house was the meeting area in preparation for the hunting day yet to come. Here it was that Elaine and Sok would prepare a feast that would nourish us for the rigors of the day's hunt. How different and sometimes funny Sok would appear dressed in his fluorescent orange jacket, pants and hood with only that smooth, dark-skinned round face with those dark angled eyes showing through. It was a sight quite atypical of most hunters in upstate New York. Yet Sok carried himself with such poise and humility that it was easy for him to fit in anywhere.

Sok Ko, you were a true ambassador of life. May those who truly knew you continue to carry with them your spirit of togetherness. I am thankful that God brought you to Amsterdam, N.Y. and that I and my family had the pleasurable experience of being taught about the goodness that life had to offer by one of the great educators of my lifetime. Until we meet again, I will not forget the mark that you left upon me for its impression will always be there. May your wonderful family always remember that you have only temporarily left them behind and that they might feel your presence wherever they go, in whatever decisions they make and always strive to live life as fully and honestly as you.

Your friend,

—*David May*
Pharmacist. St. Mary's Hospital
Amsterdam, N.Y.

Hunting and Fishing Trips with Ted

Ko and I went on several fishing and hunting trips together; these truly showed Sok in his glory. Usually there were at least four of us. One time, Rocco Conte, Earl Van Arnem, Sok and I went catfishing on the Champlain River. We had an arrangement with a landowner who allowed us to launch our boats from his shoreline and park our motorhome on his property. We drove up into Whitehall and stopped at the supermarket to get provisions for an overnight stay. We all went in and everyone chose what they thought we needed. Sok, of course, picked several different kinds of fruit and candy. (He was known for picking up more munchies than we were ever able to finish.) He also couldn't be deterred from paying when we got to the checkout. We had to threaten to leave him at the store before he would let us pay our share.

When we reached the launch site, Sok discovered that he knew the property owner and members of his immediate and distant family. (It never failed, Sok always knew someone wherever we went.) What a memory!!

We launched late in the afternoon and usually fished all night using two boats, two guys in each boat. Sok paired off with Earl; Rocco and I were in another boat. We used chicken liver which we left out in the sun for a day or so as bait. This decaying mess must be strung around the hook and ever so gently, cast into the river.

During the course of the night Rocco and I heard various lamentations from Earl: "Damn Sok!! Are you in the trees again??" or "Oh, xxxx!!" This is the case when Sok, who never cast gently, flipped that raunchy chicken liver a little too hard and most of it landed on Earl. Remember, this was in the dark of night on the river, so we used lanterns which attracted every bug in the upstate New York—Vermont area. At one point Sok commented about the number of bugs and called to us to see if we had bugs, too. Rocco, who could barely open his mouth without bugs climbing in, answers: "Bugs? No, we don't have any bugs at all." To which Sok says, "Oh, then we must be by a sewer pipe," and tells Earl to move the boat. That same night it started to rain around 2:00 a.m. and Rocco and I found some shelter under a bridge where we waited out most of the weather. Sok and Earl, however, fished through the rain. We all got back to the motorhome about the same time. (The motorhome was a 1974 Ford pick-up with a camper body that someone had built at home.) It was functional because all we had to do to clean it was hose it out when we got home.

When we finished fishing, we all climbed out of our wet clothes and found a comfortable spot to sleep in the camper—no easy task. Sok said it smelled so bad that he would rather sleep outside in the rain, and he did.

Another insane fishing trip was out of Belmar, New Jersey in January. The temperature offshore was about 20 degrees. It was the same crew: Rocco, Earl, Sok, and a few others. We spent part of the night at a motel and arrived at the party boat at 3:00 a.m. expecting to be the first ones there, but found all the good spots already taken. Rocco and another fellow began thanking Sok for taking them on such an enjoyable field trip from the "home." They went into great depth about their lives at the "home", their treatment, and how they didn't want to go back. They acted slightly demented and Sok just smiled and went along with it nodding his head. We ended up with a good section of the boat to ourselves. Good thing we did because Rocco had served ham-salad sandwiches the night before and everyone's digestive systems had been adversely affected (We were sure that he left them out in the sun the day before.) Sok, of course, was unaffected (I truly believe that he could eat anything), and even had another one on board, which made the rest of us even sicker. At one point Sok hooked a big one and started to reel him in, but just as it got to the boat, it would take off on a spectacular run. This happened several times and lasted about half an hour. Eventually someone realized a fellow on the other side of the boat was undergoing the same drama, but in reverse. Sok wouldn't believe it, refusing to let his line loose. The other fellow wouldn't either, so it took awhile to convince one of them to cut his line. But boy, that fish really gave him a fight.

The muskie Ko did catch—46 inches and 26 pounds.

Sok and I and my son, Andrew, fished Muskie Lake together many times during the summer, with Andrew ranging in age from about 8 to 12. In my mind's eye I see Sok at the bow casting with set-ups that only he thought would work—and often they did. Sometimes he fished with a fly rod and Andrew would help him untangle himself from the line when it fell all around him. You could easily tell what the temperature was by checking how much of his clothing Sok had removed. He would start in the cold morning air all bundled up, but by late afternoon he'd strip down to his skivvies. Obviously he had no problems with false modesty.

We hunted together for several years. I can remember two specific occasions.

Once he went out on watch at 6:00 a.m. on a snowy morning in his camouflaged white outfit. When he didn't return to the truck by ten, I went to look for him and found him fast asleep sitting under a tree. I almost missed him since he blended in so well with the background. He was just resting his eyes for a minute!

Another time Sok shot at a deer which he said was jumping a fence heading into the woods. When we all went down to look we found a recently killed fox shot through the rear. Sok was convinced that someone else had shot the fox and made us go into the woods to look for the blood trail of the deer. There was no trail, but he never would admit to shooting that fox, though any other scenario was unlikely.

When Ko made up his mind, that was it!!!

—Dr. Ted Marciniszyn

Not Successful at Salmon Fishing

Some of my memories of Sok were events that took place around the summer of 1985. They are typical of my recollections of my associations with him.

One of Sok's many varied interests was fishing. He once caught a muskellunge in the St. Lawrence River. He fished for bass and walleyes in the Sacandaga Reservoir and catfish in the Champlain Canal.

A fishing group that I belonged to had an opening on our annual Atlantic salmon fishing trip in the summer of 1985. The trip would include driving to Montreal, flying to Newfoundland, driving to the northern tip, a ferry across the straits of Belle Isle to Labrador and a jaunt overland to the Old Fort River for a week of salmon fishing. Knowing Sok's love of fishing and even greater love of a good adventure, I invited him to go with us. He accepted, knowing full well that he knew nothing of fly fishing, which was the manner used in attempting to catch a salmon.

I took Sok down to Brookwood Sporting Goods Store in Rexford and we got him outfitted with rod, reel, line, flies and all the other things that went with it. Of course, on the way home we had to stop for lunch at the Golden Dragon for some shrimp in black bean sauce, compliments of Sok.

In July of 1985, we headed up the Northway, our party of six, toward Montreal and the first leg of our safari. The journey progressed nicely and Sok took in all the sights with the rest of us up the coast of Newfoundland, across the Straits of Belle Isle, past floating remnants of ice bergs, and numerous pelagic birds, to Labrador and the dock at Blanc Sablon. We proceeded to the fishing camp, settled in and commenced fishing. Sok, not being familiar with fly fishing, had a hard time casting the fly. I tried to coach him about not letting the rod drop too far behind him on his back cast. It seemed like each time he cast he would drop his fly on the rocks behind him on his back cast. When we would inspect his fly, invariably the hook end had been broken off on the rocks. I would try again to show him how to avoid doing that and he would seem to get it. Then, I would step away and soon Sok would be right back at his old way, slapping the fly into the rocks on his back cast. He could be stubborn!

Sok fished hard all week and immensely enjoyed the spruce grouse, osprey, muskrat and martins that showed around us almost daily. Sok never hooked, much less landed, a salmon all week but he had a ball. He had so much enthusiasm for the whole experience—such as was his way.

Sok and I never got to fish together again, but I will remember fondly that week together up in Canada.

—Roger L. Miller, M.D.

NURSES AND SECRETARIES

Others who worked closely with Dr. Ko were the nurses and secretaries, who shared their thoughts about him.

So Kind and Caring to His Staff and Patients

The time that I spent working in Dr. Ko's office will always be remembered because he was such a special person—so kind and caring to all of us and to his patients. I'm very proud to have been one of the first people to work with him when he first came to Amsterdam. We spent many long, hard-working hours in the office, but we always had fun and there was always something that he could teach us.

—Diane Snell
Dental Assistant

Respected Professional, Educator, Employer and Friend

Dr. Sok Nam Ko was a true professional, educator, employer and respected friend. My husband and I feel privileged to have known him and to have shared a part of his life.

—Jean Cassetta
Receptionist and Secretary

Trained as a Dental Assistant Under Dr. Ko

I am presently a dental hygienist for Dr. Bialobok in Fonda. Back in the summer of 1973, when Diane Snell worked for Dr. Ko, I had the opportunity to train as a dental assistant under Dr. Ko. He helped me to get started in the dental field. He was very kind, helpful and understanding.

—Betty Devost Sanders

A Gentle Manner and Beautiful Smile

Seeing Dr. Ko in the Amsterdam Hospital X-ray Department, where I work, and his interest in patients and caring for all will always be remembered, as well as his gentle manner and beautiful smile.

—Jane Bramer

A Well Respected Gentleman

Those of us who worked with Dr. Ko will miss him. He was a gentleman in the very best sense of the word. So many of the nurses have spoken of the kindness he showed to them and their families. All who knew him respected him!

—Martha Stanton
A nurse at St. Mary's Hospital

A Top-Rate Person in My Eyes

Mrs. Ko, although you do not know me personally, I had the pleasure of knowing Dr. Ko through my 13 years of employment with Dr. Cichy. Dr. Ko was one of the few doctors who did not treat an assistant as a second class citizen, but rather like a peer. He was a top-rate person in my eyes and his presence will be missed by all.

—Cheryl Scott

I Learned from a Fine Teacher

The passing of Dr. Ko doesn't seem real. I admired and respected Dr. Ko. He not only taught me everything about dentistry, but also a lot about life itself. He was not only my employer for years but he was a good friend.

Even though Dr. Ko is not here physically, his memory will always be.

—Karen Malpass
Dental Assistant

He Administered to Our Entire Family

Our association and friendship with Dr. Ko goes way back to his initial days in Amsterdam.

One association was on a professional level, since I am an Emergency Nurse in St. Mary's Hospital. He dealt with me as a staff nurse as well as Head Nurse of the Emergency and Ambulatory Surgery Departments.

Whenever we needed him, he was always very gracious to accept our call for help. He treated us all with such respect. He was interested in our families, our ambitions and our problems. He was one unique person. I have never witnessed any outward expressions of anger in all the years we worked together. I will always remember him as a gentle, caring person.

One time, a new staff member from New York City had a dental problem and Dr. Ko saw her in the office on short notice. He was so kind and did such a great job that the next day she said to me, 'I'm going to kidnap him!' That's the way people felt about him. He endeared himself to all.

He had unique skills, also. We marveled at the way he repaired a child's face and mouth, which was torn by barbed-wire while snowmobiling. We could not believe it was the same child after repair and reconstruction was done.

My own family was touched personally by Dr. Ko. I recall when our oldest daughter just graduated from college and got a position with the County Child Abuse Agency. She was not yet eligible for insurance coverage, but needed a root canal badly. Dr. Ko reduced her bill by more than 50%.

When our son at the age of 12 and in junior high school chipped off a piece of his front tooth, Dr. Ko extended the tooth free of charge.

Our youngest daughter, now 28, has nice straight teeth thanks to his close monitoring. Her two sons were also under his care.

Just recently, our grand-daughter, age 7, was bitten on her face by her dog. Our son brought her to St. Mary's from Clifton Park. Dr. Ko sutured her and she is scarless. Our son wrote a letter to the hospital administration lauding Dr. Ko's service.

I won't even go into how long my husband has been his patient. He, too, will never forget his kindness and patience.

Other people may have other experiences to relate, but I'm sure we all share the same feelings and memories of him—a gentle, professional, caring man.

—Lillian Truax
Emergency Room Nurse at St. Mary's Hospital

A Doctor Showing Generosity and Compassion for Others As Well As Giving Us a Lesson in Sewing

Our tribute to Dr. Ko refers to our contacts with him on a professional level and occasionally on a personal level. Basically, our associations with him were during our work in the Operating Room at the St. Mary's Hospital in Amsterdam, where we served as Head Nurse, Scrub Nurse and R.N.s.

Dr. Ko came to Amsterdam in the early seventies prepared to serve as an Oral Surgeon in the local hospitals. His first office located on Pine Street was a two-family house. One apartment he converted into dental offices and equipped with second-hand furniture. We were told that he searched for sales and bargains and settled his first office with equipment that some other dentist had discarded or sold his business.

It appears that Dr.Ko was a very frugal man. With this humble beginning, he prepared for service in our community. He hired a receptionist and engaged the help of high school girls to serve as aides in his office.

In his early contacts at St. Mary's, he was obviously eager to have patients and frequently visited with us about our knowledge of potential patients who might need his services. Not having many patients at the time gave him considerable time to visit. During these lean years, we used to laugh at his unpretentious concern for clothes. On occasion we noticed that he even had holes in his socks!

As time went on, his patient load became heavier and we began to learn about this new doctor who demonstrated his compassion and sincere caring for people. We noticed these characteristics as he dealt with patients in the hospital as well as when he served members of our families; helping our sons who benefited from his special care of their needs. He never refused his services and extended his working days in order to accommodate individuals who worked late in the day and often worked on weekends and holidays. It didn't seem to matter when patients needed care, he never said, "No." He figured out some way to help those in need. Dr. Ko was especially compassionate with his less fortunate patients. He treated them so kindly, they learned to consider him as a special friend—which is not exactly the reputation that some dentists have. So many people fear dentists!

When meeting us at the hospital and/or away from his office, Dr. Ko always inquired about members of our families. He had a good memory for names and used this gift to convey his interest in others.

Dr. Ko was very sensitive to the needs of foreign students; perhaps because of his own struggles when he came to this country. For example, there was an Asian student attending Fulton-Montgomery Community College. Finding out that this student didn't know too many people and was, no doubt, lonely, Dr. Ko invited the young lad to the Ko home. Without doubt, this young man appreciated such thoughtfulness. On so many occasions, it was apparent that Dr. Ko constantly thought of others.

Adding to his compassionate ways, he was known for his generosity. He was one of the few, if not the only one, to remember us with gifts at Christmas time. We appreciated his thoughtfulness.

He took the time to recognize and attend retirement parties and other functions of interest to our staff. Mena especially remembers the lovely silver tray that Dr. Ko had had appropriately engraved and gave to her at the time of her retirement.

As we became better acquainted, we discovered that he had a great sense of humor. He enjoyed jokes, even though he wasn't an especially good story teller himself. Somehow, when he tried to tell a joke he often forgot the punch line. This in itself was funny as we watched him try to remember the whole point of his story.

A day in the Operating Room usually began with Dr. Ilagan (the anesthetist who nearly always worked with Dr. Ko) pacing the floor saying, "Where is Sok? He's late again!" Dr. Ilagan, not known for his patience, was always in a hurry, partly due to his realization that there was a busy schedule ahead. With calmness, Dr. Ko would finally appear and the scheduled operation would begin.

At the conclusion of an operation, Dr. Ko always did his paper work, checked his patient and made it a point to contact the family members, who were anxiously waiting to hear from the doctor. All of these delays usually annoyed Dr. Ilagan, who was anxious to get on to the next operation.

Dr. Ko and Dr. Ilagan made an excellent team and really complemented each other but, at times, they disagreed as to scheduling, due to their differences in nature. A heated argument might develop, but each situation was resolved amicably. The two doctors worked together so much that they knew each other's ways very well.

Signs of happiness in their work was evident as these two doctors proceeded during operations. One or the other would begin to sing and the rest of the staff would chime in. We harmonized one song right after another. Some of the favorite songs were: "Down by the Old Mill Stream," "Danny Boy," "Home on the Range" and "On Top of Old Smokey." The blending of the voices was really beautiful. It is too bad we weren't taped!

Occasionally, a funny incident occurred. One time Eleanor was helping Dr. Ko with an operation. He was pulling the teeth on a fellow who had a full mouth. Trying to get way in the back was presenting a problem, so Dr. Ko asked Eleanor to put her hand in the fellow's mouth to aid in retraction. After Dr. Ko completed the suturing, Eleanor tried to pull her hand out only to find it would not come out. She said to Dr. Ko, "I think you sewed me to this man's gums." The doctor looked up and said, "Well, there's only one thing for you to do and that's to follow him everywhere he goes!"

It was incidents like this that decreased tension and gave us a good laugh. While humorous situations were rare, when one did happen, we all enjoyed the release from the more serious moments. We really had so much fun during our work at St. Mary's.

Besides Dr. Ko's love of work, he was fond of entertaining. One time he told us about serving baked lasagna to Dr. Kim from Korea, who had never had anything with tomatoes in it. Dr. Ko delighted in serving new dishes to his friends.

One time he took us all out to dinner and introduced us to the popular pu-pu platter. We made a lot of fun of that, asking, "Are you sure that's the name of a meal?" When he assured us that it was, we dared to order the meal. Much to our surprise it was delicious and since then we have enjoyed the platter several times.

On a few occasions (and one time with our husbands) we were invited to dinner at the Ko home. We were served several Korean dishes, but perhaps the one we especially remember is the chicken prepared Korean style. It was really very delicious! The hospitality extended to us by both Dr. Ko and his wife, Elaine, will long be remembered.

While Dr. Ko never verbally expressed dedication to his work; actions proved this point. Any doctor who will work long hours each week day, go to his office or to the hospital to care for patients on weekends including Sundays, and/or get up from the table during a holiday meal in order to administer to a patient with a problem has to love his work! His dedication to his work was expressed through the enjoyment of serving mankind.

As representatives of the Operating Room Staff (now retired from St. Mary's Hospital) we have fond memories of Dr. Ko, who will be greatly missed for all the humanitarian ways he served our community.

—St. Mary's Operating Room Staff
Mena Marciniak, Head Nurse;
Eleanor Landry, Scrub Nurse;
Julie Jagielski, R. N.

PATIENTS

Especially touching are the kind words expressed by patients who took the time to say thank you for the care Dr. Ko gave them.

Willing to Serve Without Pay

I was one of Dr. Ko's first patients when he had his office on Pine Street. He was a great, kind and compassionate man. When I had no money to pay him he never asked for a penny. I will never forget Dr. Ko.

—Bob Shaffer

A Kind and Gentle Doctor

I was one of Dr. Ko's very first patients in 1972 and will never forget what a great doctor and what a wonderful person he was. He was the kindest, most gentle doctor I have ever known. I will never forget him

—Elizabeth Skouroneh

Our Family Was Touched and Made Stronger by Dr. Ko

About 19 years ago, when Dr. Ko first opened his practice on Pine Street, I was one of his first patients. I had my four wisdom teeth out. I remember how he assured me that everything would be fine. What a true professional and caring person he was!

About 10 years ago, he affected our lives in another significant way. My Dad, John Pereicich, quit smoking, thanks to the program that Dr. Ko was sponsoring. The support from this program has kept my Dad from going back to that bad habit.

Lastly, about 7 years ago, my son, J.J. Thomas was playing Little League Baseball. He was playing on third base and a young man from the other team slid into third base. How it happened no one knows for sure, but my son broke his ankle. Our team was being observed by Dr. Ko (as a spectator).

Well, this very caring person, Dr. Ko, called my house the next day to see how my son was doing. We all thought how considerate he was to call.

Our entire family has been touched and made stronger because of Dr. Ko.

—Mrs. John P. Thomas

Sit Still; Don't Move

I was only a patient of Dr. Ko. I started going to him because my wisdom teeth were giving me trouble. I first went to him when he was on Pine Street in Amsterdam. He was very nice to me and told me how difficult my tooth would be to remove. He said I gave him a real challenge!

Through the years that followed, I went to Dr. Ko for many other dental problems, most of which were root canals. He always showed me the x-rays. He always explained what he saw on the x-rays and what he was going to do for me.

When dental work was going to be done, I usually was put to sleep. One time, while in his office having work done, Dr. Ko could see that I was going to be late going back to work. (I am a cosmetologist.) Dr. Ko was concerned and said, "I'd better give you novocaine or else you will do some crazy hairdos!"

Another interesting side of Dr. Ko has to do with my 4-year-old niece, Angela. She hurt her tongue one time and he had to stitch it. She went to him about four times with different types of mouth injuries. The last time she went to him was in December 1990. She fell and hurt the upper part of her mouth and needed stitches on her gums. She told me that she couldn't feel the stitches in her mouth. When she went back to have the stitches removed, she told me that she sat alone on the chair and didn't move so he didn't hurt her at all. She told me to do this when I went to the doctor.

A few days later Dr. Ko was working on a root canal on me and I told him what Angela told me to do. He laughed and said, "She is so precious!

I will miss Dr. Ko terribly. I can't even imagine going for my root canals or other problems to anyone else. He was a great guy!

—Josephine Sperduto

Always Explained Procedures

Dr. Ko will truly be missed as a caring medical professional. He removed my impacted wisdom teeth several years ago. A year ago, Dr. Ko performed the same surgery on our son. The doctor's gentle manner made us feel comfortable and he always explained the procedure that he was going to perform.

We were the first host family for Ken Lawford from Bolivia. Ken was also greatly saddened by the news of Dr. Ko's death. Dr. Ko definitely left an impression on the exchange students and he will not be forgotten. We know Dr. Ko will also be greatly missed by Rotary.

—Darlene, John and Jeff Holubetz
Ken Lawford

Surgeon and Friend

Dr. Ko has been our surgeon and friend over the years. It has been a privilege to know him. We admired his keen intelligence, compassionate personality and great skill. He was outstanding in his field.

—Bill, Joyce, Karl and Kristen Berner

As Good As New Now

I think of the nights that Dr. Ko treated my children; they always seemed to knock out teeth at the most inappropriate times! He always reassured them with gentleness.

He had to reassure me last August, when my beautiful daughter broke her jaw in a pool accident. She is as good as new now. Thank God for Dr. Ko!

—Jessica and Suzanne Kane-Brauns

Changed Our Lives

This is the story of how Doctor Ko helped to change our lives forever.

My husband, Mark, is a recovered alcoholic. He first met Doctor Ko fourteen years ago after a terrible car accident which killed a young man driving the vehicle and my husband was seriously injured with his jaw broken in five places. This was the first time Doctor Ko touched my husband's life. Even though the accident was not alcohol related, Doctor Ko was aware of Mark's drinking problem through his frequent visits to Doctor Ko's office. My husband was not only trying to deal with his own injuries but also the loss of a very good friend. So he was drinking heavily and would become drunk and fall quite often. Doctor Ko would have to repeatedly repair damage done to his jaw due to falls. Mark felt very comfortable with Doctor Ko and confided in him about his drinking problem. Doctor Ko not only took the time to listen to Mark but he tried to convince Mark that he should get help for his problem.

Ten years went by and my husband drank and used drugs heavily during this period. He would sometimes be gone days at a time remembering very little of where he was or who he was with. The pressure was too much for our marriage to bear and we divorced. Mark and I had a daughter by this time and when I left him I tried to build a life for us without him.

We were divorced for four years and during this time he saw very little of me or his daughter growing up. I still loved him very much and couldn't give up on him. So we started dating again and things seemed to be better. We remarried and had a second child, a girl, shortly after. Things started to turn bad again. The drinking got progressively worse and we argued about it often. Mark would then be gone days at a time drinking and God only knows what else, leaving my daughters and me alone to face many financial burdens. If it had not been for family and friends I would not have survived that awful period in our lives. It finally came to a stop with another car accident in which Mark was driving drunk alone at 8 o'clock in the morning when school was in session. He hit a tree a block away from our home. Mark was knocked unconscious and broke his jaw for the second time. Doctor Ko came in to the hospital room to see Mark and gave him a real talking to; *I feel the one that changed his life.* Doctor Ko told Mark that his drinking problem could not only destroy him but more importantly, since Mark didn't seem to care anything about himself at this time, he could have killed someone else, a child. It was a school day and the accident occurred in a residential area where many school buses traveled back and forth. He spoke to my husband at length about his drinking and the consequences of continuing his life like this. His jaw couldn't take it, his family couldn't take it and, God forbid, an innocent bystander could be hurt seriously. Doctor Ko then referred Mark to an excellent counselor who helped Mark get into a rehabilitation center for alcoholism where he stayed for one month.

This was the turning point of *our* lives. Maybe Mark was just finally ready to get help, or maybe it was the thought of hurting a child, but this time he listened to Doctor Ko's words; the words that changed Mark's thinking about his lifestyle. But whatever it was, Mark has now been alcohol and drug free for *three* years. He sometimes goes to AA meetings to try and help others to turn their lives around and maybe he'll be the one to convince them to change as Doctor Ko did for Mark.

Mark and I and our two daughters now own a beautiful home; the home of my dreams and we have a normal, happy family. Our children have very few memories of their father drinking (they were so young). They only know him as a loving, gentle and kind father and we are happier than I ever thought or hoped I could be.

We thank God for people like Doctor Ko. As a doctor we realize how busy his schedule must have been, but because he had such strong compassion for others in time of need he reached out to Mark and tried to help him get his life back together when so many others would have ignored him. Doctor Ko went beyond what his professional responsibilities were in this case and saved a life. We owe him a great deal of gratitude.

When we heard the sad news of Doctor Ko's passing, my husband and I were truly heart broken. The world is a better place because of Doctor Ko and the many lives he has touched. We are honored to have known him.

Mrs. Ko sent a letter of thanks to the Colonial Club and on it was a picture of Doctor Ko. I asked for that picture and I now have it framed and in my living room. When we look at it we thank God that He made people like Doctor Ko.

—Marianne Lane

Responsive to All Humanitarian Causes

Dr. Ko was a most admired person, not only for his professional ability but also for his caring and responsiveness to all humanitarian causes. He was held in high regard with all who knew him.

My husband and children often reflected on his energy and untiring service to the community.

—Clara Partyka

A Living Memorial to Dr. Ko

I vaguely remember lying in the hospital bed during those first moments of regaining consciousness. I asked for a mirror and my father lovingly mocked me for my vanity as he sang, "You're so vain, you probably think this song is about you." Perhaps then it was about me, now the song is about Dr. Ko—a song of praise to my healer, my shliach (messenger from G-d as we say in Hebrew) in the time of need.

As I looked in the mirror I saw a face that reminded me of myself—except my jaw was hanging down over my chest. A small line of stitches appeared across the left side of my chin as well as to the left of my eye. The form of the letter "J" marked the stitches that restored my upper lip. It was as if the hand of God (so to speak) engraved the first letter of my English name "Jill" on my face. A personal invitation to look at myself, my life anew.

Actually, I didn't think that I looked so bad. Others were literally frightened to visit me. I remember hearing conversations among my family and friends, especially Dr. and Mrs. Berg. They had been interviewing an oral surgeon, Dr. Ko, who would have the delicate task of restoring the face of a twenty-year-old woman. That was me.

Through the codeine and whatever other drugs that were given me, I sensed that there was a unanimous consensus of the indisputable ability of Dr. Ko to perform the pending 7-hour operation; a light of hope in the tragic darkness!

At least I was still alive. My friend who was driving the car didn't make it. Now I was given another gift, the possibility of a complete recovery. This awesome time in my life marked the beginning of a long journey of searching for truth and meaning. Dr. Ko, the God sent healer, made my journey possible as a normal, healthy woman.

I believe that the first time I saw Dr. Ko I was surrounded by my entire family. He was explaining to all of us that he would be entering into my jaw through the same small line of stitches that I already had in order to not cause any more scarring. It seemed like a very difficult task. I never once thought that he couldn't do it.

Dr. Ko's smooth angelic face and dark intelligent eyes emitted an immovable air of confidence. He gave hours and hours of his valuable time to me and my family as he patiently explained in detail my medical situation and his procedures. Only very wise people can relate to the intelligence of others. At times we all felt like his colleague. I wasn't a passive body but a mentally active partner in my healing process. Dr. Ko's acute sensitivity to my soul reinforced my desire to continue to live.

At this time in my life I considered myself an "agnostic." I was playing it safe. Nineteen years later I find myself living already for ten years in Israel. Here I'm able to openly offer thanks for the miracles that were performed on my behalf. Of the many ways we experience God's unity the most profound way is through our relationships with each other. That Dr. Ko entered my life at the exact moment of my dire need is nothing less than miraculous.

I remember recovery from the 7-hour operation probably feeling more rested than my relieved family, who had just endured 7 hours of anxiety. I didn't feel a thing. The operation was a 100% success. Once in awhile, when the Jerusalem weather gets cold and damp and I open my mouth wide, I hear a little crack—a gentle reminder of Dr. Ko, who came to this world for too short of a visit. There are no words that can express my gratitude for having had the privilege of being the patient of such an outstanding human being.

Perhaps every time I speak—if I could just fully grasp the awareness of the moment—to say only words of truth, sensitivity and wisdom—and whenever I eat to feel gratitude for every bite. Perhaps this will be my offering as a living memorial to Dr. Ko. May his soul bask forever in the lights of the Garden of Eden, mirroring his wisdom, kindness and great deeds.

—Nechara Sarah Nadborny
Rehov Hage Olam 2
Jerusalem, Israel

CHAPTER V

COMMUNITY SERVICE

Dr. Ko was a contributing member of many professional organizations, including: the American Dental Association; the Fulton, Hamilton and Montgomery Counties Dental Society; the Fourth District Dental Society; the New York State Society of Oral Surgeons; and the American Dental Society of Anesthesiology.

He also served on the medical-dental Staff at Amsterdam Memorial Hospital, St. Mary's Hospital in Amsterdam, Nathan Littauer Hospital in Gloversville, and Johnstown Hospital in Johnstown, New York.

Korean War Veterans Memorial

In January 1986, members of the community had the idea of erecting a monument honoring Korean War veterans from Amsterdam. Richard China believed a fitting tribute to the men and women of the Korean War was long overdue. As chairman of the Memorial Committee in Amsterdam, Mr. China and a group of interested citizens (Gerard Koller, Ed Walker, Armand Giovanni, Al China, Morris Olender and Sam Zurlo) began working on the project, as reported in the Recorder on January 18, 1986. Dr. Ko learned of the efforts to erect a tribute to those who fought in Korea in the early 1950s and offered to assist the group.

Ko hoped to arrange for a gift to the city from the government of South Korea. He would make the necessary contacts. He hoped to see if South Korea would contribute a stone that could be engraved to honor local military personnel who helped defend that country during the conflict with North Korea and China. He felt that a stone to honor the veterans was "not too

The Recorder

THURSDAY, JANUARY 23, 1986

Ko offers help on monument for Korea vets

By DOUGLAS E. LANDON
Recorder News Staff

An Amsterdam dentist who is a native of Korea likes the idea of a monument honoring veterans of the Korean War and wants to help establish one.

Dr. Sok Nam Ko of 80 Locust Ave. said Wednesday he has learned of efforts to erect a tribute to those who fought in Korea in the early 1950's, and thinks he may be able to assist the group.

Ko hopes to arrange for a gift to the city from the government of South Korea. He would like to see that South Korea contribute a stone that can be engraved to honor local military personnel who helped defend that country during its conflict with North Korea more than 30 years ago.

He said he plans to meet with the Korean consulate in New York City within the next two weeks, and will ask if arrangements can be made to have a decorative stone shipped to Amsterdam from South Korea.

The newly formed Korean War Veterans Memorial Committee of Amsterdam, led by Richard China, has discussed the idea of trying to raise money for a monument, because veterans of the "forgotten war" are not recognized to the same extent as are veterans of World War II and Vietnam.

Ko said he thinks the tribute is an excellent idea that is long overdue. He said he would like to help China and his group. Ko added that a monument sculptured out of stone from the Korean countryside would be a "meaningful expression" of thanks to those who foughtin Korea.

"I think the Korean people ought to help them out," Ko said. "They owe this to the people who died in the war."

He added that 14 Montgomery County residents were killed in the Korean War, and with that in mind, a stone to honor the veterans is "not too much to ask."

China said he and his committee are thrilled that Ko came has offered to get involved in the project. He agreed that a monument from Korea would be appropriate.

"We're very greatful for him to even attempt to do it," China said. He added that the committee believes Veterans Field would be the ideal spot to place a monument to Korean veterans.

China noted that veterans of the Korean conflict should have been honored in this way a long time ago.

Ko said granite is plentiful in Korea, and marble also is available. He will ask the consulate if the South Korean government will contribute the stone and sculpt it into the shape of monument.

"It depends on what type of thing the people in Korea are willing to do," Ko said.

Recorder photo: Mitch Wojnarowicz

Dr. Sok Nam Ko of Amsterdam displays a wooden turtle hand-carved in Korea, his native land. Ko stands amid his collection of Korean artifacts in the parlor of his 80 Locust Ave. home. He plans to help to establish a monument to local servicemen who fought in Korea.

much to ask." Fourteen Montgomery County residents were killed in the Korean War. Ko suggested engraving each of their names on the monument, along with a message of tribute to all Korean War veterans from this area.

Dr. Ko made the trip to New York City to meet with the Korean Consul, General Tae Zhee Kim, to ask for the assistance of the South Korean Government in erecting the monument. The Memorial Committee had decided that a stone from Korea would have special meaning and would be of even more significance if it could be obtained from a location along the 38th parallel such as the Chosin Reservoir or Panmunjom. A memorial celebration and unveiling of the monument was proposed for June 25, 1988, which would mark the 38th anniversary of the beginning of the war.

Ko realized the problems in transporting a stone to Amsterdam from Korea. The costs would be high. So, he was not at all sure that his efforts would be successful. Several locations for the monument were discussed by the Committee including Ko's choice of Veterans Park in Amsterdam. Fund raising activities were planned in order to raise enough money for the project. Such events as a spaghetti dinner, a dinner-dance and fund drives were discussed. The monument was finally erected years later.

The Y.M.C.A. and the Amsterdam City Center

On June 20, 1984, Dr. Ko was elected President of the Board of Directors of the Y.M.C.A. He had been a member since 1979, served as 2nd Vice President in 1982 and 1st Vice President in 1983. He also served on the Program Committee and Nominating Committee.

In 1985 the Constitution and By-laws of the Y.M.C.A. were revised and the organization became known as the Amsterdam City Center. The mission of this organization is "to develop the character and usefulness of its members, and the improvement of the moral, mental, social and physical condition of the people of this community. It shall act as the center of recreational, social, and cultural activities toward the enhancement of quality of life within the greater Amsterdam area."

SCIENTIA OMNEM DOLOREM VINCIT

AMERICAN DENTAL SOCIETY OF ANESTHESIOLOGY, INC.

YMCA

CHAMPLAIN COUNCIL

PEOPLE to PEOPLE

THE DENTAL SOCIETY OF THE STATE OF NEW YORK

ARTE NATURAE SUCCURRERE

ORGANIZED BY ACT OF LEGISLATURE · 1868

THE NEW YORK ACADEMY OF SCIENCES

PER CŒLESTIS PER ÆREM PER TERRAS PER MARIA

· 1817 ·

ROTARY INTERNATIONAL

AMERICAN CANCER SOCIETY

RESEARCH SERVICE EDUCATION

DELTA SIGMA DELTA

In the 1985 Annual Report of the Amsterdam City Center, the Program Director, Kathleen Bursese-Morawski, presented a review of the year's activities as follows:

> Since coming on as Program Director at the City Center, in September of this year, a number of new programs have been scheduled (Adult Water Fitness, Scuba, Women's Volleyball, Senior Square Dancing, Toddler Gym, Youth Volleyball and Pre-Natal Exercise) that were not able to run due to insufficient enrollment. Many questions as to why these failed to draw interest still remain, however, efforts to keep the concepts alive are being explored for the future. Even with these unfortunate cancellations many successful programs were a part of the City Center schedule over the past two seasons.
>
> After-School Youth Soccer at the respective elementary schools was a huge success in the fall, only to be surpassed by the Soccer League which met on Saturdays where these respective schools competed against each other.
>
> Youth basketball was not as well followed as soccer, but tended to draw in more second and third graders. No girls were involved although they were eligible. Boys gymnastics had a fair sign-up.
>
> A racquetball tournament was held in January in the gym. Male players competed and cash prizes were awarded.
>
> Advanced Lifesaving was so successful in the fall that it was run again in the winter. These individuals will be encouraged to participate in the upcoming Water Safety Instructor course, also.
>
> Amsterdam Sea Rams, the Amsterdam City Center age group swim team, showed an initial sign-up of 35 members under the direction of two new coaches, who are the college interns that assist in the instruction of St. Stanislaus' School gym program.
>
> The "Aerial Flames", our affiliated girls' gymnastics team, is still going strong with their coach offering a variety of clinics to complement their program.
>
> The Men's and Women's Athletic Clubs saw an increase in membership since March 1984, especially due to the 1984 monthly membership.

The Lynch Middle School continues to rent the pool for modified team practices/meets from November through February.

Liberty Enterprise rented the pool twice weekly through the fall and then saw the exchange of one pool program for a music workshop in the gym, which was well received.

The Aerobics Program has seen a decline in attendance with the loss of various instructors, but hope to revive their numbers by consolidating sites.

All Senior Exercise Classes, both in the pool and gym, are still quite successful.

The Slimnastics Class shows good attendance and has been joined by Stretchersize and Forty-five Minute Workout, which are available to those women looking for a calmer exercise pace.

The Pre-School continues to be well attended in both classes.

Three non-physical programs were offered: Nutrition Class, Flower Arranging and Raggedy Ann Doll Making, which had excellent responses.

Progressive Swim Lessons found large class sizes and show promise for the same in spite of the changing to the Red Cross Swim format.

The Amsterdam City Center continues to expand upon its already vast program offerings, and hopes to encourage more of the community to become involved at the physical and non-physical level.

As the retiring President of the Board of Directors of the YMCA/City Center, Dr Ko presented the following report at the 1985 Amsterdam City Center Annual Meeting:

As one would expect, my final message to you as President of the Board of Directors will center around the financial condition of the YMCA/City Center during the past twelve months.

The restructuring of the physical structures for membership fees were successful in some ways, but caused drastic reduction of memberships. Generally speaking, the whole event was favorable for our physical problems even though we lost members.

Our capital fund-raising project was set back because of the conflict with other organizational projects in town. The fund raising project should be revitalized this year. The Wasserman Foundation, Arkell Hall Foundation, and other foundations were contacted without success.

Our cash flow appears to have improved relative to last year. Our budget deficit is less and our bookkeeping system was improved. I wish to take this opportunity to thank our finance committee, treasurer, and executive director for our successful financial improvement and our grant projects. Our special thanks go to the United Way for their dedicated support.

Our organizational change took place in 1984. The Y.M.C.A. of Amsterdam became the Amsterdam City Center. This is the first giant step toward a new adventure for the organization. We revised our constitution and by-laws. A feasibility study is in progress for future plans and new buildings. We are cautious and careful, but we are optimistic and look ahead to our new adventure in joining city government, the school district, AIDA, and other concerned groups.

Changes in our administrative staff took place in 1984. A new executive director came and new directions were given by the Board of Directors concentrating on promotion of our public relations and financial improvement as well as administrative coordination. A new program director came aboard to improve organizational programming, and promoting these programs to our community. Last, but not least, the Board of Directors were very active on committee levels, providing leadership and policy making for the purpose of reorganizing the Amsterdam City Center. The Board of Directors will be discontinued, as they were asked to join the Board of Directors as active participants overseeing the business of the organization. A general membership meeting was held and established to direct a channel of communication between management and the general membership. It was felt that this meeting should be continued every three to six months for the purpose of a two-way communication to stimulate the general membership and clarify administrative policies. Emphasis should be made that we are in the same boat and the name of the boat is 'Amsterdam City Center.'

Our future appears to be bright, and indeed, to make our center brighter and shinier we must struggle to improve the following:

a. Capital fund raising and continue to explore the possibility of improving or building a new physical plant. A growing body must shed an old cover in order to grow greater.
b. Continuously improve our cash flow for the operational fund and balance the budget. No one should spend more money than one can earn.
c. Struggle to increase membership, improve our program and upgrade the quality of services. This should include building repairs and rebuilding of the Bean Hill Day Camp site.
d. Improve community relationships. The channels of communication should be opened wide to receive and provide necessary services.

We are a very unique organization in our community. We have community-minded leaders, we are a recreational and social center, athletic center, cultural center, and a service-minded facility. We are so unique because we are the only non-profit organization with all the capabilities listed above, in our community.

We have served our community well for over 125 years, and we will continue to do so for many more years to come.

My sincere thanks to all the board members, staff members, and the general membership.

The Executive Director, Marvin R. LeRoy, Jr., concluded his report at this meeting with thanks to Dr. Ko. It read as follows:

I would be remiss if I failed to bring attention to the fine job done by our current Board President, Dr. Sok Nam Ko. It was under his leadership that many accomplishments took place, and he, along with the other officers, should be highly commended for their dedication to the organization. We are not finished with the tasks demanded of us to totally revive this agency...much work remains in a number of significant areas...but a sense of optimism is now with us, and one has to believe that perhaps, in time, we will realize our goal of ensuring that the Center will continue on into the future as a mainstay in Amsterdam.

Always Looking for Ways to Do Things Better

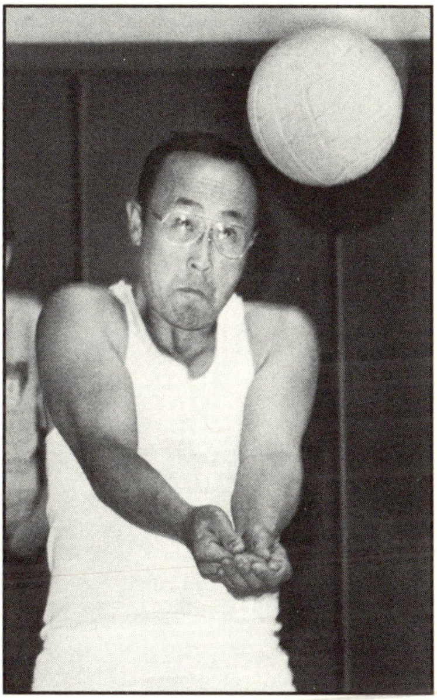

Dr. Ko playing volleyball.

I remember Sok Ko as a man who was fun to be with. He was bright, happy and willing and able to confront all challenges. It was pure joy to share the volleyball court with him and have him push up some champion set shots on difficult returns. Bright, happy but deadly serious on matters of principle. His greatest asset as President of the City Center–Y.M.C.A. Board of Directors was his constant questioning, probing, sorting and looking for ways to do things better and always finding new and more constructive avenues of response. Indeed, his probing intellect stimulated the thinking and actions of the board as they faced the challenges of the changing scene. Each of us has a part to play on the stage of life. Dr. Ko broadened the horizons and dimensions of the Amsterdam City Center–Y.M.C.A. during his term of service.

—Lionel Fallows
A fellow member of the Y.M.C.A.

Korean acupuncturist to address Arthritis Assn.

By NANCY EAMES
Recorder women's editor

AMSTERDAM — The Amsterdam Arthritis Assn. will have an expert on acupuncture as guest speaker at its February meeting.

Dr. Chang Hwan Kim, an oriental medical doctor from Seoul, Korea, will discuss recent developments in acupuncture treatment of arthritis Wednesday at 8 p.m. at Amsterdam Memorial Hospital. Dr. Kim will illustrate his talk with a demonstration of acupuncture — the introduction of a needle into the human body to cure disease.

Dr. Kim, who is visiting Dr. Sok Nam Ko and family at 80 Locust Ave., is assistant professor of acupuncture at Kyung Hee University Oriental Medical School in Seoul. Dr. Ko, an oral surgeon, studied acupuncture there under Dr. Kim in 1975 and invited him to visit this country.

"It took him six years to accept," says Dr. Ko. Dr. Kim, who has been in Amsterdam three weeks, plans a two-month stay in the US.

Acupuncture not new

Dr. Kim graduated from Kyung Hee University Oriental Medical School in 1972. He earned a master's degree in oriental medicine in 1975, and has completed work on his PhD. His specialty, acupuncture, is still new to occidental (western) medicine but has been a part of oriental medicine for a long time.

TOOLS OF THE TRADE — Dr. Chan Hwan Kim, right, an oriental medical doctor from Korea, chats with his Amsterdam host, Dr. Sok Nam Ko, left, over the tools of Dr. Kim's profession. Dr. Kim, whose specialty is acupuncture, will address the Amsterdam Arthritis Assn. Wednesday at 8 p.m. at Amsterdam Memorial Hospital. (Recorder photo by Nancy Eames)

Acupuncture is used on arthritis victims to alleviate the swelling, pain and redness that are the signs and symptoms of the disease. The treatment might be given every day or every other day for three to six weeks, depending on individual conditions.

Acupuncture is sometimes used in combination with moxibustion — the burning of fiber from the moxi plant on the afflicted area, causing white blood cells to increase and fight the infection and-or inflammation.

Oriental medicine's goal

The goal of oriental medicine, which originated in China between 320-250 BC, is the removal of the signs and symptoms of illness, rather than the cause. According to Dr. Kim, it is based on three principles:

- Both the mental and physical aspects of the patient must be considered.
- The human body is a small part of a large universe and therefore changes with the environment.
- Treatment must be based on the body as a whole, not just certain aspects of it.

Dr. Kim will be accompanied by Dr. Ko as translator Wednesday evening.

'A friendly town'

Dr. Kim describes Amsterdam as a "very pretty town, with a history and tradition of its own." He is finding people here friendly and kind, and the weather similar to that in Seoul, although he thinks Amsterdam has a "little more" snow.

He has toured the city's two hospitals and visited New York City and Boston. He hopes to visit Washington, DC, Maryland and Los Angeles, as well as Buffalo (where he has family), before returning to his wife and three children in Seoul.

Public Health Work

With the sincere slogan of "We want to wipe out cancer in your lifetime," and in accordance with Presidential proclamation and Congressional resolutions, the Cancer Society asked Mohawk Valley residents to support its work during its annual fundraiser. In April 1977, with a goal set at raising $5,000, the third annual Montgomery County Cancer Drive Telethon was aired over local cable Channel Eight. The Cancer Drive was broadcast from the Community Center of the New Amsterdam Apartments on Division and Wall Streets. Dr. Sok

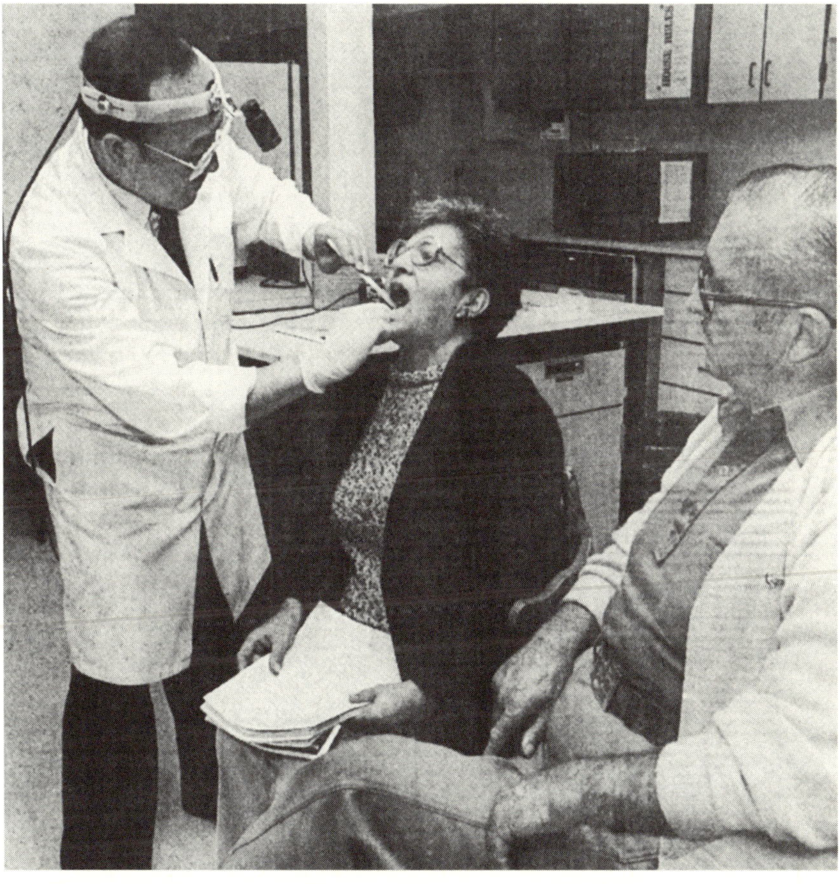

HEALTH FAIR — Dr. Sok N Ko looks into the mouth of Eve Terwilleger of Amsterdam during recent health fair at the Amsterdam High School. The fair was sponsored by the Montgomery Countywide Office for the Aging. Looking on is Eve's husband George.

— GazettePhoto — Garry Brown

Nam Ko was honorary chairman of the fund raising effort, which helps support patient aid and the administrative operations. He also served as the Special Gifts Chairman at this time.

Dr. Ko's interest in all public health led to his participation in the Health Fair at the Amsterdam High School in April 1988. The fair was sponsored by the Montgomery Countywide Office for the Aging.

Dr. Ko later served as a Celebrity Waiter at the 4th Annual Amsterdam Celebrity Waiters Charity Luncheon in 1990 for the Vermont and Upstate New York Chapter of the Leukemia Society of America. The luncheon was a great success, raising over $3,200 for local patient aid and research. The Leukemia Society continues in the fight against the #1 disease killer of children.

According to a tribute written by Sue Hemingway:

> Dr. Sok Nam Ko earned recognition, along with respect and of course appreciation, from the Montgomery County Unit. Their nomination of him for Special Tribute Volunteer stems from his ten years of service helping the American Cancer Society. Those who've worked with him on various committees cite Dr. Ko for his work far and above other professional medical men in serving our community.
>
> He served as president, public education chairman, legacy chairman for the American Cancer Society and board member of the Mohawk Valley Leukemia Society. As a maxillofacial surgeon, Dr. Ko gives free oral cancer exams at health fairs, senior citizens organizations, and he has conducted many Stop-Smoking clinics. He never turns down any duties he is asked to perform for the Cancer Society. He gives unselfishly of his time to further the causes of the American Cancer Society.

Dr. Ko was the recipient of the first Jim Hannan Memorial Service Award for outstanding service in the crusade against cancer. The award was named for an active local volunteer who died earlier. Dr. Ko was honored at a ball sponsored by the Montgomery County Unit of the American Cancer Society, which drew a large crowd and grossed close to $2,500 to be used to aid local cancer patients.

HANSON AWARD — Dr. Sok Nam Ko, recipient of the first annual Jim Hanson Memorial Service Award for outstanding service in the crusade against cancer, is congratlated by Mrs. James Hanson following the presentation of the award. The award is named for an active local volunteer who died earlier this year. (Recorder photo by Stan Eames).

Dr. Ko honored at Society ball

AMSTERDAM — Dr. Sok Nam Ko received tthe first annual Jim Hannan Memorial Service Award for outstanding service in the crusade against cancer at the Thanks-for-Giving Ball Saturday night at Fulton-Montgomery Community College. The award is named for an active local volunteer who died earlier this year.

The ball, sponsored by the Montgomery County Unit, American Cancer Society, drew 200 people and grossed close to $2,500, according to Linda Martin, executive director of the county unit. Proceeds will be used to aid local cancer patients, Martin said.

Noel Dylong and Frederico Aquano won first prize in the dance contest — a $15 gift certificate from Mario's Comedy Inn. Mr. and Mrs. George DeVito placed second and received a $10 certificate from Pepe's Restaurant.

Judges were Mrs. Patricia Ferenz, Mr. and Mrs. Steve Tierney and Jennie Sgambati. Music was by the Rex Pryor Orchestra.

Dr. William Bresonis was honorary chairman of the ball. Sal Battaglia was general chairman and Mrs. Dorothy Frascatore was co-chairman. Also in attendance were Mr. and Mrs. Herbertt L. Shuttleworth II. Shuttleworth was last year's honorary ball chairmman.

Anne Marie McKenney will continue as the unit's Voice of Hope.

Truly Made a Difference

Dr. Ko was an outstanding Volunteer of long-standing and great dedication. It is safe to say that his participation in the life and work of the American Cancer Society truly made a difference in the saving of lives through education and service. He shall be missed, and both the American Cancer Society and his community will be always in his debt.

AMERICAN SMOKE-OUT — Dr. Sok Nam Ko, left, and Mayor Mario Villa, right, symbolically break cigarettes in observance of Thursday's Great American Smoke-Out. The mayor has proclaimed the day as an "effort to encourage cigarette smokers to give up their habit for 24 hours." (Recorder photo by Cindy Livingston).

—David R. Coddington, Sr.
Executive Vice President

No Worthy Replacement

The many causes and people which Dr. Ko served and supported over the years shall never find a worthy replacement.

—Reigh Carpenter
Former Superintendent of Schools

He Wore a Tu-tu!

I have a couple of good "human" stories to tell about Sok and I would love to share them with you and the readers of your loving book:

Dr. Ko and I served together on the Board of the Montgomery County Unit of the American Cancer Society for many years. Every month, we would attend meetings and Dr. Ko, as usual, always had solid recommendations to propose or reports to be made on activities he was involved with on behalf of the Society.

Illustration Herbert A.W. Kopper.

Keep in mind, these were the days when smoking was still acceptable. Well, maybe to the rest of the world, but not Sok. As ridiculous as it may sound now, there were Board members who still smoked cigarettes. These were active volunteers and valuable to the fund raising efforts.

When he was president, however, he decreed there would be NO SMOKING at Board Meetings. Needless to say, this was not readily accepted by the smokers in the group. He was always sensitive to the feelings of others and rather than create a negative atmosphere at the meetings, he indicated smokers could smoke, but levied a fine for each cigarette smoked during the meeting. His strong feelings about the fight against cancer and what the Society was supposed to represent really acted as a deterrent for those smokers. Sure, they lit up a few times, but it didn't take long. What was really important here, was that Sok supported his ideals without creating bad feelings or losing his sense of humor.

The other remembrance I have of Sok always brings a smile to my face — and it probably does to the hundreds

Dr. Ko thanking Lou Pinella for participating in the Cancer Fund Drive.

of people who attended the very first FOLLIES sponsored by the Amsterdam Memorial Hospital Auxiliary 1981.

He and a group of other physicians agreed to take part in the stage show at Amsterdam High School. It was certainly a part that took a lot of courage and self-confidence to execute. Saving the best scene for last, he and the other doctors, dressed in tu-tus, tippie-toed out on the stage to the amazement and delight of the audience. Needless to say it was a show-stopper.

Sok was great. It was a pleasure and privilege to know him. Thank you, Elaine, for giving me the opportunity to share these stories with you and your readers.

—Jennie Sgambati

New York State Cancer Society Meeting at Syracuse, N.Y.
L. to R.: Sok Nam Ko, Greg Louganis (Olympic Gold Medalist)
and Sal Battaglia.

My Experiences as Friend, Patient and Co-volunteer with Dr. Sok Nam Ko

Knowing Dr. Ko was an experience in itself. His compassion for all people was most evident in his volunteer work.

My son, Tom was a patient of Dr. Ko's and when I met him shortly after my husband's death, due to cancer, he asked Tom if he would invite me to join the American Cancer Society's Board of Directors of which he was Public Education Chairman. Some friends and family were surprised at the invitation so soon after my husband's death...but it was exactly what I needed! A chance to inform people of cancer prevention and to help those dealing with the disease.

As part of our work, we taught "Stop Smoking Clinics" for many years.

The clinics were very stressful and I'm sure those who benefited, and today are Smoke-Free, will always be grateful to Dr. Ko.

Cancer Drive To Be April 3

AMSTERDAM — The educational and fund-raising crusade of the Montgomery County Unit of the American Cancer Unit gets under way April 3 on a hopeful note: "We want to wipe out cancer in your lifetime."

In accordance with the Presidential proclamation and Congressional resolution, Mayor John P. Gomulka has asked city residents to support the cause.

A telethon will be April 3 at the New Amsterdam Apts. Community Center from 10 a.m. - 6 p.m. under the chairmanship of Bill Pope.

On that same date the house to house canvassing throughout the county will also begin under the chairmanship of Paul Tonko. Letters have been mailed out to all industries under the chairmanship of Frank Pabis. Retail division contributions will be chaired by Mrs. Mary Insogna and special gifts are under the chairmanship of Dr. Sok Ko.

Sal Battaglia is local crusade chairman.

PREPARE FOR TELETHON — Chairmen of the annual Cancer Fund telethon to be held on Sunday, April 3, make plans for the upcoming event at a meeting at Amsterdam Memorial Hospital. From left, Sal Battaglia, cancer crusade chairman; Bill Pope, telethon chairman; Dr. Sok N Ko, special gifts chairman; Mrs. Mary Insogna, retail division chairman; Paul Tonko, county canvassing chairman and Frank D. Pabis, industries chairman. (Maroney)

A call from the school nurse at a local grade school, who was concerned by 4th and 5th graders smoking, sent him into action. We used materials and pictures available from the Cancer Society and presented our program during the last period of school. After our presentation, the children and teacher asked if we would stay for a question & answer period. We agreed to stay and were surprised that so many children were concerned about cancer—they had relatives and friends coping with the disease and their parents would not discuss it with them or answer their questions.

They felt so helpless and frightened. Quite an informative time for all of us! Dr. Ko ordered booklets to offer parents on ways to help children cope in a positive manner.

While working with Dr. Ko and having to travel to various functions, meetings, etc., many a time his wife, Elaine would call and ask me to make sure that he had something to eat—he would come right from his office and had no time for his dinner. That is true dedication!

Dr. Ko and I spent many hours together attending seminars, telethons etc., and I learned the story of his life in Korea and here in America. He was so proud to be an American and we were so fortunate to have him! His sense of humor was delightful and unique—an example:

Dr. Ko had scheduled a meeting of our Public Education Committee at his home. It snowed heavily that week and when I arrived at his home, I found I was the only one that attended. Of course, we had our meeting and while enjoying a cup of tea and fortune cookies, I said "Dr. Ko, may I ask you a personal question?" He nodded and I said "Members of our committee are both younger and older than myself, you call them by their first names yet you always address me as Mrs. Brownell. Why?" He nodded and answered, "Two reasons, First I have great respect for you. Second, I have a hard enough time pronouncing Brownell, how can I say "Shirry"! (The letters, S & L are difficult to pronounce in the Oriental languages).

The knowledge I gained from volunteering with Dr. Ko aided me in discovering my cancer early enough for me to make a full recovery now for 14 years. Again, thanks to Dr. Ko!

—Shirley M. Brownell

ROTARY

Sok became a member of Rotary in 1986. He served in various capacities and supported Rotary's many activities even before he became a member. He eventually served as Co-Chairman of the District 7190 Youth Exchange Program and was Chairman of the Polio Plus fund raising program for Amsterdam Rotary.

As Co-Chairman of the District Youth Exchange Program, he helped develop one of the the most successful programs in the district. Polio Plus was an international effort to wipe out polio around the world. Rotary International asked Amsterdam Rotary to set a goal of at least $16,000. Sok and his committee decided that the goal would be $40,000 and were successful in reaching that goal through projects completed, contributions and pledges.

Sok also supported the youth exchange program by welcoming students into his home. These foreign students came from Sweden, Finland, Mexico, Argentina, Japan, Australia, Denmark, Bolivia, Germany and Russia.

The list of exchange students includes:

1.	Eva Vestervall	1978-79	Sweden
2.	Tuija Itkonen	1981-82	Finland
3.	Magdalena Medina	1983-84	Mexico
4.	Martin Fourcade	1984-85	Argentina
5.	Chiyoko Mine	1986-87	Japan
6.	Toni Weller	1986-87	Australia
7.	Tommi Viskari	1988-89	Finland
8.	Melissa Simpson	1989-90	Australia
9.	Herwig Pape	1990-91	Germany
10.	Edward Shpikalov	1990-91	Russia

Since Sok's death, Elaine has continued to support the Youth Exchange Program by taking more students:

11.	Jesper Arkil	1991-92	Denmark
12.	Didier Flores	1991-92	Bolivia
13.	Peter Iverson	1992-93	Denmark
14.	Tobias Eriksson	1996-97	Sweden
15.	Jussi Haario	1997-98	Finland

Among the many exchange students who lived in Dr. Ko's home was Tuija Itkonen from Finland. Even though she came as an exchange student, her stay was extended to the point that Sok and Elaine helped support and pay for both her undergraduate and graduate education completed here in the States. She became sort of an adopted daughter of the Ko family. Rotary District 7190 also helped by giving Tuija a $1,000 award.

EXCHANGE STUDENTS AND THEIR FAMILIES

A Message from Germany

Without knowing Sok we all have the feeling of losing a very good friend. His letter to Herwig last year was so warm and kindly that Renate and I were absolutely sure that Herwig would have a very good year with you. All things Herwig wrote about Sok made our mind for a warm, nice and very good man.

We hope our Herwig will be helpful to you. We are sure he will. Thank you for all your kindness to Herwig.

—Renate and Anja Pape
Furth, Germany
Herwig Pape's parents

Papa Ko

"I wish Papa Ko was here to share this moment," is what I was thinking while playing ball with my 2-year-old son, Daniel, on the lawn of the Ko's house; the place I come to visit home in America, Daniel is young now, but in time he will learn from me what kind of man Papa Ko was and how he influenced—or rather changed —the course of my life.

I will tell Daniel how I first got to know the Kos while living with them as an exchange student. He'll find out how Papa Ko had seen the potential in the shy Finnish girl to grow, learn and educate herself long before she would realize it herself. Five days before the end of the exchange year, he sat me down on the couch and, with Elaine next to him, told me of their wish to finance four years of college in the United States should I wish to pursue them here. This was quite the news to take back to Finland with me. I came back to the States within a year after finishing high school in Finland and lived with the Kos for the first two years while studying at Fulton-Montgomery Community College.

Tuija Itkonen.

I also greatly appreciated the chance to come home to the Kos house on weekends and holidays while finishing my BA degree at State University of New York at Oswego. Daniel will also learn about Papa Ko's love for fishing and his decision to continue his financial support to me even after receiving my BA degree. One day, before the well-earned and much-awaited-for fishing trip to Florida, he unexpectedly told Elaine of his wish to cancel the trip in order for me to continue on to graduate school. I had chosen Massachusetts College of Art and went on to experience the excitement of living in Boston for the two years of graduate studies.

Tuija and her son Daniel Cohen.

When the time comes, I hope I will be able to convey to my son the overwhelming feelings of pride, accomplishment and gratitude I felt on the day of my graduating in May 1990. I had my own parents from Finland and the Kos next to me then. I was also full of hope and dreams for the future and very happy to share the occasion with another special person, Richard, who two years later asked me to marry him and is now a wonderful father to Daniel.

It is sad to realize that Papa Ko is not here to see and

share the fruits of his labor. I do hope that I'll be able to bring Daniel up to be the kind of person Papa Ko would be proud of; one who knows who he is, where he came from and what his goals are. Also, one who believes in his own abilities and keeps on learning, and, like Papa Ko, open-minded inclusive of different kinds of people and cultures. It is important for the generations to come as well as for ourselves, to let it be known that once a person existed and certain things are taking place now because of him. I want everyone to know what a big difference he and his family have made in my life, and I do hope that I'll find a way to continue his legacy and give the chance I had to someone else. What he did with his life was to give so many of us the courage and drive for the future.

—Tuija Itkonen
Hattula, Finland

Honor His Life and Carry on His Work

Although we didn't know Doctor Ko very well, we heard many wonderful things about him from Tuija and Richard. In the Jewish tradition any multiple of eighteen means 'chai' or life. The establishing of the Sok Nam Ko Educational Foundation is a wonderful way to honor his life and to carry on his work.

—Jane and Sumner Cohen

Magdalena Medina—Mexico—1983-1984

I remember Dr.Ko saying to me, "You are so quiet. If you don't try to speak English, you'll never learn." That encouraged me to speak so that I could learn faster. I think he was very serious with a big heart. He treated me as part of the family and I loved that. It was ten years ago that your family took me to Florida to Disney World. I am so thankful to you for these wonderful memories.

—Magdalena Medina
Mexico

Tommi Viskari—Finland—1988-1989

I had the great opportunity as an exchange student to spend a year (1988-1989) with the Ko family. In 1988 I decided to apply for a year abroad through the Rotary Exchange Student Program. I had thrown the javelin for about ten years and was really concerned as to how I could continue throwing in the United States, where the sport of track and field is not that popular—especially javelin. I even asked the Rotary Correspondent if he could find a family who would understand my interest in javelin. I don't know how I ended up with the Ko family, but it was the best thing that could have happened to me. At first I had some doubts, because Ko didn't sound like an American name. But, when I got their first letter I knew I would enjoy my stay with them.

Tommi Viskari— Winner at the World Junior Track and Field Championship, Bulgaria, 1990.

Dr. Ko was really a true sports fan. He was ready to help me to carry on my throwing. He took me to Yale and West Point to compete with the college throwers. I really enjoyed it. He was still very athletic while I was in Amsterdam. He played volleyball and took me to play, too. I will always remember when he used to give me instructions, and if I did something wrong he used to tease me. Sometimes he teased me at the dinner table by asking me all kinds of questions. I had a good time with him.

Dr. Ko thought that I would have a good chance to continue my schooling in the United States. He gave me a chance to stay another year with his family and get my high school diploma and attend college in the States. I felt very fortunate because not every exchange student has this kind of opportunity. It was a difficult decision. It took months for me to make up my mind. Finally I decided not to stay. I think I never did thank him enough for the offer of such a fine opportunity.

Dr. Ko was a very special human being and anyone who had a chance to meet him would not forget him. He will always be in my thoughts.

—Tommi Viskari
Finland

International Rotary Conference in Seoul, Korea.

Eva Vestervall
1978-79 Sweden.

Tuija Ilkonen
1981–82 Finland.

Magdalena Medina
1983–84 Mexico.

Martin Fourcade
1984–85 Argentina.

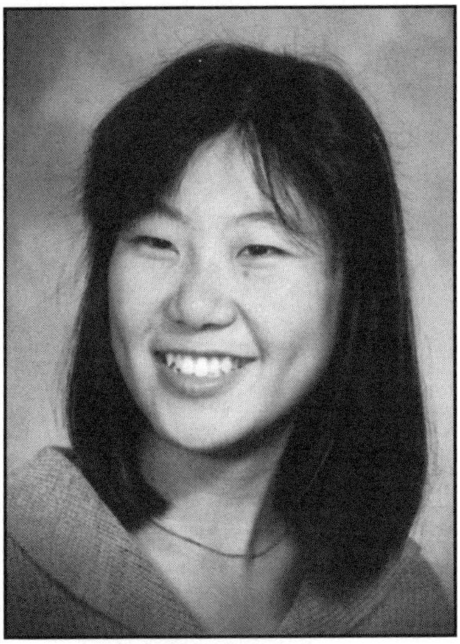

Chiyoko Mine
1986–87 Japan.

Toni Weller
1986–87 Australia.

Tommi Viskari
1988–89 Finland.

Melissa Simpson
1989–90 Australia.

Herwig Pape
1990–91
Germany.

Edward Shpikalov
1990–91 Russia.

Jesper Arkil
1991–92 Denmark.

Didier Flores
1991–92   Bolivia.

Peter Iverson
1992–93   Denmark.

Tobias Eriksson
1996-97   Sweden.

Jussi Haario
1997-98   Finland.

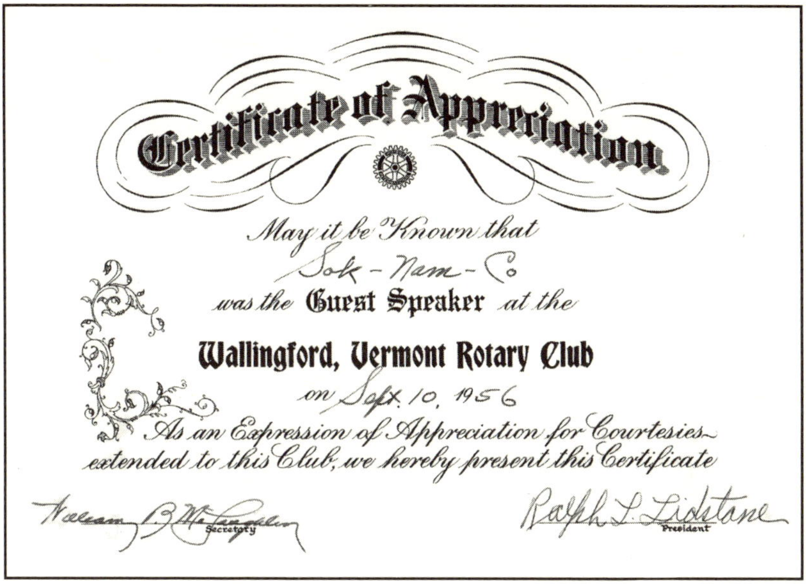

Certificate of Appreciation

May it be Known that

Sok - Nam - Co

was the Guest Speaker at the

Wallingford, Vermont Rotary Club

on Sept. 10, 1956

As an Expression of Appreciation for Courtesies extended to this Club, we hereby present this Certificate

Secretary

Ralph L. Lidstone
President

A Man With Many Visions

While it is rather difficult to pinpoint the exact time when I began to get acquainted with Sok, it was probably about the time of his 50th birthday in the fall of 1984. I had joined Rotary in the spring of 1984. That fall, Lorry and I were invited to the 50th birthday party which Elaine had planned to celebrate Sok's special day. The subject of joining Rotary was mentioned.

It was on this occasion that I learned that Sok had a sense of humor. During the evening when Sok was opening his birthday presents, suddenly the guests began to laugh. I said, "What's everybody laughing at?" Elaine lifted up a doll which was anatomically designed! That was what was causing the uproar. Sok thought the doll was unique, too.

However, it took a long time for me to feel comfortable while visiting with Sok. For some reason I was very intimidated the first few times I saw him. I suppose it was the fact that he was Oriental and he was a professional held in high esteem by those who knew him. It was at this party that I began to see his human side.

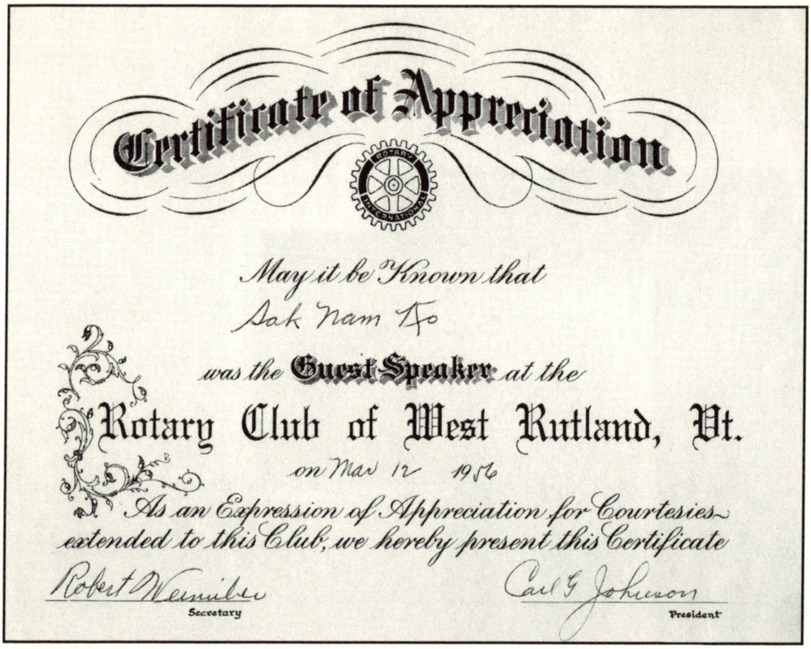
Certificate of Appreciation

May it be Known that

Sok Nam Ho

was the **Guest Speaker** at the

Rotary Club of West Rutland, Vt.

on Mar 12 1956

As an Expression of Appreciation for Courtesies extended to this Club, we hereby present this Certificate

Robert Weimiller
Secretary

Carl G. Johnson
President

At this 50th birthday party, Ben Hawkins and I strongly urged Sok to join Rotary. He seemed very reluctant to even consider the possibility, saying that he was very busy and he didn't believe he could give up the time to devote to the organization. It took Ben and me another two years to convince Sok to join Rotary. We really had to coerce and practically blackmail him into joining. With this considerable pressure on our part, Sok joined Rotary in the summer of 1986.

As time went on, Sok and I met on several occasions; at parties, etc. We became involved with the exchange student program. Before even joining Rotary, Sok and Elaine had had four exchange students in their home, so Sok became interested in working more directly with the Youth Exchange Program.

Polio Plus

Shortly after Sok joined Rotary, the Polio Plus Program began. They asked for a chairman and he agreed to work with Ben Hawkins at the District level. Rotary International sent out a letter to each club asking for money. The goal was to irradicate not only polio but other diseases in every country in the world. They hoped to raise 120 million dollars. The amount they asked each club to raise was determined by the number of members in the club. The Amsterdam Club was asked to raise $16,000. Sok's eagerness to work on this program was evident when he announced, "Well, we'll raise $40,000. Everyone thought he was crazy. He and the other members of the committee worked hard on the three-year program and our Rotary *did* raise the $40,000.

Besides this extraordinary effort and accomplishment, Polio Plus of Rotary International didn't raise just 120 million; they raised 220 million dollars. A lot of the work was coordinated through UNICEF. With this humanitarian effort, it is now possible that within a few years, nobody in any part of the world will have polio, measles, rubella or other childhood diseases.

Youth Exchange Programs

In 1987, Sok joined the District Committee for Youth Exchange and in 1988 he became Co-Chairman of Youth Exchange along with me. We served together on this committee for four years up until the time of his death. We attended local meetings and District Conferences at the Sagamore, Cooperstown and Lake Placid. Sok and I had been over to Vermont in January 1991 to set up plans for a conference over there but he died before he had a chance to participate in that conference.

Trips to Russia

Sok made two trips to Russia in the summers of 1988 and 1989. Prior to his leaving in 1989, he asked me to write letters of introduction to the Rotary Clubs in Moscow and Alexandria. I told him, "You don't need letters from me! You are Co-Chairman here."

He added, "No, no, no! You're the boss. It would be better." Now, I wasn't the boss. We were Co-Chairmen. Yet he always called me the boss. I had been on the Youth Exchange for a few years, so Sok figured that I knew more than he did. That was not the case. However, I did write a letter introducing Sok so that he could speak for our district and convey the idea

that we'd be very interested in having a Russian student come to the United States. Even though I wrote the letter, my thoughts included, "This guy is crazy. It's not going to happen, but he wants to do it so let him!" I'll be damned if he didn't succeed.

It was solely through Sok's efforts that Ed Shpikalov was brought here from Moscow. Eddie was the *very first* Russian Rotary Exchange Student to come to the United States. Tanya Larina and I flew to J.F.K. International Airport in a private jet owned by then Rotary District Governor Ed Jenner to meet Eddie. Sok had planned to go also, but as was his custom he had promised to stay in his office to help someone. Eddie thought these Americans must really be rich when he saw our private plane at J.F.K.

That was also the year when he spoke to Tanya Larina, an instructor in Russia, and invited her to come to Amsterdam for a year. Her coming had nothing to do with Rotary, but it shows his visionary acts which he pursued while in Russia.

Added to these invitations, in fact, the year following Sok's death we had another boy come here from Latvia only because of what Sok had begun.

Rotarian of the Year

Each year at our Rotary Installation Banquet, we name a Student of the Year, a Person of the Year (somebody within the community) and a Rotarian of the Year. After his year of working on Polio Plus and serving on the District Committee and Co-Chairman of Youth Exchange, Sok was chosen as Rotarian of the Year (in 1989). Sometimes it seems that he never was given the recognition he so richly deserved, but he did receive this award and appreciated it.

Korean Exchange

A vision of his which did not materialize was that of sending an exchange student to Korea. While attending an International Convention in Korea, he was laying the foundation for a possible exchange of students some day. He was always thinking, planning and challenging. I'm sure if he had lived there would have been a Korean exchange student in Amsterdam eventually.

A Personal Account Through T.J.

One year, long after applications for becoming an exchange student had been processed and assignments made, our son, T.J., decided that he'd like to spend a year somewhere abroad. Usually by the middle of November each accepted applicant knows where and when he/she is going abroad. Not so with T.J. He didn't decide he was interested until about Christmas time. When he asked me to help him become an exchange student, I felt that he was really putting me on the spot. My wife and I would be willing to take foreign students for a year if Rotary would accept T.J. at this late date. When I mentioned this to Sok, his quick answer was, "No problem!" Sok offered his home to serve as a host family, too. He didn't even mention asking Elaine first. So, with applications submitted and an assignment made, T.J. could go to Bolivia.

INTERVIEWING PROCESS

The next step was the interviewing process. By this time all the other candidates had had two interviews. T.J. was behind schedule! So in the spring he went to the District Conference at the Sagamore in Lake George, when all the out-going students were to be interviewed for the last time to be sure that everything was O.K.

Interviewers usually ask questions about family life, any possible troubles at home which might interfere with going abroad, boy friends or girl friends and if the candidate is sure he/she wants to be away from home for a year. Those were the topics I usually covered but not Sok. He would ask questions about political issues, current events, American history, etc. He felt that our students would be asked questions by their host families and he didn't want the young folks to be embarrassed by not knowing the answers.

Now, T.J. loved Dr. Ko. He thought the world of him and was glad that he would be interviewed by him. When the interview was over, I was standing outside the room where the interviews were held, talking to some other students. Tom Gould came along and was laughing heartily. I said, "What's so funny? How did he do?"

Tom answered, "Don't worry, he made it!"

This happened to be an election year. Sok asked questions about the candidates: what T.J. thought about the candidates, whether or not he thought Jesse Jackson would run, etc. But the climax was when Sok asked T.J.,"Can you tell me what the Electoral College is?"

T.J. looked Sok straight in the eye and said, "Dr. Ko, I never heard of that college!" That was the end of the questioning because Sok didn't know what to ask him after that answer! He probably shook his head in disbelief, but T.J. gave an honest answer. T.J. went on to have one of the best years of his life in Bolivia. Sok did all he could to help T.J. by showing him slides and giving him much information.

Sok was a tough interviewer. Perhaps one of the reasons was sort of a pay-back on what he had personally gone through. Sometimes his questioning would have a student in tears. I think he wanted to see how students would react under pressure. He wanted to see what kinds of habits they had and if they would answer in truthful ways. If a student didn't know an answer, Sok hoped the candidate would at least say, "I'm sorry, but I don't know the answer." He really didn't like it if a student would ramble on and on and try to answer a question in six different ways when he didn't know what he was talking about. Probably this is why T.J. got by when he admitted having no knowledge about the Electoral College.

Having a Root Canal Job Done

T.J.'s admiration for Dr. Ko was enhanced by a professional situation. T.J. had been told by a local dentist that he needed a root canal and it would take three or four sessions to complete the job. This particular dentist didn't work on Saturdays and after school appointments would interfere with T.J.'s ball playing. I suggested that he ask Dr. Ko to take care of the problem. So T.J. had his mother call for an appointment and was taken to the office. Dr. Ko knocked T.J. out, did the root canal job and eventually had the nurse call Lorry to come and get T.J.

That night when I arrived home, T.J. cheerfully said, "Hi, how do I look?"

"What do you mean, how do I look? I remarked.

To which T.J. added, "Do I look dopey?"

I continued, "Well, you normally are a little dopey. What's the matter?"

"The work's done!" was T.J.'s grateful response.

This is an example of Sok's willingness to help patients at any hour in the day. He worked in the interest of his patients and was especially kind to young people, including the exchange students who had dental problems and were so far away from home.

Wearing Out the Telephone

Working together in Rotary especially with exchange students we found many occasions when topics needed to be discussed and decisions had to be made. The telephone seemed to be our main avenue for communication. It became our principal mode for discussion. We would call each other on the phone night after night discussing many topics regarding personal and Rotary affairs. Many times our calls were made late at night and would last into the early hours of the morning. I'll bet there wasn't a day that passed that we didn't talk on the phone about something. My wife used to say she didn't know who liked to talk more on the phone, Sok or me!

Occasionally, I needed to call him during the day at his office about a decision which needed to be made. I always pictured some poor patient with his mouth wide open and with some sort of apparatus in his mouth and not being able to talk. Then my phone call would necessitate Sok answering the phone. I would say, "Am I bothering you?"

I can just hear his voice so vividly saying, "Oh, no, Tom. No, Tom!" He'd talk on and on; seemingly having plenty of time to chat when I knew better. Time meant nothing to him.

Being Late

Speaking of time, there must be many stories about Sok being late to everything. He never seemed to get anywhere on time. I used to say that he was like the South Americans who use a watch only to tell the day; not for the purpose of telling time. I think time meant even less to Sok. I don't think he ever owned a watch. He was never on time. He'd rush like hell and appear saying, "Sorry, Tom. Sorry, Tom!" Or he might say, "I got lost." But his favorite excuse was, "I had an emergency." He just never knew how to say, "No" to anyone who had a toothache or needed help immediately.

There was one exception to his habit of being late. He really wasn't too bad when it came to getting to Rotary. I think his office girls kicked him out of the office when it was time to go to a meeting. Or maybe it was because he didn't want to pay the dollar fine imposed upon a Rotarian who is late. If a person is fined, he can give any excuse which may or may not be accepted. Sok came up with some good excuses once in awhile; some real corkers! But half of the time nobody knew what the hell he was saying, so they would say, "Oh, O.K. Let him go!"

Had an Accent

Many qualities surface in my thoughts as I think of my associations with Sok during the years. His accent was apparent, yet he didn't think he had an accent. He seemed to think of himself first as American, even in the way he used the English language, and second as a Korean. So many times he would be telling me a story and I couldn't understand what he was talking about. He'd start to talk and get so excited about something. As we became better acquainted, I was comfortable enough to say, "Wait, wait! You're getting too far ahead of me. I don't know what the hell you are saying!"

There is the story about when he lived in Castleton. It was in the early fifties when you still used an operator to make a phone connection. Sok picked up the receiver and said to the operator, "I want to speak to Sam Jones (or whatever)."

The operator stated, "Line busy. Would you like me to call you when the line is free?"

"Yes, please," added Sok.

"O.K., Ko" was the promise from the operator.

Sok responded, "How you know it's me?" Now in this small town of Castleton with a population of about 600, the operator recognized every voice in town and especially one with a Korean accent!

His First Deer

One rather amusing story which Sok told me was about the first deer he ever shot. The animal practically walked up and kissed him, so Sok said, "I'd better shoot him if he's that close!" Whoever he was hunting with said, "Get going! Get out there and get that deer!" Sok did just that and got his first deer.

Generosity

Sok was the biggest, softest touch in the world for anything. He had a heart of gold. He was very giving and was always looking for some way to give something to someone. If it wasn't from his own pocket, he would find somebody else who would give to someone who was deserving. For example, when he was preparing for the People to People trip to Russia, he made sure that many dollars came out of *his* pocket. Then he went to other people in the community to raise money by saying, "Let's take the less fortunate with us, too. Let's take someone else who won't have the opportunity to go unless we help."

I noticed this type of generosity with the exchange students. He took them to many places here in the States; all of which cost a great deal of money. Then, of course, if any one of them needed dental care, he did the best he could to solve their problems without charge.

Socially, he was generous, too. There were years when he hosted lawn parties and dinners for his friends and relatives. Added to this, he was generous with individuals like me. Anytime we went to a meeting, if there was *any* way that we could stop on the way home, he wanted to have dinner at a restaurant. He'd say, "We're going to stop to eat and this will be my treat. I've got to take you out." It was like he had to give ten times more than he received. That was his way. He wanted to do that. I guess he felt as though it was an obligation. Maybe this was part of his background. He wanted to show his appreciation for the opportunities he had had in the United States.

PERSISTENCE

Another quality which aided him in helping others was his persistence. When he had an idea he would pursue all avenues needed to accomplish his goals. For example, his determination was demonstrated when he was seeking support for bringing Tanya Larina, the Russian instructor, to Amsterdam. He had met Tanya while on one of his People to People trips to Russia. He invited the young teacher to be a guest in his home for a year. While here he felt that she would be a fine addition to the school programs in this area. He went to the Rotary Club and local school boards to ask for sponsorship for Tanya, so as to get some money for her to help out with expenses. He just didn't want to take "No" for an answer. He just kept badgering and badgering until someone finally saw what he wanted; whether it was right or wrong. In *his* eyes, he was right. Again, as it was so often the case, he wasn't doing this for himself, but rather for someone else. It wasn't that he was going to gain anything personally. He didn't want notoriety; he had this hope of helping others. With persistence, he went after various groups and individuals. With more and more resolve, he went after them again and again. Finally, he got some to agree to give her a small amount of money. This made Sok happy to know that Tanya would receive about $5,000. However, as time went on, there were several in the area who never took advantage of what she had to offer. Here was somebody who had much to offer, had something to teach and show people and very few took advantage of it.

Sok Nam Ko and Iron-Eyes Cody (Espera DeCorti).

The Fulton-Montgomery Community College did invite her to participate in their programs, but the Amsterdam schools never used her services. This didn't set well with Sok at all. He *never* really got over this disappointment.

Sok was a persistent and very determined man. Being set in his ways, he often ruffled a few feathers when folks couldn't get him to change his mind about a given issue. It often appeared that he just wouldn't listen to the views of others.

Sense of Humor

Sok had a unique sense of humor. His facial expressions did not always convey this quality. Many thought of him as being very serious and that he focused on one thing—his work. However, he did have a real playful nature and was a real character.

Unpretentious About Clothes

Even though he may have been upset with me at times, I can say that we really had a lot of fun laughing about so many things. One topic which was mentioned at various times was about the clothes he wore.

He was so unpretentious, which was wonderful. Elaine said that for several years Sok didn't mind wearing Salvation Army seconds. What he wore didn't especially matter to him. He used to say, "It doesn't matter what you wear as long as your clothes are clean and they fit you." Even though he felt that way and dressed accordingly, Elaine tried to suggest changes such as not wearing plaids and stripes together or stripes and checks. He was also likely to purchase shoes or sneakers in the least expensive stores, saying, "There's nothing wrong with these shoes. They seem to fit."

It is too bad that many people get caught up in the latest fads and feel they must keep up with the styles. Yet I can remember the teachings of my mother when she said, "You can tell a lot about a man if he's got on clean clothes, wears clean shoes and has clean fingernails." I have thought about that so often. Yet at times Lorry would say, "Who the hell dresses him? Did you see what he had on today?" Sok would be walking around just as proud as could be wearing an assortment of checks and plaids and perhaps wearing orange socks or whatever. He was as happy as could be, while I am thinking, "What a way to live!" I guess the problem was mine. I was jealous of his ability to feel comfortable wearing most anything!

West Point

While Sok and I spent many times together, perhaps the most enjoyable *and* most frustrating was our trip to a football game at West Point. I had tickets to one of the Army games and I asked Sok if he'd like to go. He was pleased with the invitation and, believe it or not, was ready to go on time! Of course, I had told him that we needed to be down there in time to see the dress parade. Sok knew that if we weren't there on time, we would miss this special event. Consequently, I told him to be ready at 7:00 A.M. and we actually left Amsterdam at 7:30. Our group consisted of Tanya Larina, the Russian instructor from Rostov-on-Don, Herwig Pape, the exchange student from Furth, Germany whom we fondly called Hank, Colleen, our daughter; Sok and me. Off we went on a gorgeous fall day.

On the way I said to Sok, "I know you've been to West Point for a football game before this, but I don't know as you've been there for a parade. We don't have a pass for the stands. If you want to sit in the stands, we'll have to wait until twenty minutes before parade time. Then they'll open the stands for the general public, so we can sit in the same area as the generals and other V.I.P.s. We'll be looking right out on the field as the cadets come out." My plans were carried out and, as luck would have it, we acquired seats next to the top row and really were at a great vantage point. The parade lasted for about an hour and we enjoyed every bit of it.

After the parade, as we were going down the stairs, I looked around and Sok was gone! I said, "Where did he go? What are we going to do now?" Hank, the exchange student remarked, "Don't worry about him. We lost him for two and a half hours when we were in Washington, D.C."

I retorted, "Yeh, but the football game will start within an hour and I have his ticket!" In desperation we went from one side of the plain to the other, completely ignoring the signs which read: "Please stay off the grass!" We walked right across the plain, past the monument of George Washington. As we hurried along looking in all directions, I was sputtering, "For all I know he may be having lunch with General Westmoreland," who was there that day. This gave us an idea. We looked in the dining hall, but there were no lunches being served. At that point I concluded that he was probably in the Commandant's House with Westmoreland. Trying to suggest something practical, Hank said, "Well, what do you want to do now?"

By this time I was getting greatly concerned. It was getting close to the time for the game to begin. How were we going to find him? I was also beginning to get angry. You see, I am one who usually enjoyed being down there and I had everything carefully planned for the day. I thought every detail had been taken care of but, Sok's disappearance wasn't in my plans. Why did he do this to us?

As we looked and looked for Sok for the better part of an hour, I was getting extremely upset and angry. I kept thinking that if he wanted to go for a walk or go to see somebody or do something, why didn't he tell us so that we could make plans to meet somewhere at a given time? Finally, we stood right there at the Reviewing Stand and Hank told us the detailed story of how Sok was missing for two and a half hours in Washington. Then Tanya told us about losing Sok in Russia. He disappeared from the group. It turned out that he was in a central square taking pictures.

Knowing that I had the tickets and Sok wouldn't be able to get into the stands without me, in desperation I said, "Let's go back to our car. Maybe he got caught up in the crowd and has gone back to the car to wait for us." We turned around and started to walk in that direction. We were near Doubleday Field (the baseball field at West Point) which is next to the Parade Grounds. All of a sudden here comes Sok walking along like he was out for a little stroll in the park on Sunday. He greeted us by simply saying, "Hi!"

I said, "Hi? Where the hell have you been?"

He casually commented, "Oh, I just went over and had my picture taken with General Westmoreland. I talked to this one and I talked to that one. I didn't know where *you* went?"

Almost in disbelief of his explanation, I just shook my head and walked away. I decided there was no sense in saying anything. He blamed us! To him it was like it was *our* fault. He kept saying, "I didn't know where *you* went!"

After that we had a wonderful day. Everything worked out fine. We went through the church and he took pictures of the chapel. He took pictures of Trophy Point and got most of the game which was against Rutgers. I know he got some of the paratroopers coming into the stadium. We enjoyed our lunch right there in the stands.

I walked his butt off going up the hill to the stadium. I was so hot under the collar. After getting seated for the game I looked down and saw Sok with his shoes off. He was sitting there with just his socks on. I thought, "Well, he's probably tired after all that walking!"

Giving him the benefit of my doubts, I think Sok got so enraptured with the time and what was going on, he just didn't think. General Westmoreland was there and Sok thought he wouldn't get a chance to see him again, so off he went by himself. He may have thought he could take some pictures. He may have talked to some cadets. Only God knows where he went. He *never* told me what he did, perhaps because he realized how angry I was with his disappearance for that crucial hour before the game.

Elaine, A Very Supportive Help-Mate

So much has been said about Sok and his accomplishments. There were many the acolades bestowed—deservedly so. But, I feel it should be stressed that many of his goals would not or could not have been accomplished without the love, perseverance and dedication of Elaine. She was the epitome of the expression: "Behind every good man there is a good woman." In Elaine's case—a *great* woman. Lorry and I often reflect on all the things she did, not that Sok was chauvinistic or demanding—just assuming that Elaine would do it or wouldn't mind helping out, volunteering, hosting, or whatever he deemed necessary. The word "No" was not part of Sok's vocabulary and he felt it should be the same for his family.

At the Time of His Death

In spite of our differences, in these few short years I learned to respect and love him dearly. During his grave illness in Albany, I was attending a Rotary Training Session in Saratoga. With warm and concerned thoughts of him, I was paying tribute to him when the message came that our beloved Sok had passed away. The news produced a quiet sadness over our entire meeting. We found his death almost impossible to believe.

Sok's Parting Message compliment of the Pigeons

My grandmother used to share bits of folklore with our family. She had one story which stated that it is good luck if a pigeon drops his droppings upon you. The Irish folklore also said that somehow or in some way, when a person passes away, he will send a message eventually to those left on earth. I would like to conclude my tribute to Sok with this rather amusing story even though at the time the incident wasn't funny at all.

I was walking along the street one day with another fellow from my office. All of a sudden, I didn't have a pigeon but instead a whole flock of pigeons bestow their "gifts" upon me. I stopped in my tracks and grabbed for my handkerchief which was in my pocket. I began to wipe off my head because the "gift" was dripping down my forehead and onto my face. Fortunately, I had a trench coat on but the mess continued down on my coat, hitting my pants and even dripping onto my shoes! *One* pigeon couldn't have done all that! What a mess!

Tom Dwyer.

As soon as I got hit by the "gift" from above and began trying to clean up the mess, I thought of my grandmother's folktale about good luck. I looked heavenward and said, "I'll be damned. You really got it bestowed on me. You did a hell of a job, Sok!" You see, I know damn well he was responsible. I could just imagine him sitting up there and chuckling.

When my friend and I reached the office, I explained about my reaction to the mess. When I got home, Lorry enjoyed my story so much! In fact, she couldn't wait to get on the phone to tell Elaine. Indeed, Sok got me! He had the last laugh this time.

—Tom Dwyer
Co-Chairman of the Rotary Youth Exchange

TRIBUTES FROM ROTARIANS

Visions Beyond Borders

My special memory of Sok is watching him last year at the Board of Education meetings making presentations to bring Tanya to Amsterdam. My second grade daughter is now writing her name in Russian and speaking simple greetings in Russian. Thanks to a heart and vision that could see beyond borders and limits. How he'll be missed, but how he lives on!

—John and Kittie Bintz

Our Trip to Cheju Island

We have many fond thoughts of Dr. Ko and, of course, our most memorable ones are of our trip to Cheju Island with him and Sue. Sok shared considerable information about his ancestors with us and he made our trip outstanding by explaining so much of what we were seeing. Of course, we would have been struggling if he hadn't spent so much time to explain the many types of food and what to order. We have many delightful memories of Sok, not only from our Korean trip, but also our many other contacts with him here in Amsterdam.

—Fred and Thelma Boettger

One of the kindest

Sok was one of the kindest, most supportive and most caring people we have ever known. His commitment to his family, to young people and to Rotary were a profound example to all of us. He was a giant among us, yet he bore it so lightly as to hide it from us until we came to know him.

—Peter and Debbie Brown

A Fine Gentleman

Sok was one of the finest gentlemen we have ever had the pleasure of meeting. He will be remembered for his dedication as Co-chairman of the District Rotary Youth Exchange Committee.

—Henry and Alice Goebel

Lofty Aspirations and Enormous Accomplishments

Sok never failed to put his time and energy toward worthwhile goals to benefit all of mankind. His aspirations were lofty but justified in enormous accomplishments. Through his life he stayed the same humble, loyal and lovable man who took his satisfaction from his pride in his family.

—Ben and Rudy Hawkins

Touched the Lives of So Many People

We will always remember Dr. Ko for the great interest shown when we adopted our Korean-born children, Jared and Anne.

His work and his interest in community projects and with the Student Exchange Program enabled him to touch the lives of many. He will be greatly missed.

—Carl and Kitty Ingalls

Gave Back to the World Much More Than He Took from It

My fondest memories of Sok revolve around the effort, time and energy he put into the Polio Plus Fund Raising Program sponsored by the Amsterdam Rotary. We raised $40,000 under his leadership.

My wife and I will always remember Sok as a wonderful man who gave back to the world much more than he took.

—John R. McCune

A Giant in Our Organization

Dr. Sok Ko was a giant in our organization and a man of outstanding dedication to all good causes. His shoes cannot be filled and as an organization we have lost a real great friend who shall be very much missed. He will leave a great void but give us the impetus to go after the worthwhile causes that he always championed.

—Nate Muskin and family

EXCHANGE STUDENTS FROM NEW YORK STATE DISTRICT 7190

Looked to Him as a Role Model

Dr. Ko was a great man and did so much for all of us as exchange students. He was there when I needed him, giving me support and I looked to him as a role model.

—Edgar Rolando Cordero

Gave Us the Chance of a Lifetime

Even though I didn't know Dr. Ko well, I know he gave others and myself the chance of a lifetime as a Rotary Exchange Student. He will remain in most people's minds because of his unselfishness and because of all the things he's done for others.

—Josh Garfinkle

A Great Friend and Advisor to Exchange Students

Dr. Ko was a man of outstanding qualities; a great leader in all he did. He was a great friend and advisor to all; especially to us, the exchange students, outbound and from abroad.

—Jonathan M. Paley

The Recorder

SATURDAY, FEBRUARY 6, 1988

Rotary seeks funds to beat polio abroad

The Amsterdam Rotary Club wants to raise $40,000 toward a $120 million Rotary International PolioPlus drive to distribute polio vaccine around the world.

Dr. Sok Nam Ko is chairman of the Amsterdam Rotary Club's drive, which will occur this month. Ben F. Hawkins is district chairman in charge of the effort of the Amsterdam, Gloversville, Johnstown and Broadalbin clubs.

Ko said Amsterdam Rotary Club members have pledged to collect $32,325, and they hope the business community will contribute the rest of the $40,000 pledge.

PolioPlus is an effort by Rotary International to immunize all children in the world against polio. The organization, which has 23,000 clubs in 161 countries, wants to provide all the vaccine needed for five-year immunization projects in any country asking for help.

In order to be completely immunized against polio, a child needs three doses of the oral vaccine. Each dose costs 4 cents, so lifetime protection for a child costs 12 cents, Ko said.

"The money is not the largest problem in other countries," Ko said. "The problem is the availability of the vaccine. Almost all the polio vaccine in the world is manufactured in the U.S. and has to be shipped to other countries."

Both the Salk vaccine, an older form administered by injection, and the Sabin vaccine, liquid drops taken orally, were invented in the United States. The Salk vaccine has been almost completely replaced by the Sabin formula.

Polio has not been a problem in the United States since the 1960s, thanks to vaccine, but continues to kill and cripple people in other countries. The disease, caused by a virus, attacks the nervous system and paralyzes it.

A Kind and Caring Counselor

I was a Rotary Exchange Student in Brazil. I was very sorry to hear about the death of Dr. Ko. I met him during preparations to go abroad and he helped me and my family a lot, reassuring us about the upcoming year. In this and other ways, he played an important role in guiding me to where I am now.

During my interview he cleared up many of my family's questions and doubts. Then, at our district orientation in Lake Placid, he was honest and straightforward about Rotary rules, putting them in terms that we, as teens, could understand. He told us about using our common sense and not being afraid to ask for help.

Dr. Ko was a kind and caring counselor and we were fortunate to have him as a part of our exchange. We'll always remember him with respect and love.

—Dayna Cratty-Rich

PEOPLE TO PEOPLE

Besides opening his home to the fine students from a variety of countries, Ko served as a chaperone for about 40 students on the People to People Program going to Russia in the summers of 1988 and 1989.

It was on his 1989 trip to Russia that Ko met Tanya Larina, a 25-year-old college instructor, who specializes in teaching Russian to foreign medical students at the university in her home town of Rostov-on-Don. Tanya was invited to the Ko home to reciprocate for her hospitality toward the area youngsters on the student tour of the U.S.S.R.

Tanya's accented but flawless English made her very popular teacher while in Amsterdam. In addition to teaching junior and senior high school classes about Russia, she taught in the Fulton-Montgomery Community College's foreign language program and addressed elementary school classes about her country. While here in Amsterdam, her main goals were to improve her English and to learn as much as possible about American family life and American culture in general.

During Tanya's year in the Ko home, she had as her guest her husband, Igor, whom she married just before coming to the United States. He is a flight engineer with the Soviet national airline Aeroflot. While in the Ko home, Tanya was also reunited with the tour group she guided in 1989.

Will Never Forget the People to People Project of 1989

I regard Sok as a friend of mine, though we knew each other for a very short time when we were together on a trip in the Sovict Union — the People to People project in 1989. I'll never forget this time.

I know he had a lot of friends among the Soviets. We all are missing him very much. I shall never forget our Sok. He is staying with us forever.

—Dmitri G. A. Alehin
Krogerup, Denmark

Inside the U.S.S.R.

A Soviet visitor offers his views about homeland

By MICHAEL HART
Deputy City Editor

Because their son is here, they are here.

And because they came, about 60 members of the greater Amsterdam business community learned Wednesday afternoon that events in the Soviet Union are not as bleak as they are sometimes reported, that politics can improve ties between the U.S. and the U.S.S.R. and that business people everywhere, including those in Amsterdam, have opportunities in the land of Lenin and Gorbachev.

About seven months ago, 17-year-old Edourd ("Eddie") Shpikalov became the first Soviet student ever to take part in a U.S. Rotary Club's Student Exchange Program.

The Amsterdam Rotary Club, through its student exchange program, invited the Soviet teen to live here for a year with the family of oral surgeon Dr. Sok Nam Ko. Ko, who died unexpectedly at 56 from complications after stomach surgery this March, had promoted the visit.

On Friday, the boy's parents, Dr. Lilia Shpikalov, a neurosurgeon, and Hait, flew in to visit their son and meet Ko's widow, Elaine Ko and their three children.

After touring this area for four days, the talk, on Wednesday afternoon, turned to things Soviet and American.

Hait, a Moscow business consultant, told the Rotarians at a luncheon at the Raindancer Restaurant that he "cannot say that everything is OK at this time in the Soviet Union," but he could say that he has "hope that in time things will be resolved."

A broad-chested man with a rectangular face, brown eyes and a warm, slightly raspy voice, Hait acknowledged that the breakup of the Eastern European block last year was significant, but that "in the Soviet Union it is not a critical situation."

Actually, he found "the increased political activity of the ordinary person" — even including strikes in Bylorussia — to have good elements. For one thing, the activity suggests that Soviet President Mikhail Gorbachev's policies of perestroika and glasnost are working.

Shortly after taking power several years ago, Gorbachev began his policy of perestroika, or restructuring the country's political and bureacratic structure, and his policy of glasnost, or increased openness within the country and improved contacts without.

For Hait that was a good deal. His company, MOST (which means "bridge" in Russian), advises companies worldwide on opportunities in the Soviet Union.

Please see SOVIET, Page 11

Recorder photo: Michael Hart

Boris Hait, a Soviet Rotarian and the father of exchange student Edourd Shpikalov, speaks to the members of Amsterdam's Rotary Club on Wednesday at the Raindancer Restaurant.

Dr. Ko's efforts continue forward

By MICHAEL HART
Deputy City Editor

She's not a Rotarian.

But when the Amsterdam Rotarians stood and gave their Soviet guest, Boris Hait, a warm round of applause Wednesday afternoon, Elaine Ko enthusiastically joined in.

Ko, the wife of the late Amsterdam oral surgeon, Dr. Sok Nam Ko, had reasons other than purely appreciative for applauding.

She could see in Hait, who stood before her, and in the five young exchange students who stood behind her, some of the tangible results of her husband's life-long love affair with cross-cultural contacts.

She could also see, not in the room but in the experiences of the past few weeks since her husband's death, that her husband's work is going on.

Recently, she and others have set up a foundation to carry on her husband's cultural exchanges, and a relative has begun a biography of her husband.

For both causes, Elaine Ko has appealed for local support. Donations from the community will help build the foundation, and words and photos from those who knew Dr. Ko will move the book along.

On the day that her husband died, March 16, Elaine Ko, her family and friends set up the Educational Exchange Foundation, a trust designed to help at least one person a year to live with a family in a foreign country.

The foundation, which was loosely begun a few years ago when Dr. Ko began selling videos of trips around the world, now stands at about $12,000. It collected $3,200 at a fundraiser two weeks ago in Amsterdam.

The foundation's goal of "more than $100,000," is an ambitious one, Mrs. Ko conceded, but, she added, "We want this to go on."

Dr. Ko died unexpectedly at the age of 56 in mid-March after several operations to remove a tumor from his stomach.

Ko's love of travel and cross-cultural contacts began in a war and rose out of necessity.

When he was 15, the Korean War's 38th-parallel — the line that divided North from South Korea and set territorial sides for the conflict — virtually ran through Ko's house.

Ko's father was taken prisoner, and Ko, the eldest of seven children, ran south — until he figuratively ran into the arms of U.S. Army Captain George Harrington. Harrington, a lawyer from Castleton, Vt., had a history of bringing orphaned or unwanted children into his Vermont family, and, as he headed home, he brought the young Ko with him.

In time, the boy became a surgeon, who, in turn, would bring young people from all over the world into his Amsterdam home.

Since 1973, the Kos have welcomed 15 young foreign students into their home. This year, they invited three: Edourd Shpikalov, 17, from Moscow, Herwig Pape, 18, from Furth, Germany, both students at Amsterdam High, and Tanya Laina, 27, from Rostov on Don, in the

Please see FORWARD, Page 11

Soviet

Continued from Page 5

Making contacts, he said smiling, "is my business."

"Come to my country," he told the Rotarians, "I show you anything you like to see."

Indeed, he said, his smile growing, his consulting company is one of the "first achievements of perestroika,"

Actually, contacts are expanding. It was about a year ago that businessmen in Moscow formed the country's first Rotary Club. Hait was one of their first members.

"Everyone wants to know what are Soviet Rotarians," Hait quipped. Then stretching his arms and broadening his smile, he said, "They are the same as you. Here."

After the luncheon, Hait acknowledged that the power struggle in the Soviet Union, in which some conservative politicians and workers are demanding that Gorbachev resign, is serious.

"But I hope he does not," Hait said. "I hope everything stays as it is because Gorbachev is good for the country. He makes it healthy. The people who want to push him out are not right. The healthy part of society supports Gorbachev."

It was under Gorbachev that the Communist's socialism has begun to give way to capitalism's free market. McDonald's opened a huge store in Red Square. And Hait approved.

"Capitalism," he asked, "what is that? At the turn of the century, it was a big man in a black hat crushing and twisting the workers." Hait demonstrated, gently twisting his black, palm-sized tourist camera.

"But now it is different. Austria and Germany are more socialist than the U.S.S.R. You can't find the borders any longer. In fact, the borders are open." He smiled again. "There are no more iron scales."

Forward

Continued from Page 5

Soviet Union, who teaches Russian in the Greater Amsterdam School District and at Fulton-Montgomery Community College.

On Wednesday, then, Elaine Ko found herself applauding Shpikalov's father, Boris Hait, after Hait gave a speech to the Rotarians at the Raindancer Restaurant. Hait and his wife, Dr. Lilia Shpikalov, a neurosurgeon, had come to visit their son, Edourd. About 10 feet behind Mrs. Ko stood five exchange students that the Rotary club was sponsoring.

Dr. Ko was a Rotarian, and, with Tom Dwyer, a local stockbroker, he was co-chairman of the club's student exchange committee. The club has promoted the exchange of about 60 students since the early '70s. It was Dr. Ko who had arranged for young Shpikalov's visit last year, making the Soviet teen the first to visit the U.S. through a Rotarian exchange program.

Dr. Ko's own experience drove deep the feeling for world peace, and it taught him, his widow said, "that peace won't suddenly break out just because one person says it should. But you can build peace through education and through contact between people, one on one, all over the world. That's one way to have peace."

Dr. Ko's experiences are being recorded in a biography that Elaine Ko's aunt, Dr. Helen Smith, is writing. Smith, a former professor at the State University College at Cortland, hopes to have the book done in about a year, Ko said. Plans are to publish it privately, sell it locally, and to put the proceeds into the foundation.

People who would like to send remembrances of Dr. Ko, including copies of correspondence and photos, may mail them to Helen Smith, 3877 Highland Rd., Cortland, 13045. Donations for the foundation may be mailed to Douglas Landon, a local attorney with the foundation. Landon's address is 25 Evelyn Ave., Amsterdam, 12010.

Couldn't Believe Being Invited to the United States

I would like to share with you my memories about such a short period of time when I knew Dr. Ko. Of course, I can't compete with those people who knew him 10, 20 or 30 years, but nevertheless I am thankful of my destiny that it presented me with that one and a half year of acquaintance. I think that it is great for every person to have somebody who helped you not only to visit another different country, but to have experience of living in the family and meeting so many nice people.

My first meeting with Dr. Ko took place on July 4, 1989 when I, after sleepless night of packing my suitcase, came to Moscow to meet my first group with which we spent more than 20 unforgettable days. Dr. Ko attracted everybody's attention from the very beginning—Korean with camera. For the USSR

THURSDAY, MARCH 1, 1990 — THE DAILY GAZETTE

Teacher Would Visit Amsterdam—

Dentist Working to Bring Soviet Guide to U.S.

By SAM ZURLO
Gazette Reporter

AMSTERDAM — A city dentist hopes to make a Soviet teacher's dream of visiting the United States come true.

"It's my personal project," said Dr. Sok Nam Ko, an oral surgeon.

Ko explained he met Tonia Larina last July when she was selected to represent the Soviet Union as an interpreter and guide during a visit by 19 Amsterdam and Bishop Scully high school students. The visit was part of the People to People Friendship Caravan.

"The purpose of the tour was to promote the peace process, the cultural exchange programs and generate good will between the two superpowers," says Ko, who accompanied the group.

Larina, who is about 30, is an English teacher and faculty member of the Rostov-on-Don Institute, a college in the southeastern section of the country. She currently is involved in translating Russian to English and teaching Soviet cultural history to medical students who come from several countries to study at the Medical Institute in Rostov-on-Don.

"She speaks, reads and writes the English language fluently, however she lacks the experience of living in an English-speaking country," says Ko, who came to this country from Korea. "She feels that visiting or receiving an invitation to the United States would be a dream come true."

Her chances of visiting this country "are very good," he said, noting she has already been formally invited here. There will be no cost for room and board because she will reside with Dr. and Mrs. Ko and their children at their Locust Avenue home.

The stumbling block is costly air fare, according to Ko, who said he is now in the process of attempting to win finanicial support from area businesses and organizations to help bring Larina to Amsterdam. He estimates the cost of air fare and a "small stipend" for spending money at $5,000. Ko admits it is now a "one man effort" but is optimistic of getting local support.

Explaining she is paid 140 rubels per month, Ko said Larina would have to work almost seven years and spend nothing for food, clothing or lodging just to cover the cost of airfare.

He has approached the Amsterdam Board of Education about the possibility of becoming a partner in sponsoring her visit. The board was interested, Ko said, but has not yet taken official action on the proposal.

"It would be mutually beneficial," Ko said. "She would have an opportunity to learn English while at the same time teaching local students about the Soviet language, culture, history and recent developments. It is a very useful situation in which our children can learn about Soviet traditions and especially current events."

School Superintendent H. Alan Brown said Ko addressed the school board last week and was told his request would be given full consideration.

"We do not offer Russian language in our program, and it's unlikely we'll offer it in the future," Brown said. "If it's a question of whether we would derive some benefits by having this lady accessible to our classrooms from time to time, sure, just to come in and share what her life is like in the

Dr. SOK NAM KO
Oral Surgeon

Soviet Union. It certainly would be a learning experience for both the school district and for her."

Ko also plans to confer with officials of Fulton-Montgomery Community College about the possibility of Larina attending the college and perhaps doing some foreign language instructing.

In a letter to Ko, Larina said she welcomed the chance to be the tour guide because it allowed her to communicate with Americans.

"Thanks to my work with Caravan, I became more free in my outlook," Larina wrote. "I am sure that we in the USSR must take all positive experiences from the USA and other capatilist countries, communicate with Americans in order to make friends and know each other better, and really build a friendship bridge which is of great importance for both of us."

Larina noted there has been much discussion in her country concerning a session of the Supreme Soviet about cooperative activity, saying "many people consider that it is a very hard time for the USSR and many of them don't believe in reforms. It's difficult to have a definite image about the future. We hope for the best but most of the people don't want to listen to rumors, they simply want to have results, they are tired of talk."

Reflecting on her tour with the Amsterdam delegation, Larina said, "Americans are very proud of their country and more sure in their future than we are now. All the American children in Caravan '89 had no fear of the Russian people. They don't consider foreigners super as our kids usually do."

Ko is confident that a visit to this country would be a great experience for Larina, adding that seeing stores stocked with meats, plenty of canned goods and staples will be an experience in itself.

The dentist foresees no problem in Larina getting a leave of absence from her teaching job, saying "opportunities like this are very rare. I'm quite certain she'll get that opportunity."

While working to bring Larina to this country, Ko is looking forward to July when he will return to the Soviet Union with a group of local students as part of the 1990 People to People Friendship Caravan. Ko suggested she reapply for a guide job and ask to be assigned to the Amsterdam group.

As for Ko, he is optimistic that Larina's dream to visit the United States will come true.

many people have a very strong image of American man—such as a blond, tall, blue-eyed, strong guy. Only when you visit the country, you understand that this is a mixture of people of different nations. It was very interesting for every guide as to how he came to the USA and why he decided to visit the USSR.

When we ate, leaders of our group sat with us at the same table. Dr. Ko was probably the most curious among them. He asked about everything and you had to constantly follow the line of his conversation. Dr. Ko liked to talk with those guides who expressed their opinions freely. It was very important to him. It was very interesting for Dr. Ko to communicate with common people, listen to their ideas, try to understand their lives. Thanks to his wide outlook, he looked at things from different sides.

He was constantly keeping his camera ready in order not to miss an interesting moment. Once it was in Moscow (July 14, 1989) after our dinner in the restaurant "Arbat" he was lost. We made several circles around the restaurant. At last we saw him with his camera, standing in the street and looking for interesting moments.

In Novorossisk, I invited Dr. Ko to my grandmother's house. At that time I couldn't realize how important this visit was for him. He told me later that that meeting reminded him about his own grandmother.

In summer 1989, he asked me several times if I'd like to go to the USA. But I never took it very seriously. I thought that he invited me for a private visit for 2-3 weeks. You can imagine my surprise when in spring 1990 I began to get his letters with all the documents. He wrote that 2-3 weeks—it is really nothing. For many people in the Soviet Union it was difficult to imagine and understand such an invitation. But when I came and knew better Dr. Ko, his family, and Rotary, I understood it's quite natural and even necessary for such people to help others, to take them from their "closed space" in the other different world.

When I was leaving Moscow I thought, "What are you doing? You don't know that country and people!" But from the very beginning in the Ko's home I felt myself very safe.

Our everyday discussions at the table were on the one side an amusement, but from the other helped to develop not only language but also an understanding of life and events. I miss these discussions very much.

I miss Dr. Ko and I am really sorry that my children will not have a chance to meet him. They will know about Dr. Ko, see his picture and the thankful memory about him will live in our family forever. There are only a few people in the world who are so much connected with people from other countries and who will be remembered in so many places all over the world. Thanks to Dr. Ko and the whole family that year was the best one in my life. The memory about Dr. Ko has a very special place in my and Igor's hearts. It is very secret and it is difficult to express and describe all my feelings but I am very thankful to the God for meeting Dr. Ko, Mrs. Ko and all their children for such a feeling that far away from Russia. On the other end of the world I have my American family so dear to Igor's and my heart.

—Tanya Larina
Rostov-on-Don, Russia

(Gazette Photo - Garry Brown)

ACADEMIC EXCHANGE — Soviet Professor Tanya Larina and Dr. Sok N. Ko exchange information about their cultures at Dr. Ko's Locust Avenue home in Amsterdam. Mrs. Larina will live with Dr. Ko and his wife for the next year while teaching in Amsterdam schools and at FMCC.

In Amsterdam—

Soviet Tour Guides Plan Long Visit

By TIM RUMBERGER
Gazette Reporter

AMSTERDAM — If it were a movie, a good title might be "Moscow on the Mohawk."

Soviet citizens Tanya Larina and Vadim Goubine, who guided groups of area youngsters on student tours of the USSR, arrived in the United States this week on visits of their own. They promptly made their way to the Rug City, which has quickly become something of a second home to them.

Vadim, a 20-year-old Leningrad native, and Tanya, a 25-year-old resident of Rostov-on-Don, are currently staying at the Locust Avenue home of Dr. Sok N. Ko, a chaperone on the tours, who invited the former guides to the United States to reciprocate their hospitality.

For Vadim, who arrived Sunday, the stay in Amsterdam is temporary. He'll spend a week and a half here before journeying on to the West Coast and elsewhere in the States. A student at the Leningrad Economic College and veteran of the Afghanistan war, Vadim, who is half Korean on his mother's side, is excited but a little nervous about traveling so far on his own. He'll also have to make his money stretch. He arrived with only $300, the maximum amount the Soviet government allows travelers to carry abroad.

Tanya, who arrived Wednesday, is in a different situation. She will stay all year to teach in the Greater Amsterdam School District and at Fulton- Montgomery Community College.

Tanya is a college instructor who specializes in teaching Russian to foreign medical students at the university in her hometown, and said the trip is a dream come true for her.

"It was my dream for a long time to go to an English-speaking country," she said in heavily accented but flawless English. She'll receive a $5,000 stipend for her efforts.

Her schedule for the coming year promises to be busy. In addition to teaching junior and senior high school classes about current Soviet culture and events, she'll teach in FMCC's foreign language program, and will address elementary school classes about her country too. She will also offer Russian lessons "if somebody wants to study it," she said.

Tanya said she's excited about the opportunity to teach, especially because of the opportunity it gives her to practice speaking English.

"My main goal is to improve my English," she said. "I also want to learn all about American family life, and American culture in general."

Both Tanya and Vadim said they find Amsterdam to be an attractive city. "I can see, in comparison to New York City, it's very quiet here," Tanya said.

Perhaps the biggest impression on the visiting Soviets so far has been American stores and shopping. Tanya said she visited Crossgates Mall with Dr. Ko and his wife Elaine when they arrived back in the Capital District after a whirlwind tour of New York City after she landed there.

"I was greatly impressed by the markets," she said. "Compared with our shops, our shops do not have so many things. In your shops, you have an opportunity to choose. In ours, we have no consumer goods."

Vadim was equally astounded. In less practiced English than his fellow guide, he explained with Mrs. Ko's help his first trip to an American supermarket, where he gazed in awe at the shelves full of fresh produce and other goods.

Back in the USSR, Tanya said it was difficult to arrange the trip because one must receive a formal notarized invitation from a U.S. resident in order to go. Thanks to Dr. Ko's efforts, she said, the letter finally arrived and she received her permission. Clearing the trip with officials at her school was no small feat either, but she eventually was granted an unpaid leave and the assurance that her job will be there when she returns next year.

Another problem was leaving behind her husband Igor, whom she just married June 30. But Tanya said Igor, a helicopter pilot with the Soviet national airline Aeroflot, will come stateside to spend the holidays with his wife and the Ko family, with whom she will stay for the year. A reunion with her tour group, which she led in 1989, is also planned at that time. Vadim, who led this year's expedition, has already gotten together for an evening with his group.

CHAPTER VI

THE OFFICE

The success of a professional business largely depends on the dedication and competence demonstrated by the office staff. The efficiency with which each member of the staff does assigned tasks keeps a business functioning smoothly. Dr. Ko was fortunate in having conscientious "office girls" to carry the operation of his oral surgery practice.

Dr. Ko's private office, 80 Locust Avenue, Amsterdam.

Most of the time that Dr. Ko and his staff spent in the office was devoted to serving the many patients who came for dental work. However, through the years of working together, incidents occurred, some of them quite funny. For a person like Dr. Ko, who had a somewhat unique sense of humor, it is not surprising that in planning for his autobiography he wanted a chapter on "Humor in the Office." After his death, while looking through the contents of his office desk drawers, a few 3" x 5" index cards were found on which he had written about incidents which he planned to include in his book. The cards were dated between 1971 and 1988. These are some of his stories and others from the staff.

OUT THE BATHROOM WINDOW

A Tryon School juvenile hall youngster was brought to my Pine Street Office. Part way through my work on the kid's teeth, he asked to go to the bathroom, which was located upstairs. He didn't come back... and he didn't come back. Everyone finally realized there was a problem and did some checking. We discovered that the boy had gone out the window. Somehow he managed the jump from the second floor window and got away.

-Sok Nam Ko

TERRIBLE HEAT

A middle-aged patient came to my office with a large facial swelling caused by a tooth abscess. After my examination I prescribed some antibiotics and asked her to return in five days so I could remove the offending tooth.

The following day she called and reported that she was in "terrible heat." Then she proceeded to describe her signs and symptoms. She said she was restless, couldn't sleep, and was excited, irritable, and had hot flashes all over and it was my fault. I told her that I could treat her tooth, but that she should talk with her physician about this new condition.

- Sok Nam Ko

THE TATOOED LIP

A patient was involved in a fight with his girl friend. He remarked, "She was mad at me and hit me with a metal chair!"

My examination revealed that three teeth were broken off and there was a hairline fracture of the alveolar bone. As I examined inside his lower lip, I found a tatoo. When I raised the question as to how it came about, the patient said that he and his friends were drunk and a friend tatooed his lip. I guess they were pretty drunk. It said, "Fuch off."

- Sok Nam Ko

WHIPLASH

I worked for Dr. Ko when he first moved here and set up his office on Pine Street. I was very young (about 19) at the time and he was training me. I always got the impression that the headlight he wore with the attached cord which went to the wall was a new piece of equipment. It appeared that he hadn't worn it very much because every single time he used to walk out of the room, he would forget it was there and give himself a whiplash.

Illustration Herbert A.W. Kopper.

This sort of fascinated me. He used to walk very fast. Every time, whoops, he forgot the light on his head. I would go home and report to my mother every night, "Ten times today, Mom. *At least,* ten times he walked out of the room. It's a wonder the man does not have to wear a neck brace!"

—Susan Minch

A SERIOUS PLACE

While the office was a serious place most of the time, we did take time to laugh quite often. Sometimes simple actions would set us into gales of laughter.

One particular time I remember. The doctor needed to get into his safe for something, so he came to the receptionist's area where I was working. Naturally, I stepped out of his way. As I was standing nearby, waiting for him to finish what he was doing, my ears began to itch. I said, "All of a sudden my ears itch!"

He said, "Oh, you've got the seven 'ears itch, eh?"

At this we began to laugh. The harder he laughed, the harder I laughed. The girls in the other rooms thought that Dr. Ko and I were crazy. They began to ask, "What's going on?" But we were laughing too hard to tell them.

—Jean Gabryluk

ON THE WAY TO RECOVERY

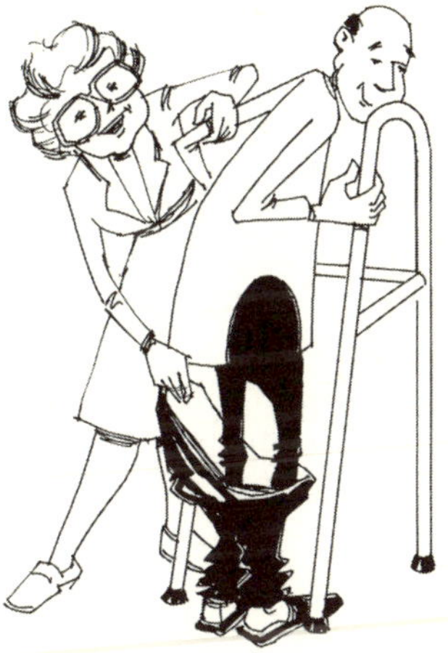

Illustration Herbert A.W. Kopper.

It seemed that Norma was always left to take a patient from an operatory to the recovery room. The story on this particular day was no exception. Dr. Ko finished his work on this patient and was filling in his chart. I had gone to develop some x-rays. Norma was left to help this man who was very dependent upon his walker. With his hands firmly gripped on the walker and Norma hanging on to the man, they began the journey to the recovery room. They had progressed to the middle of the hall and all of a sudden the man's pants fell to the floor. They went right down around his ankles and he was wearing red and white striped long underwear. He didn't seem inclined to do anything about his situation except to hang on to his walker. Poor Norma, she didn't know what to do!

Karen was in another room hiding behind a closed door and laughing hysterically.

Dr. Ko appeared and noticed Norma down on the floor near the man with his fallen pants. The doctor said, "What are you doing, miss? Have you lost a leg?"

Norma, in this predicament, looked like she was ready to kill. She kept urging the man to help her. But he just stood there clenching his walker and leaving the job of pulling up his pants to Norma. She finally got the man to the recovery room, but to this day, those who saw the incident still laugh about the fallen pants.

—*Susan Minch*

LOSING MY TEETH

While working on a patient one day, Dr. Ko sent me after a little case which contained two rows of plastic dental caps. There must have been a thousand of them in the container. While returning to the operatory, I hit something and dropped the case. The little plastic teeth flew all over the room in all directions.

About that time Dr. Ko walked by. Here I was on the floor on my hands and knees scrambling to retrieve those hundreds of caps. He looked at me as if to say, "Now what have you done?"

The next time the caps were needed, Dr. Ko said to me, "Do you *think* you could get some of those caps out of that box for me without spilling them?"

—*Norma Stellato*

HOT FLASHES

As you might expect, Dr. Ko encouraged patients to report to him if anything seemed to be wrong following any service he rendered. When Mrs. Jones had hot flashes and a fever, she returned to the office to complain. The doctor was on the phone when she came in so she explained her problem to me at the desk. She wanted to know if the medicine she was taking could be making her have hot flashes and a fever.

When Dr. Ko turned away from the phone, he said to Mrs. Jones, "Can I help you?"

She responded as to how she felt and added, "I feel like I'm in heat!"

Putting his hand over the receiver of the phone, he showed some surprise and sort of shock and laughed with his mouth wide open. He said in a comforting tone, "Well, that doesn't sound too good!" He was still laughing as he turned back to his phone call.

Knowing that the medication she was taking would not be the cause of her problem and realizing that the doctor was busy on the phone, I tried to take care of the situation by saying to Mrs. Jones, "I don't think penicillin would do that! But ask Dr. Ko if you should stop taking it!"

—Jean Gabryluk

"MAY I HAVE A VOLUNTEER"

Most of our patients came with clean teeth but there was one man who came to the office who didn't brush his teeth *ever, ever!* It looked as though food had been on his teeth for months. All of us girls would sort of hide in the kitchen and argue as to who would go in to help the doctor. He would call, "Somebody! Somebody! Come and help me!"

While he was calling, we were in the kitchen fighting over who had to go. We really knew that someone had to help but *that* man with the dirty teeth, oh my! It was disgusting! Of course, eventually one of us gave in and assisted Dr. Ko. I really don't know how he stood it to work on such teeth.

—Karen Malpass

FLIP HER OVER

The funniest thing that *ever* happened to me while working with Dr. Ko was during an emergency case. This heavy-set woman came in and needed to have a tooth pulled. It was necessary to put her to sleep.

Now, ordinarily, there were two girls on duty who assisted Dr. Ko in such cases but as it was, he and I managed to do the job.

Being late in the day, the doctor was on his hurry up bit. He was anxious to do the job and get her to the recovery room where we could lay her down. With Dr. Ko on one side of the patient and I on the other, we proceeded to help this *very* stout lady out of the chair in the operatory. Now, this woman was not awake, not really awake. We managed to get her to the office area. Jean was at her desk with her back to us so she didn't see anything. And the woman's husband was out in the waiting room so he was unaware of any problem.

Illustration Herbert A.W. Kopper.

All of a sudden in the middle of the office hall, the patient's knees began to buckle and she fell to the floor on her belly, face first in the rug and we were on top of her. Of course, this set both Dr. Ko and me to laughing. As we were scrambling to get up, Dr. Ko said, "Oh, dear, I wonder what we did wrong!"

This very stout lady was sprawled on the floor, still out like a light, and dead weight to lift. I asked, "What do we do now?"

Dr. Ko responded, "Well, let me flip her over!" With considerable effort on his part, he did manage to get her turned over. He continued with a plan, "You take her legs and I'll take her arms."

Since all this happened behind the reception area, neither Jean nor the woman's husband in the waiting room had any idea as to what had happened.

Dr. Ko and I discussed how to get this woman from the hall to the recovery room. Following the plan we managed to get the woman off the floor a little but still her butt was only three inches off the floor. Both of us laughed, oh how we laughed! We struggled to gain strength to lift her as we dragged her and dropped her, dragged her and dropped her to the Recovery Room which has an area of not more that 3 1/2 square feet and the bed was about two feet off the floor! My next question sounded like the first, "Now, what do we do?"

Straighening up and beginning to regain his composure, Dr. Ko said, "Well, we're going to have to swing her!"

I responded, "In this small space?"

"Yes, and on the count of three we'll throw her onto the bed!"

Building up all the strength we could muster, we prepared for the mighty heave. "One, two" and then he goes, "three!" The plan worked. But with the exertion of the lift in this very small area and being a little off balance, Dr. Ko landed right on top of her. Scrambling to his feet, he and I hastened to position the fallen lady so that she would be comfortable when she revived.

Then, as if nothing had happened, Dr. Ko straightened up, very calmly adjusted his smock, squared his shoulders, and prepared to leave the sleeping patient. He walked out of the little room like he didn't have any part of this episode. As for me, I was hysterical, reviewing in my mind what had happened within the last fifteen minutes. As Dr. Ko walked out of the room, he looked at me as if to say, "Don't you *ever* mention this to anyone!" I never did until now and he *never* mentioned a word about it again, *ever, ever!* As for the patient when she revived, thank God she didn't remember anything. Like most cases, she asked, "How did I get over here?" Oh, my, if she only knew!

—Susan Minch

JIMMY ARCHY

My favorite story is about Jimmy Archy. When AIDS started to become widely known, all of us in the office were like nuts wearing the gloves and taking the precautions recommended at the time, because we were worrying about contracting AIDS.

One day when I was working with Dr. Ko, he said, "Well, Jimmy Archy died."

I said, "Oh!" I didn't know who Jimmy Archy was, I didn't think it was a friend. I continued, "Who's Jimmy Archy?"

He said, "Well, you know him."

So I thought, "Oh, he must be a patient, so I added, "What did he die of?"

"Died of AIDS" was the prompt reply.

By now I was getting very nervous. My palms were starting to sweat and I was so nervous. Consequently, I kept pumping him for more information about Jimmy Archy. I just couldn't remember him. I asked, "I know him, huh?"

"Yeh, you know him."

I said, "Well, what did we do for him?"

Dr. Ko said, "What did *we* do?"

I added, "Yeh, has he been here?"

With this the doctor kind of looked disgusted as if to indicate, "How stupid can you be!" He then said, "He played the piano with the candles on it!"

At last it dawned on me and I said, "Liberace?"

"Yes!" came the response.

Here I am thinking that this person had been a patient and that I was going to get AIDS and that I was going to die. Instead he was talking about Liberace. As for me, I was a nervous wreck. After that he often referred to Jimmy Archy and I think he forgot that his name was anything else.

—Karen Malpass

WHO'S PATACHINI?

Dr. Ko had a creative mind when it came to naming people. Perhaps his originality was due to not being able to remember a name or in his subtle way he might have been actually trying to be funny. At any rate, there was a patient who, while being treated, seemed to be hyperactive. His arms kept popping up and had to be tied down. Then his leg was up and at the same time he pulled the IV out. Dr. Ko was finding it a little difficult to work on this patient. Finally, he turned to me and said, "What do you think his name is, Patachini?"

Norma (another assistant) and I looked at each other as if to say, "All right, who's Patachini?"

Dr. Ko continued, "Gee, this guy can get out of everything!" Again Norma and I questioningly looked at each other, "Do we know Patachini?"

Eventually we figured out that he meant Houdini, the famous escape artist. Occasionally we would walk out of the room and say, "How long has he been in this country?

—Karen Malpass

A LOVELY VOICE

There used to be a song that went, "Please, Release Me, Let Me Go!" Dr. Ko loved that song. He would go around the office singing, "Please, Re-Rease Me, Ret Me Go!"

—Susan Minch

GIVE HIM HELOWEIN

Sometimes patients came in with definite ideas as to what they wanted. One guy came in wanting a specific drug. He said, "I can't have Tylenol. I don't want Codeine. I need Percodan," which is a potent and habit-forming pain killer. He rambled on saying he couldn't have this and he couldn't have that.

Sue went to confer with Dr. Ko and told him, "He knows all the drugs. He doesn't want just anything. He wants Percodan."

Dr. Ko answered by saying, "Give him Helowein!"

While looking at her pad, intending to write the instructions, Sue said, "Helowein?"

"Uh, huh!"

Sue positioned her pad ready to write and said, "How do you spell that?"

I was working with the doctor and had been listening to the conversation. I whispered to her, "Heroin! He's making a joke. He means Heroin!"

Sue said to Dr. Ko, "Oh, Heroin? Why didn't you say that then? Why didn't you say Heroin?"

He answered, "I did!"

In situations like this, Dr. Ko would look at you with an expression that said, "What's wrong with you?"

—Karen Malpass

WHO GOT IT?

When a Medicaid patient came into the office, he/she would always have to get approval from the state for any dental work that needed to be done. Dr. Ko would explain the procedures; how we would have to send in for approval. As the patient left Dr. Ko (and because of his accent) the person always acted like he hadn't really understood a word the doctor had said. As the person was walking down the hall he would say, "Well, er-a-er-a, are you going to call me and let me know?"

Dr. Ko's answer was, "If you hear from them first, you let us know. And if we hear from them first, you let us know."

Even though the patient would say, "Oh, O.K." we really wondered if he actually understood Dr. Ko's joke.

—Susan Minch

THIS ISN'T GOING TO HURT A BIT

Dr. Ko's words used in explaining a procedure were often not that clear. When telling a patient about the procedure used to put him to sleep, the doctor would sometimes use words that weren't exactly what he meant.

Patients often ended up being rather uneasy after hearing his description of what he was about to do them. I was so used to the way the doctor talked, I didn't notice this happening until I had worked in his office for a couple of years! I'm sure it must have startled patients considerably to hear the doctor say, "I'm going to put a needle *through* your arm!"

—Susan Minch

IF THE TEETH FIT...

One day two sisters, Mary and Marion, came to the office together and they each carried a box containing their dentures. They were both going to have their top teeth out and these dentures were ready to be put in.

So, Mary was escorted to the operatory, put to sleep, and her teeth were taken out. We then put her dentures in and brought her into the recovery room. So far so good!

Next, it was time for Marion. The procedure was repeated except that this time, things didn't go so well. Marion was put to sleep and all her upper teeth were taken out. With dentures in hand, Dr. Ko proceeded to check for fitting. With his thumbs pressing against the dentures, he rocked his thumbs back and forth. Obviously, the dentures didn't fit. He removed the plate, looked carefully at it, frowned a little, and tried the fitting procedure again. Realizing that something was wrong, he turned to me and said, "Go get the other one's teeth!"

Somewhat shocked I said, "You want me to do *what?*"

"Go get Mary's teeth!" came the order.

Quite astonished at such an order, I said, "If she's awake, what am I supposed to tell her?"

He replied, "Don't explain. Tell her I want to see her dentures for a minute!"

So, as instructed, I went to the recovery room to get the teeth. "Mary, I need to check your teeth for a minute." I took her teeth out, took them into the kitchen, washed them and disinfected them. Returning to Dr. Ko, I said, "Here!"

He put the teeth into Marion's mouth and went through the testing for fit. Going through the rocking motion again, he said, "Oh, gee, these are no good either." Turning to me he added, "Wait a minute! Take Marion's teeth and see if they fit Mary!"

So now I'm rinsing teeth off again. I don't know who's got what teeth. I took Marion's teeth in for Mary and said, "Here you are!" Only this time it was Marion's teeth which didn't fit Mary. I quickly said, "Wait a minute, I'll be right back!"

I went back to Dr. Ko and said, "These aren't the right teeth." So I washed them all off again and took Mary's teeth back to her.

As for Marion, Dr. Ko was mumbling, "Oh, geesh." He did the best he could to make Marion's teeth fit by doctoring them up. He put in a ton of powder, but in the end we had to send the dentures back to the company that made her teeth.

—Karen Malpass

ROTARIANS WILL REMEMBER

Dr. Ko rarely told us anything about his experiences away from the office. But this particular time he had just returned from a Rotary Meeting. While there, he was asked to lead the group in the song "America." Obligingly and reverently, he stood up, placed his hand over his heart and began, "I predge arregiance to the frag!" Obviously the Rotarians burst out in almost uncontrollable laughter.

In concluding his story, Dr. Ko said, "I was *so* embarrassed. After all, I *do* know the difference. Added to this embarrassment, I was fined a dollar!"

—Karen Malpass

ORGANS FOR SALE

One day during a conversation with a patient, I learned that she had musical instruments—organs—for sale. I said to Dr. Ko, "Mrs. B has organs for sale. Would you like to buy an organ, Dr. Ko?"

He responded, "I cannot use any organs that she has. They wouldn't fit me...What kind of organs does she have?"

—Susan Minch

THE APPOINTMENT BOOK

A patient had been told by Dr. Ko that she needed a frenectomy. She came to my desk on her way out of the office and said, "You know, Jean, I've got to have a hysterectomy or whatever."

It was written in the appointment book just like she

said. I imagine Dr. Ko had a good laugh when he read that one.

—Jean Gabryluk

"NO-MA" AND "OTHER GIRL"

Dr. Ko often worked after hours. He frequently used this time to examine x-rays in preparation for scheduled surgeries. One day he was examining the x-rays of a man who had a badly broken jaw. Being eager to share his discovery, he called, "'No-ma' and other girl, come in here!" He never knew my name.
I was "Carolyn." I was "other girl," I was "what's-her-name." So, he called us to observe the x-ray. As he held it up and looked at it carefully, he said, "Look at this broken jaw. The guy is going to talk like this the rest of his life if I don't fix it. (At this, he twisted his jaw like it was broken.) As he described the problem and explained what needed to be done, he continued to talk with a twisted jaw. He must have talked like this for ten minutes or more.

Now while the broken jaw was not really funny, the way Dr. Ko was describing it was hysterical. Norma and I knew we shouldn't laugh but ended up doing just that. I made my exit by saying, "I gotta go!" Poor Norma didn't know what to do. Tears of laughter were falling down her face. She got some Kleenex, patted her eyes and pretended to blow her nose. It was so hard to refrain from laughing when Dr. Ko did something that was really funny.

—Karen Malpass

YOU'LL HAVE TO LET IT DRIP!

Dr. Ko maintained an office in Gloversville for a while. While we were working a scheduled day up there, Dr. Ko had a bad cold. He apparently felt that he should be wearing a mask or doing something about his drippy nose. At times like this he usually wore a mask but there were no masks at the Gloversville Office. While I was getting a patient ready for the doctor, he disappeared. Soon he returned from the bathroom with two cotton balls stuck up his nose to eliminate the drip. He looked *so* funny that I burst out laughing and said, "I can't work in here with you wearing those cotton balls up your nose. You've got to take them out!"

Illustration Herbert A.W. Kopper.

Obligingly he said, "All right!" And he left the room. He was gone for a few minutes. But, when he returned, he looked even more ridiculous. He had decided to make a mask out of a 4" x 4" piece of unwrapped gauze. He had taken two rubber bands. hooked them to each end and tied them in a knot so that there were loops. He hooked one around one ear which wasn't too bad. Then he went to hook the other one around the other ear. When he let go, both of his ears were thrust forward, "boing". Bursting into laughter again, I exclaimed, "That's it. I'm not staying in here with you looking like that. You're going to have to let your nose drip!"

—*Susan Minch*

UP AND DOWN HALL

One of Dr. Ko's patients had to have many fillings done. She insisted that we put her to sleep for each filling. Now this really wasn't necessary and the assistants weren't too happy about having to go through the procedures fifteen or more times. But Dr. Ko would put her to sleep as requested.

One time I can remember in particular. I was standing over her trying to see what I was doing. All the while she was rubbing Dr. Ko's leg while he was trying to work. He'd take her hand and put it back on the arm of the chair but she immediately repeated her actions.

Eventually Dr. Ko said to the patient, "Oh, you've got to stop that. I've got to run up and down hall. You're going to get me all excited." Turning to me, he said, "I'm going to run up and down hall! Hold her arm! Strap her arm to the chair!"

—Karen Malpass

HE GOT IT

One day I had to get something out from under a bed in the recovery room. I lifted the top up and there was a nest holding a mouse with her tiny babies. I started screaming. Dr. Ko came running, saying, "What are you so excited about?" There I am screaming about the mouse. While he very calmly said, "No problem. Where is it?"

I said, "Well, there's a mouse and a lot of babies in here!" I don't know what he did to kill the babies while the mother was running back and forth, back and forth across the floor. He calmly picked up a pencil and went after the mouse. I said, "What are you doing?"

With perfect aim he stabbed at the mouse and got it. He looked at me as if to say, "What's wrong with you? So what, it's dead. It's only a mouse and I killed it!"

—Karen Malpass

SHE'S NOT DEAD—YES, SHE IS

Dr. Ko was perfectly willing to accept various animals from farmers in exchange for his services. One particular time a patient offered payment of a rooster and some chickens toward a bill. One night I went down into the cellar to turn the tanks off. It was dark down there. When I opened the door and flipped on the lights as I entered the room, something screeched at me. As to be expected, I jumped and screamed. I hurried back upstairs and said to Dr. Ko, "*What* is in that cellar?"

Quite casually, he said, "It's a rooster and a chicken."

I admonished, "You can't leave them in there together!"

"Yes, I can."

I continued, "Won't they kill each other?"

He replied, "No, they won't."

The next day, I went down cellar and found the chicken dead. I returned upstairs and said, "Do you know that rooster you got down there?"

He said, "Yeh."

I added, "Do you know the chicken that was with him?"
He said, "Yeh, he's not going to kill her, is he?"
I returned, "No? Well, she's dead!"
"No, she's not."
"Yeh, she is!"
Dr. Ko's theory didn't prove true this time.

—Karen Malpass

CONDITIONS OF EMPLOYMENT

The employment of staff stayed rather stable down through the years with the exception of the time when Dr. Ko had the Gloversville Office. When he tried to run two offices he had to get more girls. That's when he went through about twenty new employees in a very short time.

There was Patty whose feet hurt, so she was always sitting down. We'd look for her and find her sitting in a chair somewhere, sort of out of sight, resting her feet!

Then there was the girl who was hired without knowing much about the conditions of her employment. Dr. Ko told the girl to come to the office a certain day to meet with him. When they met, he said, "Oh, how do you do? Well, you can put my lab coat on and get to work." She did just that and started working.

I asked her one day, "What hours are you working?"

She replied, "I don't know."

I continued, "Did you talk to him about what days you are working?"

"No, I've been here for months. The man has never said a word to me about my hours. He just said, "Put this lab coat on and here I am!"

—Susan Minch

SNIFF, SNIFF, SNIFF, SNIFF

Even though the office staffing was quite constant, a variety of girls were employed by Dr. Ko from time to time. One of them had been in the army. She was big and tall. She used to come to work wearing black nail polish! She sometimes wore a black slip under her white uniform. In various ways she used to irritate Dr. Ko something fierce.

For example, she would be suctioning and obviously was in close proximity to the patient and Dr. Ko. One time she was going sniff, sniff, sniff, sniff. He was becoming increasingly annoyed. Finally, he turned to me and said,

"Give her a Kleenex!" I produced the Kleenex and handed it to her. Instead of using it for her nose, she looked at me in a puzzled fashion and then decided that she must do something with it. She took the suction out of the patient's mouth, used the Kleenex to wipe off the suction and put it back where it was in the first place.

In desperation, Dr. Ko looked at me as if to say, "Oh, God, help me!"

—Karen Malpass

HE FLEW

A series of errors seemed to be Linda's claim to fame. One day she was suctioning. We finished and she was still cleaning up the patient's mouth. Dr. Ko walked around in front of the chair. He put one leg up over the suction hose. As he pulled his other leg up, she pulled the hose up. He went flying. He flew out of the orange room into the hall and landed on all fours!

I was in the next room. Even though I didn't see the accident, I knew what had happened. I decided I couldn't go out in the hall because I was laughing so hard.

Dr. Rad, who was with us at that time, was busy charting. He glanced up and saw Dr. Ko flat on the floor. Dr. Rad inquired, "Are you all right?"

Curtly with some tones of disgust in his voice, Dr. Ko said, "Yes, I'm going to be just fine!"

Linda, realizing that she had caused the accident, thought she'd never live through the day. I suppose she wondered what Dr. Ko was going to say. But as far as I know, he didn't say anything.

—Karen Malpass

...AND NEVER CAME BACK

Some girls really had no idea what the office was like. Their preconceived ideas were sometimes very odd. One day a girl came to apply for a job and worked the day. The next day she came in and said to me, "Where do you go on these vacations with the doctor?"

I answered her, "I haven't been on a vacation with him."

She said, "You haven't?"

I replied, "No!" She quit that day and never came back.

—Jean Gabryluk

A PERFECTIONIST

When I first started working for Dr. Ko, I was afraid of him–not afraid because he was mean, but because *he* wanted perfection. If you didn't give it to him, he would speak sharply, "When I'm in, you're out and when you're out, I'm in. When I'm over here you're supposed to be cleaning that up so that I can turn around and get back in there." These directions referred to the best utilization of time and space in the operatory while working on a patient. He wanted every move to count. It took me three or four years before I was confident in my ability to function as he expected.

One day as Carol was suctioning, Dr. Ko gave her the same orders as mentioned above. With a feeling of hopelessness, she turned to me and said, "Here, you do it!" Then she proceeded to walk out of the room. There is no doubt about it, he wanted procedures done *his* way and it was our jobs as assistants to learn those ways. I am sure he figured that he was serving his patients better by being precise.

—Karen Malpass

HOW TO TAKE X-RAYS

Dr. Ko was very patient in teaching us how to take x-rays. He was determined to make us competent in each task. The first couple of years it was rather tough working for him. But the end results were that we became very proficient in taking x-rays. Once he was satisfied that we were accomplished in each task, he never criticized us if we did make a mistake. He seemed to react that it was no big deal if we made an isolated mistake so long as we really knew what we were doing.

—Susan Minch

MADE ME LEARN

Dr. Ko taught me to do things I didn't think I could do. He made me learn to suction with my left hand explaining, "Don't cross your arms!"

I kept saying, "I can't flex the hose that way!"

To this he would say, "Yes, you can!"

In the beginning I would have the suction in my left hand. It would be going in several directions, up a patient's nose. down below his chin and who knows where?" But with Dr. Ko's insistance I learned.

—Karen Malpass

WRONG TOOTH

Dr. Ko was rarely wrong about procedures in his office, but I can remember a couple of times when he almost made mistakes. As he was preparing to pull a patient's tooth, he said, "Now, I must take this tooth out and that tooth out." But he had the forceps on a wrong tooth!

I didn't *dare* say, "That's not the right tooth." I felt, "Who am I to tell him that he was getting ready to pull the wrong tooth?" I usually came up with some stupid comment like, "Ah, gee, would you look at the x-rays again?"

At this point he would look back at the x-rays and you'd see him move his forceps to the right tooth. With a sly grin, he'd add, "O.K. we're all right now!" Being only an assistant, I didn't dare tell him he was poised to pull the wrong tooth. Yet, I tried to let him know that he'd better check his intended action. Naturally, neither he nor I wanted to make a mistake. But again it was hard to tell him anything!

—Karen Malpass

BACKING UP ON THE BELTWAY

One could easily get nervous and annoyed when traveling with Dr. Ko as the driver. Karen and I accompanied him and his wife, Elaine on a trip to an x-ray convention in Massachusetts. At one point he missed his exit on the Beltway. Much to our surprise, shock actually, he simply backed up saying, "Oh, I'll just get right back on."

So he zoomed backwards to the spot where he was supposed to get off.

The two of us in the back seat were strickened with fear as we thought, "Where on earth *is* he going?"

According to Elaine, he often solved his errors that way.

—*Norma Stellato*

COULDN'T TELL HIM ANYTHING

A situation occurred during our vacation trip to Sanibel Island. Debbie and I were in the back seat trying to read a map so as to figure out where we were going. Elaine was *trying* to tell Dr. Ko where he was supposed to go but he didn't pay any attention to her. I was sitting in the back saying, "Tell him. Tell him we've got to get off here!" It turned out that you couldn't tell him anything. His ego interferred with his making accurate decisions when driving in strange territory. He would never admit that he was lost. Consequently, he wouldn't stop to inquire for directions. Therefore, he would go many miles out of his way before finding where he was supposed to be. What is it about some drivers who will never admit they are wrong?

—*Susan Minch*

COME ON, CLIFF, LET'S GO!

Dr. Ko was inclined to believe that some rules didn't apply to him. My husband, Cliff, and I were vacationing in the Bahamas with Dr. and Mrs. Ko. One day Dr. Ko wanted Cliff to go snorkel diving. As they were walking down the beach, they came upon a nude beach. A little bit further down the beach the men saw a sign: "RESTRICTED AREA DO NOT ENTER"

Completely ignoring the sign, Dr. Ko said, "Come on, Cliff. Let's go!"

Believing in signs, Cliff said, "Gee, Doc, I don't think we can go in here!"

"Yeh, we can," reassured the Doctor. He seemed to think he could go anywhere.

Cliff, being very naive, went along with the doctor's suggestion. As they continued down the beach, they looked up on the roof of the casino nearby. There were shotguns pointed at Cliff and Dr. Ko. There was no question that they had to get out of the area. They came to find out later that the Shah of Iran was there. He had been given the use of the casino by the owner. This time Dr. Ko *had* to obey the sign!

—Karen Malpass

WHAT DID HE SAY?

Dr. Ko's ability to communicate with people unfamiliar with his accent was, at times, limited. After working with him for several years, those of us in the office understood him fairly well. Yet, there were times when even we would be a bit puzzled. We began to know how his mind worked and what was expected of us. He would frequently be walking down the hall, mumbling away to himself. His voice would trail off and we would try to figure out if he was saying something that concerned us or a patient. Frequently, he would give some directions to a patient who, in turn, would come to me asking, "What did hc say? What does he want me to do? How do you know what he wants?"

Of course, if I really didn't understand, I had to go to Dr. Ko for clarification so as to enlighten the patient. Fortunately, over the years I learned how to be the interpreter for Dr. Ko's sometimes unusual way of expressing himself.

—Jean Gabryluk

WALLERS

One time when Dr. Ko and the office staff were returning from Gloversville, we stopped at a Burger King for lunch. The doctor asked us, "What do you girls want, fish sandwiches?"

Receiving affirmative nods, he stepped up to the counter and said, "I'll have three wallers!"

The girl at the counter, in a confused tone, said, "Excuse me?"

Dr. Ko repeated, "Wallers, three of 'em! Wallers!" Then with a faint smile on his face, as if being delighted that he had confused the girl, finally clarified his order by saying, "Yes, three fish fillet sandwiches!"

—*Karen Malpass*

WO-WO

When on a business trip to look at a computer for the office, Dr. Ko took Eileen and me to a Chinese Restaurant on the way back. Now we knew that he got his "L's" and "R's" mixed up and didn't always understand why people couldn't understand him. But this time he got some of his own medicine.

A Chinese-speaking man tried to convey a message to Dr. Ko by saying, "Wo-wo, wo-wo!"

Dr. Ko misunderstood and thought he was appropriately replying when he said, "No, I'm Dr. Ko."

The gentleman repeated, "Wo-wo, wo-wo?"

Again the doctor replied by giving a little additional information, "I'm Dr. Ko. I'm from Amsterdam."

This exchange went *on* and *on* and *on.* Eileen and I wanted to laugh. We kept looking out the window and pretending we didn't hear the banter back and forth.

Finally, Dr. Ko caught on to what was being said. The man apparently was impressed with Dr. Ko's car outside in the parking lot and he kept saying, "Whose Volvo? Whose Volvo?"

—*Jean Gabryluk*

Illustration Herbert A.W. Kopper.

WALKING ON WATER

Dr. Ko exhibited an air of confidence when he walked. One day while at the beach, he appeared to us and waved as he walked by. Dressed in his sneaks, socks, and T-shirt over his bathing suit and sporting his baseball cap on his head, he proceeded down the beach toward the ocean. Without a pause in his stride, he walked right into the water, stepping along as if he could walk on water. We thought he had really flipped this time and said, "He thinks he's the Lord; walking on water!"

As it turned out, he was actually looking for shells. He wore his sneaks to prevent cutting his feet on the numerous sharp shells on the rocky shoreline. He was really very practical!

—Norma Stellato

NO USE FOR WATCHES

Dr. Ko hated watches! He didn't like to wear a watch and he certainly didn't use one. Consequently, he was always late for everything. He'd plan on going to a ball game. It would get so late, we'd ask him if he was still going. Oh, yes, he was going, But, I don't think he ever got there until the last part of the game; the last of the ninth maybe.

He'd have to catch a plane in Albany at 5:30 and at 5:00 he was just getting around to leave the office. Late as he was, he always made it.

The only time he ever missed his plane was in Houston, Texas on his way back home from Cancun. There he stopped to go to the bathroom and missed his plane. That was the only time that I know of that he ever missed a plane. He built up quite a reputation for being late for everything.

—Norma Stellato

DREAMED OF A FARM

Dr. Ko always said he wanted to live on a farm some day. In fact, he often mentioned that there was one farm chore he had always wanted to do and that was to milk a cow!

At one time he was very much interested in a piece of property up at Sacandaga Lake. He was eager to find out who owned the property. He said, "I think I want to retire up there on a farm."

How sad that this dream of his never came true!

—Jean Gabryluk

CHAPTER VII

FAMILY

An Exceptional Man Named Ko
A Light of My Life

As a young girl growing up in northern Vermont, I attended a nearby summer camp for ten years. Each year there was a special guest present who shared information with the campers about his culture and homeland. For some reason I was always magnetized by the guests from such countries as Holland, Norway, China, Korea and Angola. Little did I realize how much these contacts would become a major fascination and a strong influence in my life.

During high school, I decided that I wanted to attend college. After graduation and having been accepted at Castleton Teachers' College (now Castleton State College) I began to prepare for entering school that fall.

The summer of 1956 found me at Lake Dunmore Hotel working as a waitress earning my board and room and $10 a week plus tips. At that time, the state college had no tuition if you promised to teach in the State of Vermont for a number of years equivalent to the time you attended college. So, I was earning money to pay for board, room and books.

While working at this job, I lived in an employees' cottage across the road from the hotel. Most of the other waitresses roughing it with me were college students equipped with hair dryers, make-up bags and college yearbooks. One girl who was going to be a college sophomore had a 1956 Castleton Teachers' College Yearbook. As we were looking through the book, the picture of a young man stood out from all the others.

Family Portrait. Back row: Andrew, Timothy, Stephen, Suzanne Front row: Sok Nam, Elaine.

I was interested, but to my disappointment the girl said he was planning to transfer to the University of Vermont that fall.

When summer was over, and with board and room money in my pocket, I left for college. Now, way back then all freshmen had to go through a week of "initiation" which included wearing a little green beanie. (That was a felt hat you had to make yourself with a brim and a piece of felt.)

The Welcoming Committee was made up of upper classmen, and you were supposed to serve at their beck and call.

The first night on campus, a group of us freshmen were on our way down a narrow corridor in Leavenworth Hall heading for the dining room. As we quietly met a group of noisy upper classmen leaving the dining room, we recognized the men as being upper classmen because they wore no beanies. What to my excited eyes—there he was! He had not gone to the University of Vermont after all!

This shy, timid girl spoke right up and said, "Hi, Ko!" He turned and looked at me as if to say, "Who are you? You look new to me!" However, he politely said, "Hi!" and kept right on going. I thought, "Huh, I'm going to get to know him better." That was the beginning of my life with an exceptional man named Ko.

After that I watched him like a hawk. I would often see him in the Leavenworth Recreation Room with Ed Pritchard, his closest friend at college. Frequently, they would be watching TV or playing ping pong. At this time Ed was just starting to date. Eventually, Ko asked me for our first date, which was to be a trip to a movie in Rutland via a rattly old bus; double dating with Ed and his girl friend. Before the date took place, Ko learned that Ed might not go. This lead Ko to say that he might decide not to go. It was like one wouldn't do anything unless the other was going to do it too. However, we did go to the movie.

Ko graduated from Castleton two years ahead of me, but the last two years he was at Castleton, we enjoyed going to square dances (which he preferred to round dances), going to movies in Rutland, watching TV at the Harringtons (Ko's home in Castleton) and attending college formal dances occasionally.

One dance I'll never forget! You know how girls got all gussied up wearing a new ball gown and wrist corsage and displaying a new hairdo; the works! I prepared for this very special occasion only to have Ko show up in a pick-up truck! Butch Holden, who also lived in the Harrington home, had asked for the family car first. Being late was a trait Ko had all his life.

The custom after a dance was to head for the Roma in Whitehall, New York to indulge in a pizza and ginger ale or pepsi. We did not imbibe any alcoholic beverages like some of the

First formal 1956 — Elaine and Ko.

college students did. Stopping at the Roma became a habit we followed years later when we were passing through that part of the country. Dining there always brought back fond memories of our college days.

In the summer of 1956 Ko completed the training program at the National Aquatic School at Camp Tevya. He used this training for many summer waterfront jobs.

Ko participated in every sport offered at Castleton. He was a very good tennis player and a great short stop or second baseman in baseball. Once a competitor broke Ko's leg sliding into a base. Ko was a quick ball handler in basketball (a talent which was perhaps inherited by his son, Steve) and a long distance runner on the college track team. His favorite sport in Korea was soccer, but he couldn't get the coach interested in starting a team when he

Ko at Camp Tevya Aquatic School —Breastroke Test Summer, 1956.

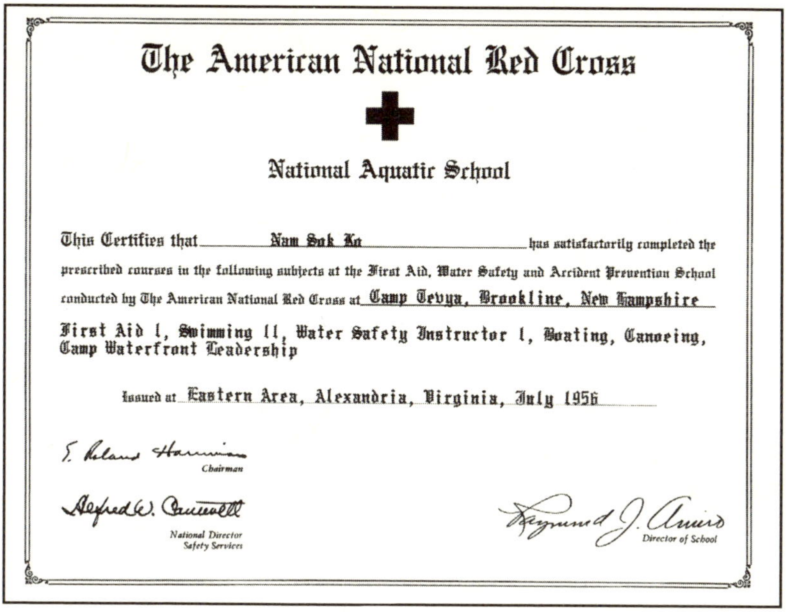

The American National Red Cross

National Aquatic School

This Certifies that Nam Sok Ko has satisfactorily completed the prescribed courses in the following subjects at the First Aid, Water Safety and Accident Prevention School conducted by The American National Red Cross at Camp Tevya, Brookline, New Hampshire

First Aid I, Swimming II, Water Safety Instructor I, Boating, Canoeing, Camp Waterfront Leadership

Issued at Eastern Area, Alexandria, Virginia, July 1956

Chairman

National Director Safety Services

Director of School

American National Red Cross Certificate.

was in school in Castleton. Ko was fast, agile and a quick thinker on the playing field; talents which he carried all his life.

In his junior year, Ko was supposed to go out student teaching. The college wouldn't let him go on an assignment at this time because they claimed his English wasn't good enough. They made him go to Columbia University for a summer to take English. He grumbled a lot about having to go to Columbia. Having no money, he had to wait tables in order to support himself. He did all of his student teaching in his senior year of college.

While Ko was a senior at Castleton (in 1958 and still not a citizen yet) he was drafted into the Army. He had been going to National Guard Training in Rutland, Vermont. Though I'm not sure why, unless he felt it was his obligation to his new country. It was there that he met Ben Hawkins, who now lives in Amsterdam, New York and who became a good friend many years later when we moved to Amsterdam, New York. These National Guard experiences were the beginning seven years of service in the Army Reserves.

Castleton Teachers College Baseball Team.
First row: Lyle Raymond, Robert Slaminen, Hugh Goldsmith, Hugh Perkins, Ralph Williams. Second row: Harold Feiner, Ko, Pat Fallon, Gerry McKean. Third row: Coach Taddonio, Tom Fitzpatrick, Walter Freeman, Owen O'Brien, Donald Perkins, Edward Pritchard, David Pearson.

Castleton Teachers College Basketball Team, 1955.
Back row: Robert Richardson, Wendell Powers, Walter Freeman, Charles Antonetti, Coach Taddonio, John O'Day, Owen O'Brien, Ned Jeffreys, Frank Brown. Front row: Carl Rice, Jack Cioffi, Frank Bizzarro, Sok Nam Ko, George Cross.

Castleton Teachers College Cross Country Team, 1955.
Back row: Thomas Nugent, Walter Freeman, Dalton Athey.
Front row: Coach Taddonio, Sok Nam Ko, Edward Pritchard, Richard Myers.

Reminiscing About His Life

Over the years when we were together, Ko told many little stories as they popped into his mind. He shared them in his quiet and sometimes off-hand way. In mentioning his early life, he always spoke fondly of his Grandmother, who was the matriarch of the family. His grandfather, Heung Bong Baek, who was a twin died as a young man. Ko's father, who grew up as an only child, was a landowner, a producer of rice and a cloth merchant. Ko was the oldest of seven children and had the responsibility for the family when his father was away from home on business.

The family lived in Kaesong, a city of 100,000 people,but they also had a store and a second home farther south. In caring for the family, Ko had to pull the "honey cart" to the appropriate places, take care of the family finances and still go to school. He found time to play soccer and he loved to go fishing when he visited his cousin, Chu Yul Kim, in the country. He became a good student in school and was skillful at Taekwondo.

When the war came in December 1950, Ko told about wanting to leave after the invasion. But, his mother and grandmother asked him to wait awhile. His father was missing. Ko was sent to find him. When Ko went to the store, neighbors told him that the North Koreans had taken his father away. He was never seen again.

Kaesong was in the south and on the border of what is now North and South Korea. Whenever the Chinese or North Koreans came into Kaesong, Ko would hide in the mountains, eating berries (or whatever was available) until they left. Then he would go home. The Allied troops were in and out of Kaesong a number of times and on one such occasion Ko left with the troops as they headed south. He spent much time with the U.N. troops and at one point was with the 8th Army, 17th Field Artillery. Here he met George Harrington, a young Vermont lawyer turned Captain in the U.S. Army. George was impressed by Ko's cleverness in beating Harrington's fellow army buddies in cards and his quickness in learning.

During this time, Ko decided to try to return to his family in Kaesong. As he was about to cross a bridge, airplanes came, striking the bridge and ultimately blowing it up. Ko ran for cover on the side of a hill and was never able to reach his family on the other side.

Captain Harrington was about to return to the United States and asked Ko, then age 17, if he would like to study in America. Since Ko had lost his family, he decided it was a good opportunity. So after George left, proceedings were begun to get a passport, visa and passage for Ko. Seoul and every other part of Korea was in a turmoil at that time. But with the help of dear cousins, he was able to find passage on a freighter sailing to Seattle, Washington.

Upon arrival, his papers were not in order, so immigration held him in detention an extra day to settle the problem. He finally was on a bus headed for Albany, New York, where the Harringtons were to meet him. A story Ko loved to tell was that enroute he thought someone was following him, so he'd run and hide at every bus stop. Come to find out George had asked the Red Cross to watch out for him crossing the country. Ko's English was limited and he didn't ask questions. He often said he had soup and eggs all the way across the country.

His October 1952 arrival at the Harringtons must have been interesting to all and especially to folks in Castleton, where he was the only Asian and became known by all in a very short time. Ko entered Fair Haven High School and many newspaper articles were written about him.

Back to Experiences While in Castleton

After graduation from Castleton Teachers' College in 1958, Ko did spend six months of Army basic training at Fort Dix, New Jersey. I remember taking a bus from Rutland to Fort Dix and visiting him at that dusty, old base. He drove a jeep for the commanding officer, was clerk of his unit and in his spare time watched lots of movies. He was a good marksman and won awards for marksmanship. He often hitch-hiked home to see me. At least, I believed that was why he came to Castleton.

When the six months of training were up, Ko decided to attend the University of Vermont to try to get another degree and ultimately to be a doctor. Of course, getting an education never comes easy. First, you need money; secondly, courage to face the hierarchy and mounds of paper work; and, thirdly, you need an active brain. Ko had all but the first, money, so he looked around for jobs that included room and board. His first step was the YMCA; a temporary place to sleep while he started at UVM. He eventually lived in the home of the President of WCAX-TV in Burlington, Vermont.

At this time he looked for a teaching position in the Burlington area. He was hired at the South Burlington Central School to teach junior high school math and science. Mr. Ko never had much trouble with discipline. Much to the chagrin of

Miss Stebbins, the principal, both he and the students were called into the office occasionally. He firmly believed that he was in the classroom to teach, the students were there to learn and come hell or high water he meant to accomplish just that.

We dated through my four years at Castleton and in December 1959, as my Mom, Aunt Helen and I were saying goodbye to him at Christmas time, Ko gave me my diamond. Our engagement was now official and we began making plans for our wedding, which would take place after my graduation.

We were married in the Castleton Federated Church on Sunday at 2 P.M. on August 14, 1960 by Rev. Olof C. Johnson. His wonderful and talented red-haired wife, Elizabeth, played the organ as our attendants walked down the aisle. Ko and I exchanged our vows to love, cherish and honor each other until death do us part.

George Harrington was Ko's Best Man. Taking part in the ceremony were several people, one of whom I didn't know very well. He was Larry Labarge, a pilot whom Ko met in Korea. Larry's family owned the Labarge Flower Shop in Burlington.

Wedding Day, August 14, 1960.
Left to right: George & Betty Harrington, Ko & Elaine, Gyneth & Ruthford Hogaboom. Federated Church, Castleton, Vermont.

Other attendants were: Chyun Shik Park, a close friend from Korea; Ed Pritchard, his close college friend; Andrew Johnson, the minister's son and Bobby Titemore, my cousin.

Priscilla Titemore, my cousin, was my Maid of Honor. My bridesmaids were high school and college friends: Barbara Bergeron, Betty Coleman, Sylvia Alcorn and Ramona Butterfield Snyder. The flower girl was Heidi Gee, a neighbor of Aunt Helen's, and the two ring bearers were young George Harrington and Aunt Helen's son, Bruce. Another little boy, Larry Stone, had a part in the service, too.

After the wedding and a receiving line on the steps of the church were over, we all gathered in the reception room where punch, cookies and wedding cake were served. Our guests were given tiny groom's fruit cakes that had been

Wedding Party, August 14, 1960.
Front row (left to right): Wedding Day, August 14, 1960.
Bruce Smith, George Harrington, Heidi Gee and Larry Stone.
Second row: Betty Coleman, Priscilla Titemore, Ko, Elaine, Barbara Bergeron, Sylvia Alcorn, Ramona Butterfield Snyder.
Third row: Larry LaBarge, Andy Johnson, Chyun Shik Park, Bob Titemore, and Ed Pritchard.

made and gift wrapped by my Mom. This little package was to be put under your pillow so that you would dream about the person you were going to marry.

Someone blocked our get-away car. My Dad said, "Ko, how are you going to leave?" Ko calmly answered, "Well, I don't know. Guess we'll have to wait until someone moves!" This response foreshadowed our future.

When we finally were able to get away, we drove to our new apartment at 24 1/2 Brookes Avenue in Burlington for the first night, before we left for our Maine honeymoon. We had a guest (Ko's good friend Dr. Chyun Shik Park) for that night. This was another inkling of what our future held. I remember how delighted George Harrington was to see us back from our one-week honeymoon. We had brought some lobsters with us, so the family enjoyed a feast.

Ko had to leave soon for the service and was stationed at Fort Drum. I went to Liverpool, New York to visit my cousin Carroll and his family. While there we received the news of George's death. It had been only two weeks after our wedding when George, at age 42, went into the hospital and died after surgery. Ko had lost his mentor and his dearest friend.

Ko and I returned to our home in Burlington immediately. I can remember going down to Poultney for the visiting hours and attending the funeral. Ko was grief-stricken by George's death. George was like a father to Ko and many of his ways in later life were molded and adopted from George's teachings. I only know of one other time in his life when Ko was so completely overwhelmed emotionally. This was described by our son, Andrew, when he and his father went to North Korea the first time in 1985. It was tough to see him really fall apart. On that first trip it was just the two of them. It was a terribly emotional time. Traveling so far to find his "lost" family and finding his sister and brothers after 30 years of separation and learning that his grandmother had died, his closest sister had been killed by a bomb when she was trying to get food to their family, and his mother had died just months before he returned to Korea—all were very traumatic bits of news to accept. By the time that the rest of the family made a second trip to North Korea with him, he knew what the situation was, so he wasn't like that at all. I'm so glad he had a second chance to visit his brothers and sister after so many years of separation.

Ko taught at South Burlington Central School during the school year before we were married in 1960. I, too, had a position in this same school teaching third grade. Our first investments that fall were a 1960 blue Saab and a collie-German shepherd mix that we named Boots and who chewed the woodwork in our rented apartment. When the landlord found out, he gave us an ultimatum the dog or us. So, we bought a house at 27 Mary Street in South Burlington, which was just a block or so from our school.

Some rather unusual events happened during our early years together. The first year of our marriage, I came home to our tiny apartment to find six guinea pigs grunting in our bath tub. Needless to say, they were hustled off to school the next day, where they were used in experimenting with different diets, and after which some lucky students took them home.

Boots. Photo: Sok Nam Ko.

Another type of experimentation was when Ko started a science club with his students and began a new project. He reconstructed an entire chicken skeleton by boiling the meat off the bones and then carefully assembling all the skeleton with wire and glue. I don't know how he ever had the patience to do it. He was quite artistic and patient! Can you imagine how many sessions of boiling chickens and assembling tiny bones it took to prepare the complete skeleton? He put the creation on a base and we carried that thing every time we moved; seven times in fourteen years!

While at the South Burlington Central School, Ko coached the boys high school baseball team and the girls basketball team; winning the championship one year. He was really proud of these young people and was pleased to learn about their accomplishments down through the years.

First home, 27 Mary St., South Burlington, Vermont.

In 1961, when he returned to teach another year, he applied for admission to the UVM Medical School. He actually applied to quite a few medical and dental schools. He felt that if he didn't get into a medical school, a dental school would be acceptable.

In those Burlington years, summers were filled with Reserve duty, being director of a summer camp and doing course work at college. His work ethic was always there without question. He knew he had to work to get whatever he wanted. Nothing came easy.

It was in the summer of 1963 that Ko and I served as co-directors of the Camp Fire Girls for the Greater Burlington Area at Camp He-Ya-Ka, an Indian name meaning "Camp Among the Mountains." An article in the Burlington Free Press dated August 3, 1963 entitled "Area Camp Fire Girls Receive Awards After Session at Camp" contained the following information:

> Sok Nam Ko, who with his wife, Elaine, was co-director of camp presented awards and spoke to the girls of their week at Camp He-Ya-Ka and complimented them on their achievements.

Mrs. Elaine Ko (who with Mr. Ko has been a teacher in South Burlington) taught music and was assisted by Judy DeGraff. Arts and crafts classes were directed by Mrs. Thomas Snyder. The girls made rings, bracelets of beads and plastic bracelets. A 10-hour First Aid Course was taught by Ko, with help from Mrs. Ko, a Red Cross Instructor.

Senior staff members were Mrs. Gyneth Saulters (nurse and camp cook), Mrs. Antoine Mcgowan, Mrs. Ramona Snyder and Mrs. Jean Brown, counselor.

In mid-August of 1963, Ko was away doing his Army Reserve Training when Andrew decided to be born. Ko arrived home in time to take me to the hospital. However, from complete exhaustion he promptly fell asleep in the waiting room having confidence that Dr. Boardman and the staff at the Mary Fletcher would take care of everything.

Ko enjoyed his teaching years, four altogether, but his goal was still ahead. By the time Andrew was born, Ko had been accepted at Temple University Dental School and UVM Medical School.

After every summer of attending the National Science Foundation Summer Schools from Howard University in Washington, D.C. and/or taking classes to get his BA from the University of Vermont, he finally was on his way to medical school.

Now, to digress a little—years ago in Korea, Ko met Dr. Zbikowski, a dentist. The doctor was very kind to Ko and at one time bought Ko a gray flannel suit to replace the one-and-only blue one. Dr. Zbikowski impressed Ko because the doctor always checked the labels in clothes. Ko used to say that whenever he went to Dr. Zbikowski's, the first thing he would do was to take Ko's jacket and look at the label on it. Ko said, "I didn't dare tell him I got it in the Salvation Army Store!" Now it was actually Dr. Zbikowski who helped Ko get into Temple University in Philadelphia. He took Ko to the Dental School and introduced him to the Dean. Dr. Zbikowski was a graduate of that school so was interested in getting Ko enrolled in a dental program.

Ko accepted the UVM offer of admission, but decided however that he'd better keep that place at Temple, so he asked for an extension of time and the request was granted. So, that

Elaine, Andy, Sok, Boots at their first home, 27 Mary St., South Burlington, Vermont.

fall after Andy was born, Ko started his studies at UVM Medical School. We rented a room to another med student and the work began. Ko spent many hours in labs working on cadavers, etc. but continuing at UVM was not meant to be. At that time a student had to have grades of 78 or higher in all courses. Ko was below that in a couple of courses. Therefore, he decided to take advantage of his deferred year at Temple. I know he never regretted this decision and once enrolled at that college he gave it his all.

Moving to Pennsylvania

With the decision made, we packed our belongings, rented our house, said goodbye to our friends and family and headed for Haddonfield, New Jersey. We lived there while Ko commuted into Philly to attend classes at Temple Dental School. It was hard to leave our little Cape Cod home on Mary Street. However, we borrowed my father's car and hooked a U-Haul on the back of it. By that time in July, I knew that I was pregnant with Timothy. I really wasn't feeling all that great. At the end of August we took Dell, a friend, to help us move. We had this great big potted plant placed between Dell and Ko in the front seat of the car and a mattress on the back seat for baby Andrew. With the dog and me in the back, we left for our new home, dragging the U-Haul trailer behind the car.

On a previous trip, we had found a rental in Haddonfield and I acquired a teaching position. So, we knew where we were headed. As we were driving down the New York Thruway, I was saying, "I'm going to miss my orientation meeting with the superintendent. What am I going to do?" Sok said, Wait a minute. We'll stop and we can call him." So I stopped on the Thruway and called the superintendent. He was so mad at me! He said, "What! You're not going to be here!" I tried to explain by saying, "I'll be there, but I'll be a little late. We're on our way down now." He was not very understanding. I thought, "Oh, boy, this is great! Here I am pregnant. I'm not going to tell him that right now." Finally we got to the apartment and I had on all these old clothes and old shoes. I thought, "Oh, my gosh, I've got to get some clothes to wear to the meeting." Now I happened to have some clothes in the back of the U-Haul, but my shoes were way in the front of the trailer. The boys, Ko and Dell, weren't going to be able to get the thing unloaded before I had to leave for the meeting so I ran downtown trying to find some shoes to buy quickly. I didn't know the town of Haddonfield very well; I had never been there long enough to drive around. But, I finally found a place and I bought some shoes, which turned out to be too small for me. I'll never forget because my feet hurt all day.

By the time I got to the orientation meeting, the teachers were all coming out of the Auditorium. I thought, "maybe I can just kind of melt right in with the other teachers and go with them to the school and this is just what I did. We were supposed to go from our meeting to our classrooms. I met the principal who was really nice to me and the teachers welcomed me, too. Everybody was really nice and I set up my classroom that day.

From that September, when school started, until I left Haddonfield, we found it to be a very nice village. I liked it there a lot—until I finally had to tell the superintendent that I was pregnant. He wasn't very pleased at my announcement. He said, "Did you know you were pregnant when I hired you?" I could honestly say, "No, I didn't."

It was very difficult for Ko while living in Haddonfield, because he had to drive from there into Philadelphia every day to attend classes. He had to cross the Benjamin Franklin Bridge, combat the traffic and plan for the time involved in driving and parking. So, he wanted to move closer to his school. We found a rowhouse rental right behind the Temple Dental School at 3257 Park Avenue. We lived there for the last 3 1/2 years of Ko's schooling at Temple.

Timothy Allen Ko was born in March of 1965 and when I thought I had to go to the hospital, of course, Ko was in school taking an exam. I knew he was busy so I couldn't bother him. I had my neighbor take Andy and I walked down to the Temple Hospital, which was just three blocks down the street. I called the doctor and told him that I was on my way. He said, "Are you sure it is time?" The description of my situation let him know that it was time. I added, "Maybe you'd better call my husband at the Dental School and tell him, because I know he is there taking a test."

When I returned to teaching that fall, Ko and I would each take a boy to a baby sitters. We couldn't find one baby sitter for both boys. I taught at the Rockledge School and eventually transferred to the Simon Muir School on Allegheny Avenue. I liked the Rockledge School, but it was quite a drive from our apartment so I made the change. Ko also kept his hand in teaching by substituting at the Strawberry Mansion Junior High when he could, especially after college closed in the spring.

It was while we were at Temple that Ko's name changed. People were aghast that I called him by his last name. So, as my Mom had done for years, I began to call him Sok.

By this time Sok had already received his honorable discharge from the Army and had joined the Navy, graduating

Fourth home, 3257 Park Ave., Philadelphia, Pennsylvania.

from Temple as a 2nd Lieutenant. Upon graduation from Temple, even though he had applied to various graduate schools, he had not heard from any place in a positive way. So he decided to enter the Navy on active duty. The moving van came to take all our belongings to Newport, Rhode Island. We were about to pack the boys and dog into our little black Valiant in preparation to head north. Well, now, a phone call came through to Sok while at school and he rushed home to tell me that there was likely to be a change of plans. He asked what I thought about going to Boston instead, because he had been accepted into the Tufts Oral Maxillofacial Program at the Jamaica Plains Veterans' Administration Hospital for three years. He would be working under the guidance of Dr. Charles McCann and Dr. Salvatore Esposito.

Andy — 2 years,
Tim — 6 months.

Of course, we were elated. But, by this time our clothes, furniture and all our belongings were on their way to Rhode Island and we were about to leave for Boston. I had a cousin in Quincy, Massachusetts who kindly put us up for a couple of days until we found a home in Weymouth Landing. As we had done before, we had to 1) find a home, 2) find a job for me, 3) find a school for Andy, and 4) get Sok acclimated to his new work. All this had to be taken care of by the end of August. Things had always worked out, so we had courage and hope. We found a home and slept on the floor until the Navy graciously brought our furniture from Rhode Island. I found a teaching position in Wollaston and we found a kindergarten program for Andy. Our neighbor, Dorothea Higgins, was the teacher. Sok began his drive into Boston in bumper to bumper traffic. Those three years were wonderful ones for our family.

Sok bought a 18' fishing boat that he and the boys took out into the Atlantic from the Town River Yacht Club every weekend. He loved taking his friends out fishing, too. Sok was always looking for good deals and he found a number of whaling boats that were Navy surplus. He bid on three or four, thinking he might get one. Much to his surprise, he got all of them and then didn't know what to do. He was also always looking for used dental equipment; preparing for opening his own practice some day.

Fifth home, 53 Kingman St., Weymouth, Massachusetts.

During our stay in Weymouth, on a very snowy night on December 12, 1970, Stephen Olin Ko came into the world. Stephen's names form the initials S O K. This very special event occurred at the South Weymouth Hospital.

After Sok's three-year residency in Boston, it was time to look for a practice. Sok found one in Framingham, Massachusetts. We sold our little renovated Cape Cod house and bought a split-level home in Holliston, Mass. It seemed like a good place for the boys. They had a stream in the back yard on which they could skate in winter and the Crow family's children across the street became very good playmates. We moved into this house in July, but moved out the next April when we decided to find a place where Sok could expand his practice in oral surgery.

In October 1971, my Dad had an auto accident on the Turkey Farm Road in Vail's Mills, New York. After visiting him, Sok asked me to look over the Amsterdam, New York area as a possibility for setting up a practice. As instructed, I drove to Amsterdam and stopped at a dentist's office to ask about opportunities for an oral surgeon. I was told that there really wasn't a bit of demand for one, since the local dentists either did their own oral surgery or sent patients to Schenectady. I drove right back home to tell the "boss" that he wouldn't want to go to Amsterdam. As to be expected, the next week Sok drove to Amsterdam to check out the hospitals and the dentists and to look for a place to set up an office!

He found office space that he was informed Urban Renewal would eventually be tearing it down. Sok set up shop on Pine Street next to Mr. Fonda's Bicycle Shop, even though he knew he'd have to move soon. Our faithful cousin, Harland Titemore, came from eastern Vermont every weekend for months to get the office ready for use. The office was a far cry from a modern professional building, but Sok was persistent in providing a sterile atmosphere and in training his staff well.

Andrew — 8 years, Timothy — 6 years, Stephen — 11 months.

Sixth home, 50 Travis Road, Holliston, Massachusetts.

Business was slow in the beginning. The patients he had in those early years remind me that they went to his office on Pine Street and they were still his patients after many years. So Sok must have served his early patients well!

While Sok and Harland were busy getting the Pine Street Office ready for use, I drove with the children most weekends from Holliston to Amsterdam to see Sok and to help paint and paper the office. On Sundays I returned to Holliston so that the boys could go back to school. By April, Bill Bashwinger, a local realtor, took us to look at a wonderful house on Locust Avenue.

Moving to New York State

With the help of our neighbors' VW bus and a U-Haul, we moved our children, the dog and all our belongings to 80 Locust Avenue in Amsterdam. The house, a three-story Victorian, was built by industrialist Luther L. Dean around 1895. There was plenty of land for the boys to play ball, and up the road there was a park where Sok and the boys could spend a lot of time. The older boys entered school. Little Stephen, age 1, came down with the red measles and was a sick baby. Dr. Christine Bolane came to the house to see Stephen twice. We were very grateful to her and Steve recovered nicely.

Soon after moving into our Locust Avenue home, Sok began planning how the carriage house out back could be converted into dental offices. Cousins Harland Titemore, Willard Mahoney and others came once again. Eventually, the old carriage house became a fine modern set of dental offices, which served well during all the years of Sok's oral surgery practice.

Office, Pine Street, Amsterdam, New York.

His practice grew steadily through the years. He was on call 24 hours a day, seven days a week. There was no answering service and the phone was never taken off the hook. The whole family became secretaries. In answering the phone the "secretaries" were instructed by Sok to take name, telephone number and the time called. Sok worked hard to serve patients night or day and even on holidays. His fees were sometimes paid in chickens, pigs and dogs. We acquired white German shepherds in this way and later bred them.

While Sok was still serving as a Lieutenant Commander in the Naval Reserves, he wouldn't much more than get down to the Albany Armory when an emergency call would come in and he'd have to return home. Although he enjoyed the two

Seventh home, 80 Locust Ave., Amsterdam, New York.

weeks of Reserve Training, he finally decided to go on inactive status. By 1990, he had asked for his discharge from the Navy. The formal certificate with his picture in uniform came a month after Sok died. He served in the United States military practically all of the years that he lived in this country; nearly 40 years!

Winter Snow — 1989.

After coming to Amsterdam, we were blessed with the birth of our only daughter, Suzanne Elaine Ko. She was born on June 9, 1975 and Sok finally had a daughter. By this time I had given up teaching at the Bacon School here in Amsterdam, realizing that there was plenty for me to do in caring for our family and helping with the dental practice.

Sok believed in education and never ceased being a teacher in his office, at home and on the ball field or gym floor. He encouraged his dental assistants to get more education, even if it meant losing a good assistant.

Sok expected a lot from his children and especially from our eldest son. Sok's motto was: "Teach the oldest and the

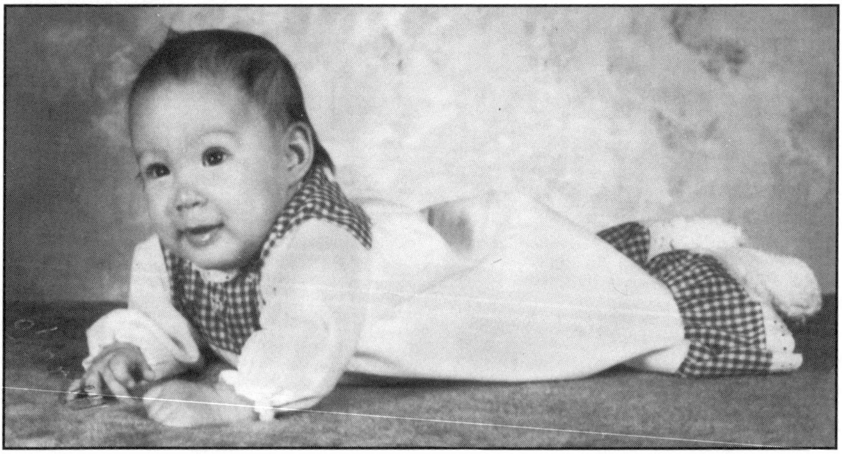

Suzanne Elaine Ko.

others will follow." That might have been true in the old country, but it doesn't always work in our society. It is tough to be the first child. Sok gave me the directions and I was supposed to snap the whip. I tended to be soft-hearted, which he didn't appreciate much. Unfortunately, he ended being the whip because I was more of a mediator. No one said bringing up children was a snap. As we had more children, it did seem to be easier. Once I remember very clearly he called a family meeting to tell all that we were to help each other, do our jobs and support each other. He didn't put up with nonsense!

Sok was proud of young George Harrington's accomplishments at IBM and he watched with interest the activities of George and Susan's children: Nathan, Matthew (who was called Ko's "Hulk"), Merenia and James. Sok was also pleased to see the accomplishments of his own as well as other children. Many basketball games were re-played in the car on the way home from a game. He supported his children's choices of colleges, but the rest was up to them. He rarely visited the schools. That was left up to Mom.

Sok was not only hard on his children; he was even more demanding of himself. He was constantly searching for more knowledge about his profession. Somehow, it seems as if he knew life for him was going to be brief. He crammed

The Harrington Family — George, Merenia, Nathan, Susan, James and Matthew.

People to People Ambassadors from Amsterdam with Congressman Mike McNulty. Dr. Ko top row.

so much into his few years. His greatest passion was for the wonders his mind could imagine and pursuing education, education and more education. He was not afraid to take a position and stay with it, even if it meant ostracism from his peers and standing alone. Sok made his decisions based upon logic, but he could debate on either side of an issue. At times, you'd think he was an ultra conservative. Then again he might express a view that was socially liberal, wanting the most for himself and all others.

He sincerely wanted to contribute to the world community and searched for ways to communicate. Rotary International and People to People Ambassadors provided avenues for service. During our years in Amsterdam, 15 Rotary exchange students lived in the Ko home. All were very special to us. Some returned after high school to attend college in the United States. Sok was able to help some pay their tuition and our home was always theirs. One girl, Tuija Itkonen from Finland, graduated from SUNY-Oswego and received her masters degree from the Massachusetts College of Arts and Sciences. Sok attended both graduations and met her husband to-be, Richard Cohen. Unfortunately, Sok died before their beautiful marriage services were held in New York and Finland.

Besides his enthusiastic interest in many sports, he was fond of taking pictures. He was a shutterbug dating back to his prize possession of a camera when he first arrived in the United States. First, he had a brownie box camera, moved on to an 8 mm, and then a video and 35 mm. With an eye always glued to a camera, he would get lost in his picture taking.

Sok loved life and made the most of his 56 years. It is still too painful to recall that last month of his life from February 16th to March 16th. It certainly was a nightmare for his family, but his spirit is still guiding, scolding and spurring us on to the opportunities he opened for each of us.

With Loving Memories,

—Elaine H. Ko
Amsterdam, NY

Volleyball Champs, Amsterdam Recreation League, 1977. Back row: Joe Lemanski, Randy Kowalski, Tom Kowalski, Buck Buchanan. Front row: Jerry Skiba, Frank Szyjkowski, Dr. Sok Nam Ko, Chuck Poole.

Sok taking movies of Catherine Laurilla holding Kathleen Dwyer, 1990.

Elaine and Sok Nam Ko, 1991.

Fishing with Dad

My obsession with fishing amuses my friends, just as my preoccupation with my father entertained them when we were in school. I doubt any of them really understands how one is a continuation of the other and that, in an absolutely literal sense, I go out fishing to be with my father.

The memory of my first fishing trip with him is so clear that it seems impossible that it was over thirty years ago. I was four or five years old at the time, my father younger than I am now. It was the late 1960's at a pier on the southern shore of Boston Harbor. We must have been an odd sight for the deck crew, a young Korean-born dentist and a little boy walking aboard what seemed like a marginally seaworthy fishing boat on a drizzly, cold morning. I'm not sure if my father got seasick that day, as later became his habit. I know that it was the one time in my life that I did feel the waves. Spending most of my time below deck (neither of us knew any better back then), I don't even know if he caught anything. He later decided to buy the family a small wooden boat, and over the next four years we motored out of Quincy's Town River Yacht Club to terrorize the flounder and cod of Massachusetts Bay.

My younger brother always went out fishing with us after that first trip. I've often thought that Tim must have resented being left behind on that initial outing. He took his revenge on every trip over the next 20 years by pointedly catching more fish than my father and me combined. Some times our mother, Elaine, would come out, other days it was just Dad and the boys.

Fair weather or foul, few weekends went by that we didn't fish. We would have an early morning breakfast of fried eggs and toast, spiced with the lingering stench of dishwater coffee and stale cigarette smoke that permeated the marina's greasy spoon diner. We first learned there that the combination of fried eggs and a glass of orange juice would cause my brother to barf before he had even left the table. It was a stunt that he performed many times over the years.

After eating, we'd head out of the harbor in our little boat, with lemon drops and cans of soda, to see what we could drag up thrashing from the depths. It was never clear where our father thought he was taking us or where we would end up. He seemed to enjoy looking for a place to fish more than finding it. On some trips, we would end up floating quietly on a smooth sea, the sun as hot as summer on glass. Other times, we'd lower our lines among swells high enough to hide our small boat. Each crest made it feel like we were casting from the top of a mountain. The fishing was always exciting and mysterious for me as a little boy, and it was always with Dad.

Later, when the family moved inland, we continued to fish. We traded in the broom-stick-stiff saltwater rods for flimsy freshwater gear and started catching trout and bass. We paddled across lakes and waded streams, instead of bobbing among the sea swells. Though the scenery changed, the ritual remained the same: choke down a crummy breakfast, pick up some lemon drops and sodas along the way, and head out looking for a place to fish.

As he got older—or maybe as I got older—I began to understand that what my father really loved about fishing was the brief, but intense, hours of freedom. For my brother and me, who assumed then that the point of fishing was to catch fish, these wanderings were frustrating. But wandering in anonymity was even more important to Dad than casting to fish. That was probably just as well, since in truth he never quite mastered the mechanics of angling.

I never really understood my father's need to be apart from his daily life until just before I left home for college. We had been driving all over the central Adirondack Mountains looking for a trout stream to fish. After Dad turned up yet another dirt road to nowhere, we parked by a culvert over a tiny stream. My brother and I followed him as he tripped through the brush where the creek trickled under a dark canopy of trees. Eventually, the stream broke out into a broad, grassy meadow. It was obvious to us that we weren't going to find any trout there in the bright sunlight and breezy warmth, so we called to him that we wanted to move on. But he was too deep in his anonymity to respond to us, or even care. He just kept walking through the meadow until he found a spot that looked good to him, and he stopped. Then, to our horror, he took off all his clothes and silently stretched out naked in the sun.

Andrew and Sok fishing, 1970.

After I left home, the opportunity to go fishing with my father came less frequently. When I began law school, our trips became even more rare. He and Tim got out occasionally, especially after my brother discovered the steelhead rivers of Lake Ontario. When I made it back home on vacation, we'd sometimes head into the mountains to find a pond or stream to fish. But those days somehow felt different. Only a narrow thread seemed to connect them to earlier trips. Maybe it was because I had started my own wanderings and, without either of us really acknowledging it, I wasn't his little boy anymore.

When my father became ill, I was buried in thoughts and wishes that I worried would crush me and tear my connection to him. Some were the usual thoughts of a son whose life and choices were dominated by a father's demands, others were less obvious concerns that I still do not fully understand. One desire, however, consumed me when I finally realized that my father was about to die. I wanted us to have one more day to go fishing. We never got that day.

Since then, fishing has become almost a need. It was always fun, but it is now somehow different and more. My father, with his ideas and expectations, is inside of me. After I left home and had met some of those expectations, I was able to shut him out when I chose. I can't do that anymore. My father made it impossible for me to ignore him by dying.

So, I go on with the fishing and wandering. In the fall of 1995, I drove my mother's distressed pickup truck from New York City to Alaska. That also amused those friends I mentioned earlier. They seem to know that fishing has become something that I not only want to do, but vaguely sense that I should do—as if it were a responsibility. I am not sure how else to describe it. Fishing has become the last remaining time that I can be alone with my father. My own anonymous wanderings have taken me from the Adirondacks to British Columbia and many startling places between. Each time, I was looking more for my father than for fish. Some days the fishing has been good, others not so good. But, always, I have found him there waiting for me.

—Andrew William Ko
Seattle, WA

His Calling

It was a special weekend. Uncle Ronnie was visiting from wherever it was he lived. Being four years old at the time, addresses weren't important to me. What was important was that we were all going fishing on my father's boat. In 1969, the highlight of my week was our Saturday/Sunday fishing trips around Massachusetts Bay. My father, older brother Andy, and I would load our rods and the lunch my mother made for us in the station wagon and head out. As I said, this weekend was special. Since Uncle Ronnie was fishing with us, mom was going to fish with us too.

Uncle Ron was quite tall, pear-like in shape, and had dark curly hair. I didn't realize it at the time, but this was his first time deep-sea fishing.

Timothy and trout.

We stopped at the tackle shop to get some frozen clams, squid, and of course the infamous bloodworms. I was happy that mom had thought ahead and had already placed a 40 pound bag of Boots' dog food in the car. For those who are not familiar with ocean fishing, dog food used as chum can be sprinkled overboard to attract fish. It works especially well on mackeral. From the tackle and bait shop, it was off to the Town River Yacht Club.

We arrived at the docks and dad went to see Cannonball, the proprietor of the yacht club.[4] I'm not certain that Cannonball was actually his name or if he was just given this nickname after swallowing a cannonball. Either way, he had a really big belly and we all knew who he was.

Andy and I loaded up the boat, and as soon as dad got back, we shoved off for a fun day of fishing. Even though it was early in the morning, it was very sunny and warm. As we taxied through the traffic around the harbor, our 18-foot boat pitched from side to side. My dad noticed that something was making

[4] Cannonball didn't actually own the yacht club, but he had fun telling us kids that he did.

Uncle Ron nervous. He was very observant. In his doctor's voice, he asked Uncle Ron if he wanted an injection for sea sickness. Uncle Ron said that he would be fine as soon as we cleared the harbor. The harbor always smelled of fish, algae, and diesel fumes.

I started to tell Uncle Ron about bloodworms. "You see bloodworms have pincers inside that come out and can really hurt. So what we do is grab them behind the head and when their pincers come out, we chop them off with a knife. You see that way…" As we neared the Hull gut at the mouth of the harbor, Uncle Ron's eyes got really wide. And the closer we got, the more pale he became. The gut was the narrow channel to Boston Harbor. It could develop quite a strong current and become very violent when subjected to tidal changes. The Hull gut was particularly scary that morning.

At this point, dad spoke up, "Tim go sit next to your brother." My father had a small placard that he had riveted in place on the boat. It read. "The Captain's Word Is Law." So,

Ko's boat. *Photo: Sok Nam Ko.*

I walked back over to speak with Andy, leaving Ron alone.

Andy told me that Uncle Ron was seasick and that he might throw up. I hated throw-up. It sounded terrible and smelled worse. For the rest of the fishing trip, I stayed clear of Uncle Ronnie on the off chance that he did have to heave.

My dad, however, seemed to be checking on him constantly. I couldn't understand it. Dad loved to fish almost as much as me. Yet he was not really taking the time to concentrate on catching the big one, but instead was making sure Uncle Ron was okay.

The trip was a bust, but I learned something about my father that day. Treating the ill wasn't just a way to make a living for him. It was his calling.

—Timothy Allen Ko
Syracuse, NY

You Have to Eat

When I was a little boy, maybe five or six years old, my father told me a story about his life soon after he was separated from his family by the war. Dad must have been sixteen then. He told me of chasing a small deer across a minefield and catching it at a river, where he grabbed the animal and drowned it in the water. He told me this story during the height of the Vietnam War. So, even at that age, I knew all about minefields, artillery and body counts. It frightened me to think of my father placing himself in danger, and it shocked me that he would kill a deer with his hands. When I asked him why he had done such a thing, he seemed surprised. Then he said, very quietly, "You have to eat."

- Andrew Ko

We Become Our Parents In The End

In our family, there was one kind of hair cut: the kind that dad gave us. Growing up in Korea and twenty years as a naval

Tim in Austria, 1987.

reserve officer had molded my fathers views on the subject. As a DDS, much like the dentists of old, he moonlighted as a barber. I'm not going to go into detail. Let it suffice to say that hair length was an issue at the Ko house.

My first job after graduation was as a sales associate for a large public radio station in Albany, New York. Every day, I would go to the corner of our block to buy a sub for lunch. The owner was a young man named Daryl. From behind the counter, Daryl would wait on customers, bake rolls, and make sandwiches.

One lunch break, after paying for my seafood on whole wheat, I noticed a pony tail under Daryl's baseball cap. I thought to myself "he's a hard working young man, all he needs is a hair cut."

—Timothy Allen Ko

Goodbye Minty Ko

Webster's Collegiate Dictionary defines the word "epiphany" as "an intuitive grasp of reality through something, as an event, usually simple and striking."

Magical days fishing on the New York's Salmon River are not common. The timing is very difficult. To be at the right spot at the right time when a large school of salmon is present requires that one be on the river every day, have a good (and I mean good) friend with current information. But, sometimes it is enough to be just plain lucky. The second weekend in

October 1988 found my father and myself just plain lucky.

It had been a couple of years since we had fished the Salmon River together. My graduation from college and searching for a job, along with his busy practice, had conspired to keep us from the river.

Getting to the spot that we wanted to fish was difficult wading. We locked arms and with some effort made the crossing. Being more than five inches taller than my father made me the stronger wader, so I was up stream breaking the current.

From 8 o'clock in the morning to 8 at night, we caught and released no less than 30 chinook salmon weighing from 15 and 30 pounds. We fought fish until our wrists and arms ached. We talked, laughed and we acted strangely like friends.

Finally, when our arms and backs could take no more, we started back for the parking lot. As we loaded the car, my father asked about my new job at the radio station, if things were okay, did I need some money to pay rent? I assured him I was doing fine and didn't need the money (even though I did).

After dropping him off in Amsterdam, I continued to Albany. And as I reflected over our magical day on the river and how happy I was for the chance to spend it with my father, tears began to well up in my eyes. I wasn't a little boy anymore. I was a man. I really felt like I had made it.

When I finally got to my apartment and began to unload my fishing gear. As I reached into my coat pocket to get my fishing license, I could feel something that wasn't there before. When I pulled out a fifty dollar bill, I realized that some things hadn't changed. I was still his son.

—Timothy Allen Ko

A Skunk, A 2x4, The Birth of Xtreme and My Dad

At first, I thought I'd write about my father's involvement in team sports. But I've decided to write about something a little bit different. My father's accomplishments as a baseball coach are fairly well recorded. One need only go to back

Stephen in France.

volumes of the Amsterdam Recorder to tally up the city league baseball championships won in the mid to late-1980's. But, less well documented is his introduction of a grass roots sports craze that has become quite en vogue since the early nineties. I'm talking about Extreme Sports ("Xtreme").

It is a little known fact that my father was one of the early pioneers in what has become a popular form of self-expression in sports. It is generally believed that Xtreme was invented by grungy flannel-plaid-wearing, alternative-music-listening, not-quite-athletic-but-still-full-of-energy Gen X-ers: kids who were looking to jump out of a helicopter to ski down a glacier. But, they were all followers. Their clothing (flannels, plaids, drab colors), their alterative musical tastes (my dad found underground "muzak" stations in every county from Upstate New York to Dade County Florida), and their answer to the need for sensory stimulation came from this incident involving my father, me and a skunk.

My father's creation of Xtreme was born from a need to liven up just another one of those slow Sundays. Dad had some wild notion about cleaning out the office in Gloversville. Even worse, he woke me up at some godawful hour (it must've been 1 p.m. at least) to bring me into his 7-day work week. I went downstairs and showered. I wanted to be clean when I got dirty! My dad was dressed in his Xtreme gear. An unbuttoned plaid flannel shirt, t-shirt, seer polyester striped pants (the stripes played wonderfully off the plaid), socks pulled up to the knees, and a pair of workboots. My mom came along too. A half hour later, we pulled into the driveway at Kingsboro Avenue. It was still light out, which irritated me greatly. We started by cleaning out the main floor. There were various things: books, trophies from city league baseball championships, volleyball trophies, garage sale purchases, and other stuff. It all looked okay to me where it was. Then we went for the basement. My mom wisely stayed behind to look over the accounting books and outstanding invoices. My dad was first to the cellar door.

It was here that Xtreme took off, and a new life-style for sweating pubescent youths was born. A skunk had managed to make its way into the cellar. By the time I got down the stairs, my dad had the animal pinned momentarily between a wall and a piece of plaster board. Dad and the skunk were on a small landing on the stairway to the basement. I was told to hold the skunk down while my dad began to search for some sporting way to "take care of the skunk."

Out of nowhere, Dad came up with a 6' long piece of 2x4 lumber. My father drew back and let it fly like a wooden javelin. Here was where the "natural high" associated with Xtreme really grabbed our senses. I had never been sprayed point blank by a skunk. I, being merely a spectator, ran out the back door gagging for fresh air. Dad, Father of Xtreme, stayed in the basement to finish off the trespassing skunk with his piece of wood. An hour later, the skunk was dead, the office was clean of debris and freshly fumigated, and a new sport and its alternative lifestyle was born.

—Stephen Olin Ko
New York, NY

My Father

My father affected nearly every aspect of my life—often in ways that I haven't always understood. He was born in Kaesong, Korea and emigrated to America in 1952 during the Korean War, bringing many of his morals and cultural beliefs with him. Growing up as my father's child meant many things. Along with the obvious American influence that surrounded my brothers and me, ours was also a very strict Confucian-style upbringing. We were expected to listen and learn before speaking, and to be respectful to everyone. Education was all-important. Combined with hard work, education was the key to success, my father taught. When caught watching TV after school, which wasn't allowed, I was told to do my homework or read a book.

Sok and Suzanne.

Dad felt that the best way to become informed about a culture was to actually visit a country and gain experiences firsthand. We travelled to many different places, from the Dominican Republic to Russia and North Korea. He always wanted to give us a broader view of the world and of people in general. He wanted to give his children the benefits of what he gained from being both American and Korean.

Dad had other sides to him as well. He was intensely competitive. Sports and fun were rarely one and the same. After every basketball game or tennis match, a compliment that I had played well was quickly followed by advice that I should work on my shooting or serving. He always wanted to see me improve in whatever I did.

Of all my father's personal qualities, I hope that I have inherited his perseverance and sense of responsibility. He would continue doing something that he felt important until it was finished, no matter how difficult or odd it might have appeared. My father's unwillingness to give up often made life difficult for his family, but I came to admire all of the things that he accomplished with this attitude.

Sok and Suzanne rollerskating. Rotary Weekend, December, 1990.

As a man who had made a comfortable life for his family, he felt a responsibility to give back to the community in small ways and on a larger scale. I remember one time when he had worked on a patient who owned a small farm and did not have very much money. Dad worked out a special payment agreement with the farmer and the next thing I knew we had a couple of chickens and a rooster in our garden. My father also felt a commitment to our broader community. He not only served as an oral surgeon, but in many other ways as well. I have only recently begun to really understand the affect that he had on our town.

I learned many things from my father. I believe that education and hard work are keys to a successful life. I also learned that goals would be meaningless to me unless they actually helped someone or made a positive difference. Even the fact that I am Korean by my father and of European descent by my mother has shown me the senselessness of racism and all other forms of bigotry.

When I first decided to spend my junior year of high school in Denmark, my parents were almost as excited as I was. But, four months before I was to go, my father died. I had to decide whether to go abroad or to stay at home. I went to Denmark because I knew that my father was proud of me and wanted me to take advantage of this opportunity. I can't really

Suzanne Ko, Cornell University, October, 1993.

describe how homesick I was or how much I missed my father and family while I was abroad. But now, I think that the whole experience and the things that I learned from my father made me stronger and more able to face his death. It has all helped me to realize that my father is still with me.

—Suzanne Elaine Ko
New York, NY

CHAPTER VIII

RELATIVES AND FRIENDS FROM KAESONG

Memories of Sok Nam

My memories go back to our days in Korea. My father and Sok's mother were brother and sister. The way relationships are figured here in the United States, Sok and I would be first cousins. But I have always been referred to by his children as "Uncle" Kim.

When I was a little boy, I would spend vacations visiting the Ko home. My grandfather and I walked or sometimes would ride a wagon pulled by oxen to the Ko home. Their home was a big and well-to-do home in the city of Kaesong. While there I would play with Sok and his sister. I was a year younger than Sok. He would take care of me and fight anyone who bothered me. Sometimes, however, he would tease me. Then his mother would yell at him to stop picking on me. I remember Sok's mother as being very pretty as a young lady. She was the hard worker in the family. I was afraid of Sok's grandmother, who was the matriarch of the family.

The Ko family had a cloth factory where looms were used and people were hired to make cloth. The family members were land owners, too. They had ginseng fields and rice fields all over the countryside. Sok's father was gone much of the time supervising the farmers who were tending the fields.

Sok's father had another wife in the country. In those days a man wasn't a man unless he had more than one wife. My father had two wives, too.

My family lived in the country. Sok's mother and her sisters would often visit my family for a few days. When they came, it was like a family reunion. Or sometimes Sok would come alone. He had to walk for about two hours to get to my house.

Whenever Sok came to my house, we used to head for the river near Panmunjom. It was a long walk to the river and we would get hot. So as we got near the river we would start taking off all our clothes, piece by piece, so as to be ready to jump into the water as soon as we got there. Sok was a good swimmer.

Sometimes, while at the river, we fished with a single wood pole and a hook. Sok also liked to hunt. He was good at whatever he tried. Sok liked many sports as a boy. He was a very serious player. In fact, he was serious about everything he did. In this way he was like my brother.

Sok and I were known for playing some risky games. There were fields of watermelon in the countryside. These fields were watched by a man who stayed on a little platform covered with straw overlooking the fields at night. Sok and I would take off our clothes and creep into the orchard at night to get a melon. The man would see us and yell, "Thief! Thief!" We would get scared and run. There wasn't anyone else around so nothing would have happened, but we were afraid and would run just the same.

In the first year of high school, students were taught karate, gymnastics, tumbling and fencing using bamboo sticks. The Japanese were there in Korea for 36 or 37 years, so their language was learned by all the children. They would not allow Korean to be spoken in the schools. One would be physically punished if they were heard speaking Korean. Some students would tell on you if they heard you speak Korean; even your cousin might tell on you. Then you would be punished. The way the Japanese punished was to put you outside the classroom and make you hold your arms up over your head for about an hour. The Japanese could not control what was spoken in the family, so Korean was still spoken at home.

Left to right: Ho Nam Kim, Alissa Kim, Sharon Kim, Chu Yul Kim, Kum Soon Kim.

There were no Christian churches—maybe one—in Kaesong. There was a Christian School which was a very good high school.

A few miles out of Kaesong in the mountains were many houses where the Buddhist monks lived. They prayed and people thought they brought good luck. The monks would come down from the mountains and ask for food from all the farmers at harvest time. They had places in the mountains (like little temples) where you could leave coins for the monks. That is how they survived. They did not support Christianity.

Before the invasion of Kaesong, the guerillas would come out of the mountains at night and put their flag up the city flag pole. Then they would retreat into the mountains before daylight. During the day the city belonged to the civilians of Kaesong. Then the guerillas would come down from the mountains again at night. When the invasion of Kaesong came, we would run into the mountains to hide so that we would not be conscripted into the North Korean Army. We would not have anything to eat sometimes; only berries or whatever we could find. This went on for two or three months. The North Koreans had a lot of big Russian tanks and armored carriers. When they invaded Seoul, I was there going to high school. My mother and I lived in Seoul at that time. I watched as they killed people and burned buildings. One student said, “Come, join us.” I said, “Maybe tomorrow.” Instead I left the area.

My mother went back to Kaesong and I was going to follow her but then I could not get back across the lines. Both Sok and I thought we would be leaving our home for just a few days, but we lost our family because we could not return.

During the war I worked for the United States Army stacking ammunition containers near the railroad tracks. One day as the train was passing, a jeep appeared on the other side of the tracks. HCO George Harrington was sitting on the front seat of the jeep. He was wearing an army uniform and hat. Sok was sitting on the back of the jeep. He was holding a yellow manila folder with all the American Embassy papers in it. I didn't know then, but now I know these were signs that Sok would be leaving Korea eventually. As the jeep drove by, Sok called to me and said he was going to America and he would write to me, as soon as he could. Later I was told that he did write to me but I never saw the letters because I moved around so much. I spoke a little English which helped me later on.

As it turned out, both of us left Korea. The last time I saw Sok was in the summer of 1952. That fall Sok came to the United States, but I didn't come until 1978. I thought Sok was in Los Angeles or perhaps in New York City. Later, in letters from family members in Korea, I learned that Sok had visited Kaesong twice. Finally I was told he was living in Amsterdam, wherever that was! Through information given by a telephone operator, I got Sok's number. I was so excited as I dialed the phone hoping that my search for Sok was over. Stephen answered the phone and told me that his father was there. At first I could hardly believe the news. After 35 years of waiting, my search was over and my dream of finding Sok had come true.

—Chu Yul Kim

Cousin Chu Yul Kim and Sok Nam Ko.

After Years of Separation

(Spoken at the Memorial Service for Dr. Ko)

My father and Dr. Ko are cousins and grew up together in Korea. They were separated during the war. When my father came to America, he tried to find Dr. Ko. Eventually he got a letter from North Korea in 1987. They wrote in Korean — "Amsterdam." My father didn't know where there was an Amsterdam in New York. The only Amsterdam he knew was in the Netherlands. When he learned differently, he called New York information. They looked up Amsterdam. In about fifteen minutes my father was in touch with Dr. Ko. Hearing Uncle Sok whom he hadn't seen for thirty-five years made my father so happy. You see, my father doesn't have any other relatives besides our immediate family. All of us are so grateful to you for keeping Dr. Ko until we found him.

—Lissa Kim
(Daughter of Chu Yul Kim)

SOK N. KO, D.D.S.
PRACTICE LIMITED TO ORAL SURGERY
80 LOCUST AVENUE
AMSTERDAM, N. Y. 12010
TELEPHONE (518) 843-0382

This letter is written with the hope that you might help me with a personal problem: the relocating of my family in North Korea.

I came to the United States in October, 1952 and became a United States citizen in 1962. My hometown was Kaesong, Korea, presently a city in North Korea. I left my family during the Korean Conflict (1952), when I was a fifteen year old boy. I had three brothers, two sisters, parents, and a paternal grandmother (a list of my family is attached). We have had no communication since 1951 and were separated for thirty-four years without knowing the existance or where-about of each other.

I arrived under the sponsorship of Attorney and Mrs. George Harrington of Castleton, Vermont in 1952. Since then I have graduated from Fair Haven High School, Fair Haven, Vermont in 1954: Castleton State College, Castleton, Vermont (B.S. in Education - 1958): University Of Vermont, Burlington, Vermont (B.A. in Zoology and minor in Chemistry - 1963): and Tufts University School of Dental Medicine and Boston V.A. Hospital, Boston, Mass. (Oral and Maxillofacial Surgery Internship and Residency - 1971). As you can see, my soul purpose for coming to the United States was for my education and I have fulfilled this objective.

I taught Junior and Senior High School in South Burlington, Vermont and also taught at Tufts University School of Dental Medicine, Boston, Massachusetts.

I have been in private practice for Oral and Maxillofacial Surgery in Amsterdam, New York, U.S.A. for fourteen years, since 1971. I have been married to my wife, Elaine Hogaboom, since 1960. We have four children: Andrew is a twenty-one year old graduate of Tufts University, Boston, Mass., and will be attending New York University Law School; Timothy is a twenty year old student at Syracuse University, Syracuse, N.Y.; Stephen is a fourteen year old high school student; and Suzanne is a ten year old grade school girl.

Now, I am fifty years old and anxiously looking forward to finding the family I left behind in Kaesong, Korea thirty-four years ago. I am sure that my family would be very disappointed and sad if they never learned of my outcome since the conflict. I would be very grateful if you would assist me in finding my family in any shape or manner.

Enclosed please find my home address in Korea, list of family members, relationship, age, etcetera. Also enclosed is my present address and telephone numbers.

I would appreciate your assistance very much in this manner, and sincerely hope my family reunion will be soon.

Enclosures

Sincerely,

Sok Nam Ko DDS

Sok Nam Ko, D.D.S.

Letter requesting permission to visit family in the Democratic People's Republic of Korea.

MY KOREAN ADDRESS: (조선주소)

개성시 고려동 229 번지의 9호

開城市 高麗洞 229 番地 9号

229-9 KO RYO DONG, KAESONG, KOREA (PEOPLES REPUBL

MY U.S. ADDRESS: (미국 주소)

DR. SOK NAM KO
80 LOCUST AVE
AMSTERDAM, NEW YORK 12010
U.S.A.

FAMILY LIST (가족)

FATHER	아버지	高晉明	고진명	70 세
MOTHER	어머니	金三玉	김삼옥	68 "
GRAND-MOTHER	할머니	白興봉	백흥봉	90 "
SISTER	여동생	高英洙	고영주	48 "
BROTHER	동생	高錫東	고석동	46 "
BROTHER	동생	高錫根	고석근	44 "
BROTHER	동생	高錫元	고석원	42 "
SISTER	여동생	高[illegible]洙	고[illegible]주	38 "
MYSELF	나자신	高錫南	고석남	50 "

Travel Itinerary sent to the Democratic People's Republic of Korea's Embassy in Beijing China September 18, 1985.

To Dr. Sok Nam Ko

We have the honour of inviting you to visit the homeland. Your families and relations at home are all faring well, and they are impatiently waiting for your visit to the native land.

As for the necessary formalities for your home visit, you are requested to contact the Embassy of the Democratic People's Republic of Korea in Peking or Moscow. They will serve your conveniences.

Hoping that you will want to visit the homeland at any time convenient to you, we would be much obliged if you let us know at the earliest possible date the exact time of your coming.

Committee for Aiding Overseas Nationals
of the D.P.R.K. Pyongyang

July 9, 1985

Text of Letter granting permission to visit family in the Democratic People's Republic of Korea.

SOK N. KO, D.D.S.
PRACTICE LIMITED TO ORAL SURGERY
80 LOCUST AVENUE
AMSTERDAM, N. Y. 12010
TELEPHONE (518) 843-0382

September 18, 1985

Embassy
Democratic People's Republic of Korea
Beijing
People's Republic of China

Dear Sir:

This is to inform you that I will be departing the United States of America on September 30, 1985 to reunite with my family in Korea.

I will be arriving at Beijing Airport, People's Republic of China on Thursday, October 3, 1985 at 2:10 P.M. via London, England, on British Airline. I am looking ahead to a speedy reuniting with my family.

I sincerely thank you for the kind cooperation of the Committee for Aiding Overseas Nationals of the D.P.R.K., other officials for making this event possible, and my long dream come true.

Sincerely,

Sok Nam Ko

Letter informing authorities of dates or travel to the Democratic People's Republic of Korea.

North Korea 1985

In October of 1985, my father and I traveled to North Korea. It was the first time that he was allowed to return home to see his family in more than thirty years. Millions of Koreans were killed, wounded or went missing during the war. Until just a few weeks before we flew out of Montreal, Dad had no idea if any of his family had survived the war and hardship that followed the cease-fire. I can't imagine what he must have thought and felt on the day he got permission to return home. But, for all his excitement and anticipation, he clearly did not want to make the trip alone, so he asked me if I would go with him. I've always wondered if being separated from his family in Korea accounted for my father's unwillingness to travel any distance without his wife or at least one of his children. Traveling with Dad, I had many questions answered.

I kept this journal as we traveled together through China and North Korea that October. Obviously, it wasn't written for this book, and on the surface it might seem more about our trip than about my father. But, it was a big event in his life, and it certainly changed the way I saw him and our relationship. I began writing while we were on a flight from Beijing to Pyongyang.

<u>October 6, 1985 2:00 p.m.</u>
Somewhere Over China — "Stand Please"

At around 1:45 p.m. we boarded a small, Soviet-built twin engine plane. I was a little worried by the thought that the North Koreans probably only have this plane because the Russians didn't want it anymore. I was also a bit concerned when they didn't just stamp our passports, but instead took a quick look at our photos and kept them.

The pilot decided to communicate with us directly in English during takeoff. Dad didn't even have to translate; I just assumed that the pilot's instruction to "Stand please" meant that I should take a seat and buckle up.

The flight attendant and crew must think that I am a little crazy. I keep thinking about our first day in Beijing and can't help laughing out loud. We had flown British Airways the long way around the globe—it is the Ko way. When we arrived in Beijing, we had been up for at least thirty-six hours since leaving Amsterdam (New York), having landed in London, Rome, the Middle East and Hong Kong along the way. We both felt okay, so we had some food and then settled in at the Airport Hotel outside of Beijing. I was exhausted by then and already felt vulnerable enough, not knowing any Chinese. So, I told Dad that I was going to stay in the room and get some sleep. But the excitement of being in China and the anticipation of seeing his family had him lit up with nervous energy, so he went out to take some photos. He came back a few hours later and said he wanted to get dinner. The trip had hit me pretty hard by that time, but he seemed to be holding up. We went down to the hotel restaurant, and he ordered shrimp with black bean sauce and his usual cola. I had something not so memorable and a big Tsing Tao beer to wash it down.

We were eating and talking, then something must have snapped between my father's ears. He started mumbling something odd about the waitress looking funny. I wasn't quite sure where that was coming from until he started dribbling black bean sauce down the front of his shirt. Then I realized that crossing more than twelve time zones had finally caught up with him. My father was elsewhere, and I was having dinner with Dr. Jetlag. He then pointed to the big green bottle next to my plate and asked, "What is that?" I said, "It's beer, Dad," pretty much expecting to get a lecture on alcohol consumption. Instead, he vaguely mumbled, "Give me some." I told him that I'd order him another Coke and looked around for the waitress, but he just kept waving his empty water glass at me, demanding that I fill it up. I did, and he drank it all down without taking a breath. At that point, I paid the bill and we got out of there.

Maybe I should have leaned him against a wall while I got our room key from the front desk, but I left him standing — sort of — in the middle of the small lobby. As I tried to get the Chinese desk clerk to understand that I wanted our room key, I noticed the man looking over my shoulder. I turned to see what had caught the clerk's attention and saw Dad swaying in a strange circular pattern. His shoes seemed like they were nailed to the floor; no matter which direction he tilted, his feet stayed firmly planted. He defied gravity. I smiled at the clerk, he smiled back and gave me the key, and I got Dad upstairs.

In our room, Dad demanded his toothbrush, forgetting that he had put it in the bathroom when we arrived. As I tried to hand him the toothbrush, he was busy struggling with the cellophane wrapper of a new one. It was all too much for my poor father. Before he had even gotten through the wrapper, his eyes rolled up into the top of his sleep-deprived head and he slowly fell backwards. He seemed to float as he descended. It was so completely peaceful that it didn't even occur to me, until too late, that I should try to catch him. Fortunately, he landed gently on the bed — his little Korean legs dangling over the end of the mattress, the half-opened toothbrush box clutched to his chest. Dr. Jetlag was done for the evening. I couldn't stop laughing until I fell asleep myself.

That was a few days ago. Now we're in a two-engine plane going to North Korea. The pilot is a good flier, and for a plane of this size, the ride is smooth. The engines hum along, as my father talks with another passenger in Korean. He seems to be an air force officer or some sort of pilot. He is very friendly and they seem to be enjoying their conversation.

I've never flown over countryside like this. The closest landscape was the Black Hills of South Dakota. Below us, the Great Wall winds endlessly, disappearing into the distance. I can see the guardhouses connected by the links of wall, and beyond I think I see mountains. It looks very dry down there. Browns and grays. (Dad just reminded me that I forgot to mail some letters.) Villages, scattered between dusty mountains, are connected by curving dirt roads. Those isolated communities seem strange, as if the houses had been set on top of the mountains and then slid down the sides to collect in the valleys.

Earlier, the young stewardess joined in the conversation with the officer and Dad. I showed them a picture of Dad and Suz. Though I can't understand their words, I know that they are talking about the family. I feel a bit guilty, since the flight attendant seems to be taking better care of us than my father's new friend and the other passenger. She's offered us everything from candy, to cigarettes, to beer. She has a smile that would melt even Bobby J.'s heart. As they speak, I hear "Tufts" and "Syracuse" and "NYU." They look at me and smile. I smile back. I guess the airforce guy is a pilot, since he just walked forward to the cockpit. Whoa, here comes a bit of turbulence, Dad's knuckles are going white.

A half-hour later we've begun to leave the mountains behind and are over what must be Manchuria. Below are fields, probably dry grain. The farmland seems to be cut out of the mountains that we just left behind, as if the tops had been scraped off to grow a little food for the unlucky people who live down there. It looks dry, there is no water (or very little) in the bare riverbeds. It looks very dry — brown and dry.

Farther along, I see that the decapitated mountains were probably that, because we are immediately over other mountains with their lids still on. No trees, just man-made plateaus and mountains, isolated towns and immense dry riverbeds. The river channels are huge, and I can see the dry courses of their tributaries stretching into the hills. They must be terrifying when the snow melts in the mountains each spring.

My father just pointed out a power generating plant below — a rather incongruous pair of silos among the mountains. I also see a large town below. Actually, it's more of a small city. Through it winds a river, which flows with water. Green fields surround it, which are themselves surrounded by bone-dry country. Twenty minutes later we're over mountains again, but a different kind. They are rocky and sharply ridged. They appear speckled with white, though I don't think it's snow. Evergreen forests cover some of the slopes.

Later we bounce along above flat croplands. Here the expansive plain and turbulent atmosphere are real. Before the storms that we sailed through on *Westward,* this might have bothered me a little. But, after two weeks of being thrown around by the Atlantic, this doesn't seem so awful...yet.

Thirty or so minutes later, we're away from the farmland. Through the clouds I see what seem to be mining pits and large lakes. Maybe I wasn't seeing Manchuria before, but instead northern China. Through the dense clouds it is hard to say.

Great Wall of China. *Photo: Andy Ko*

Slowly, we're turning east, not directly crossing the sea between China and North Korea. That's fine with me. Through a break in the clouds I see more mountains. But these have more forest cover, and the huge riverbeds contain more water. The soil is a richer brown. I feel better seeing increasingly more trees and water. Covering the clouds I see a pale rainbow— very odd. And within the arc rests a small circular rainbow, just as pale.

October 6, 1985 4:18 p.m.
Over North Korea

We're in our descent, lots of turbulence (as you can see from my handwriting). Red tile roofs, fields and factories. A large, milky green river. Thatch covered houses. The fields are a hundred (or so) colors, not just tan or brown. Large, gray, hazy mountains loom in the distance. Tree-covered hills separate farming valleys. It is a very nice change after the barrenness of northern China. It seems like a fairytale land in this strange gray light.

October 6, 1985 4:49 p.m.
A North Korean Airport

We land with a bounce, skip and a big thump. As we came down, we seemed to be gliding over the tarmac. I couldn't tell if the wheels were on the ground or not. My father turned to me and said, "Smooth landing, huh?" Then we hit with a jarring thud that made us both sit up straight. Dad turned to me and shook his head.

October 6, 1985 4:51 p.m.
Party Officials and Little Flower Girls

After a thirty-kilometer ride we are in Pyongyang. I am fascinated — not by anything in particular, but by it all. The reality of being here is a very strange sensation. The small airport was deserted when we landed. It was very nice, but didn't seem to be all that busy. I saw very few planes of the size that brought us here, though there were some smaller planes and a few helicopters. It was no JFK International Airport — not even an Albany County Airport. But it was nice. The gray, drizzly weather cast a gloom over the city and the outlying area.

Two men met us at the airport terminal. My father spoke with them and then turned to me and introduced the younger man as our guide, Mr. Lee. The older man, who seemed to be his superior, was some kind of communist party official. I never caught his name, but he seemed pleasant. With them were two cute little girls who gave us flowers. Of course, I wasn't able to participate in their conversation as we were driven in a Volvo sedan to our hotel. I only later learned that Mr. Lee speaks Russian, having spent six years in the Soviet Union as a student.

Pyongyang is a massive assortment of large apartment buildings, parks, stadiums and construction sites. There are lots of trees, but few people out and about. The hotel is beautiful by any standard, and in developing Asia it almost seems unreal, with its medium fridge, nice bathroom, television, anteroom, living room, bedroom, and balcony. (I just noticed all the Volvos out front.) I'm sure that much of this is intended to impress us — which it has. I am a little surprised at how much it all reminds me of southern Korea. I guess thirty years of separation is almost insignificant in comparison to a common culture and history going back a few thousand years.

China was impressive in its vastness. But there is something else that is fascinating about Korea. Even though the nation has been divided for more than thirty years, Koreans in both halves seem like they are somehow interconnected. One minute everything is still and everyone seems to be standing around; then, like someone pushed a hidden button, everyone is up and rushing around. Then everything is still again. Maybe it's my imagination. I'm still at bit disoriented from being in this place that I thought I'd never see.

<u>October 7, 1985 8:00 a.m.</u>
Pyongyang

Mr. Lee and the older man took us to dinner in the hotel last night. The meal was a very good chicken Kiev. Our balcony overlooks the city. I'm sure that we were placed in this room with the intention of creating a certain impression. It doesn't really matter, the view is spectacular. Mist swirls through the willow trees along the river. Athletes do their morning warm-ups in the parking lot. As in China, a glowing orange sunrise outlines the high-rise apartment buildings. I'm not sure what exists behind the green, yellow and orange tile facades of the apartment buildings, but everything is clean and orderly outside, even if spartan. School children have just begun to sing in the distance, as they march to school. I remember the little girls who gave us flowers at the airport. It's strange, but the city's trains, children, street cleaners and trucks all seem to have started up within the last two or three minutes.

Last night the older man said that he hoped to change my view of the North as formed by "propaganda lies in the South" (my father's translation of the man's words). My father is too excited about seeing his family to be overly cynical. He seems dazzled, but I think it is more likely that he isn't even completely here. In his thoughts, he is obviously already in Kaesong with his family. For now, all that I'm willing to concede about North Korea is that everything has been too expansive and felt too surreal to be staged just for us. Certainly the black smoke pouring from the factories to my left, as I stand on the balcony, is real enough. The early mist seems to have turned to smog. This country is going somewhere fast, like its nemesis. Where, I'm not really sure.

They still have our passports. Hmmm.

October 7, 1985 4:12 p.m.
Pyongyang

After a very nice Western-style breakfast, the younger guy, Mr. Lee, met us with a different party official. He and my father talked for quite a while. As with the older man from last night, this guy was a charmer. Sadly, he seemed to suffer from Parkinson's disease. Dad and he spoke for hours about life, Dad's family here, and our family in the states. Mr. Lee didn't participate in the conversation, as he had at breakfast this morning when we were alone with him. The older guy referred to "The Great Leader Comrade Kim Il Sung" with every breath, according to my father. Still, they have all been very nice here.

After another wonderful meal—Korean this time—we went to the birthplace of "The Great Leader." We were met there by a guide who conducted her tour in English. If George Washington had been born in a thatched hut, this could have been a tour of Mount Vernon. The guide had every line of the story memorized, from bedroom, to ox hut, to the family's noodle press. When she spoke off the script, her English was really quite good. I don't much care for cults of personality, whether our "personalities" or theirs, but the grounds were beautifully kept. Maybe that's the tradeoff. I did find that the groups of little school children, who were either frolicking with their teachers or staring at me (as if they'd never seen a 6'3" curly-haired half-Korean before), made things a little more fun.

Within a block of the shrine at Kim Il Sung's boyhood home was an amusement park. In the four Asian countries that I've now visited, three have shown me their amusement parks. While the Japanese might have a slight edge over the others, the North Korean park compared favorably with the other that I've seen in Asia. A few families, school groups (actually, they

Dr. Ko, Andrew and Mr. Lee, their guide.

were probably Young Pioneer groups) and young soldiers were enjoying the park, but overall there weren't many people there that Monday afternoon. There were no lines to get on the rides. In fact, there was an entire section to the park that was not being used that day. I was surprised by how many young soldiers were there, as compared to other groups. I suppose that made sense; young men must serve in the army from the age of eighteen to twenty-four. Everyone stays in the reserves after that, but I'd guess that very few sign up for more than the mandatory six years of active duty.

I found myself wondering if the frivolity of the morning was a ploy to keep us occupied, so we wouldn't keep asking about travelling to Kaesong. But, I don't really think so. It seemed more like a simple attempt to show us that they enjoy the same things that we have in the States. They are wasting a lot of energy trying to impress an American dentist and his son.

On the ride back to the hotel, we passed some farmland. Every bit of land is tilled here, with most of the acreage in wet rice. Since the rice harvest is already in, farmers are doing odd jobs and maintaining their fields. I really wanted to see some development projects. Unfortunately, we didn't stop.

As everywhere here, people are out working. On the drive down to the shrine, a woman was in the middle of the road sweeping with a big handmade broom. No sooner had she swept some leaves toward the side of the road than some vehicle would come and blow them back in her face. There seem to be no private cars or homes here. Average citizens live in Soviet style apartments and travel en masse by bus or truck. As we drive along in the Volvo, people at the roadside stare as if we were Texans in a huge Cadillac limousine with cattle horns on the front, or maybe clowns riding an ostrich. I'm not sure what they see when they look at us. At any rate, it seems right that in a society as poor as this, where the material needs of the people are still not being fully met, that private cars and homes are being left for the future. I hope they are anyway. Such things seem obscene in a country still working to feed and house its people. A couple Americans, their guide and driver rolling down the street in a state-owned Volvo may not be much better.

Back in the car, I began to feel a little sorry for the guide at Kim's house. She was very nice, but I was only able to keep a straight face through some of her presentation. I hope I didn't offend our Korean companions by not taking any pictures at Kim's monument. I took so many of the small children and their mothers in the amusement park, I think they must be wondering why I wasn't more interested in their leader's home. My father tells me they're planning some sort of reception tonight. (Dad just "broke wind", which was almost as loud as his snoring. At least we both got a laugh out of it, the snoring just keeps me awake all night.)

<u>October 8, 1985 7:45 a.m.</u>
"Obey Orders"

We're late as usual. Last night we met with the big cheese, Mr. Kim-Lee-Something-or-Other. We spoke with him — at least my father did — in one of the conference rooms and then had a traditional Korean dinner (except for the western-style hamburger with the egg on it). The man who met us the first night and the younger Mr. Lee were very deferential toward this guy, so I assume he must be somebody in the Party. He reminded me of Marlon Brando in "The Godfather." When he addressed me through my father, he emphasized the need to study history, ancient as well as modern. He asked me, through my father, "If there is a war, you will probably be drafted, and you will have to fight against your cousins. What do you say to that?" I told him I probably wouldn't go. He smiled but I don't think he really understood why I gave him that answer. Before eating, we toasted "The continued progress of the DPRK." I didn't know what the stuff was, or that I only was expected to take a sip, so I sucked it all down. It was "rice liquor" that was close to vodka and much stronger than soju. On an empty stomach it didn't settle as well as it could have.

This morning, younger Mr. Lee took us around town. First we saw Kim's torch, which is an enormous tower that was erected on his seventieth birthday. He was born around 1911. Quite a view from the top, but not an especially modern elevator. It was so quiet that I thought they were putting us on. Then the door opened and we looked down over the city. The guide spoke in English, as she pointed out various highlights in the distance, such as Kim Il Sung's Arc de Triomphe. "Three meters taller than Napoleon's," she pointed out. Its lines were much simpler than the one in Paris — more tasteful maybe, notwithstanding the lame attempt to one-up the French. I'm sure that these statues, monuments and towers are important to someone — maybe Kim and his son. But, the waste is disturbing. These ornaments produce no tractors, no buses, no apartments and no rice. Of course, neither does my car at home.

Before returning to the hotel for lunch, we went to a tailor shop that is reserved for the foreign diplomatic community here. There was quite an assortment of products and my father clothed himself, ordering a tailored suit. There were also plenty of Eastern Europeans. One would probably have found it tough to swing a dead cat without hitting a chubby Russian.

Later, we went back to the hotel and saw a double documentary on reconstruction and post-war aid that the government claims to have sent to South Korea. Most of the footage portrayed a much younger, but already rotund, Kim Il Sung personally overseeing reconstruction with broad sweeps of his arms. At one point during the film my father made a snorting sound. I leaned over and asked him what had happened in the film. He told me that a row of banners behind Kim in the film read "Obey orders." I asked him what else they said. "Nothing else," he answered, "just 'Obey orders.'" My father, the American, was offended.

October 9, 1985 1:45 p.m.
Pyongyang: At the Train Station

We were up again this morning by 6:00 am and out the door by 7:30. After breakfast we did some running around: People's Study Hall, a hospital, a noodle joint, the subway, and a kindergarten. In between these stops we checked on my father's suit and bought TV's for his siblings' families. Tonight we're off to Kaesong by train. We'll leave around midnight and arrive seven hours later.

The People's Study Hall was an enormous library and teaching complex of marble and granite in the western classical style. The card catalogue was about twice the size of the one in Tufts' undergraduate library, but we only saw a few books, about two Wessell Library rows worth in this huge building. Maybe the architect was looking toward the future (it was built in the early 80's). I'm not sure why they didn't have more books. They said that the stacks were in back, but I don't think even my father believed that. The library staff demonstrated the system for getting a book from the circulation desk. This involved a card for the call number and title, the librarian punching the number into a keyboard, and the book coming from a back room on a conveyor belt. They were obviously well prepared for our visit, since the three books that came out were old medical and biology texts. Dad said something like, "Hey, pretty good, huh?" He looked amused. The building also contained a language center, lecture halls, audio rooms for music study, and a cafeteria. Kim seems to put considerable emphasis on education. The building contained a collection of his and his son's writings, works of DPRK writers, and translated texts in a separate room. From a balcony in the library, we saw thousands of students in a nearby square rehearsing for a pageant commemorating the fortieth Anniversary of the Korean Labor Party. An impressive sight that I doubt could be orchestrated in the U.S. The differences between our societies are interesting.

The hospital was also quite large. It was ten stories and very spread out. My father thought it was a noodle factory when we first pulled up. It took us a couple seconds to realize that the doctor in his white cap who came to give us a tour was not the noodle maker. The hospital was mostly a maternity and pediatric facility. We were shown quite a bit of medical equipment, from an ultrasound apparatus to a modern oral surgery with three chairs. Dad said that their setup for doing blood counts and urinalysis testing is less automated than the methods presently used in the U.S., but that our systems for prenatal and maternal care are quite similar. We even watched a cesarean being performed. As with the Juche Tower, the People's Study Hall and others, this building was erected on the occasion of one of the Premier's special days. Every patient can look up to see his portrait as she is being administered to, which I am sure is a great comfort during labor.

The noodle joint — the one without operating tables — was set at the top of a hill. The whole area is a sort of park. Within the park was an old theater house. Before the construction of the Juche Tower and other large structures, this hill was the highest point in the city. From the top, visitors have quite a view of Kim's huge statue and a number of other rather lofty monuments. We didn't visit any of those, though they seemed bizarrely interesting. We also missed the War Museum, though I expressed an interest. I expect we might have "missed" them for similar reasons. The noodles were good.

After the noodles we took a ride on their subway, which is vintage Soviet. It consisted of two intersecting straight trainlines. Each stop had its own revolutionary theme and an enormous portrait of Kim Il Sung. It was a peaceful ride, since we were basically the only ones on the train.

The kindergarten, on the other hand, was the most traumatic experience to date. The munchkins and their teachers were well prepared for our visit. They sang us songs, danced for us and showed us toddlers at play in the recreation room. The children gave us a wild sendoff by crowding around and pulling on anything within reach — which was more than a bit disturbing. The weird part was the fake smiles that the little kids kept plastered on their faces the whole time that they were singing, dancing, and pulling. It was like they knew some big secret, and they weren't telling. The kindergarten teachers were what you'd expect: patient smiles and genuine sweetness. It's been interesting to see how this society perpetuates itself politically, from pre-K onwards, with its programmed patriotism and adoration of Kim. I suppose we do the same thing with money. Friday night is when the parents pick up their kids. The cars parked outside were mostly Mercedes. I had a feeling that this was not an ordinary preschool.

We are now heading to Kaesong by train. My father's suit still wasn't ready.

October 10, 1985 10:00 p.m.
And Even More Crying in Kaesong

I woke up this morning at 6:30 a.m., when the train that we boarded at 1:00 a.m. slowed to a near stop. Getting on the train last night was a bit of a hassle. A conductor, or some sort of official person, got all pissed off as we were about to board. When he began his fuss, a female train conductor who had guided us across the tracks came to our defense. She got between him and us and yelled back in his face. The aggravated-one yelled back at her until our guide, Mr. Lee, took him by the arm and walked him down the track. I've no idea what Lee said to the dude, but when they came back he was very polite. Lee's a smooth guy and I still refuse to believe that he's just an ordinary guide. He gets too much respect from everyone we meet. He clearly has some sort of authority, though much of it may simply be his personality. Who knows?

At 6:30 a.m. we were passing through a small town in the mountains. In the predawn glow, I could see silhouettes in the windows of the apartment buildings near the rail tracks. The dim light inside the buildings didn't seem to be coming from electric light bulbs. Neither were there any electric streetlights outside. The rail yard held only a motionless steam engine that looked like it had been pulled off an American western movie set. The rice paddies on the edge of the town had been harvested. Farther on, we passed traditional Korean homes tucked around a large hill with a rock face engraved with billboardsized slogans.

At 7:00 a.m. we arrived in Kaesong and the oldest of Dad's younger brothers and their little sister met us on the train. Tears flowed. (I'll write about that with a bit more care someday.) Soon the pace of things picked up. A list of the days activities:

Met aunt's husband and three of my cousins (son and two daughters of first uncle) at first uncle's apartment;

Emotional (to say the least) reunion and catching up in common room, ate, napped, meeting in small room (more tears);

Second uncle arrived (more crying, tears and catching up), lunch (second uncle explains the beer industry in the North, though he doesn't drink);

An evening visit to Kim Il Sung's statue on the hill, we're handed flowers to lay at the statue's feet—okay, why not;

Children's performance at a local school: orchestra, chorus, tumblers, patriotic skit, twelve string folk instrument called a "kayageum," special seating with Party officials. The kids had the same prefab smiles, but were incredibly skilled on their instruments. As we left the concert hall, the smallest children ran us out of the building like the kindergarten kids had in Pyongyang, laughing and jumping all over us;

We had supper with the Kaesong regional Party secretary and his assistant. The Party guys challenged first uncle to drink a water glass full of ginseng whiskey. It made me woozy just to see him do it. Aunt wouldn't come in to eat with us until one of the officials insisted. She seemed to be a bit shocked when they brought her a chair. The Party secretary was the consummate politician and was mirrored in his manners and speech by his subordinates (both of them);

Home with the family (whole family stays over). We watched TV; they laugh and I smile. We all slept Korean style — I like a log soaked in ginseng whiskey.

<u>October 11, 1985 8:40 a.m.</u>
Kaesong

After a big breakfast, we're off again. My father said that we'd first go to the graves of his mother and grandmother, but we may not have time today according to Mr. Lee. Dad wants to see his family's old homes. His family lived in three different houses. Mr. Lee and the family don't seem eager to take Dad to see any of the houses where he grew up, and he's starting to think that something must have happened to them. The road that we're driving down is too bumpy to write, so I'll have to finish this later.

October 12, 1985 7:40 a.m.
Kaesong

Actually, after breakfast on October 11th we went for a drive. As we drove south, I started to wonder where we were going. When I asked my father, he kept looking out the window and quietly said, "Panmunjom." He knew I was going to be furious, because I had told him over and over again that I wouldn't go there to have my picture taken by U.S. soldiers as I stood on the North Korean side of the border! But, they had asked him if we wanted to see Panmunjom, and he hadn't been able to tell them no. Neither had he found a way to explain that we did not want to be their propaganda tools or that Americans generally think it is a bad idea to do things that will win them the distinction of a CIA or FBI file. But, as he kept looking out the window, we drove closer and closer to Panmunjom. And yes, the US troops did come out when we appeared on the North Korean side. And yes, they did take many, many photographs of us.

As with the US/ROK propaganda on the southern side, much of the DPRK propaganda is loosely based on fact. But, there were some pictures in their little museum that I know were being used out of context. The Margaret Bourke-White photo of an ROK soldier holding up the decapitated heads of North Korean troops was taken during the Korean War, not the Japanese occupation. I didn't think it was a good idea to set them straight on that one. Similarly, some exhibits failed to tell the whole truth or tell it accurately. In an incident in the 1970's, a truck full of North Korean soldiers attacked American personnel who were cutting down a tree in the DMZ. The North Korean captain who was leading our tour said that a truckload of U.S. troops had attacked four North Koreans. He quickly changed the subject when I asked him if it was true that no Korean troops were hurt, but that two American officers were killed that day by North Korean soldiers with axe handles. Then we went to the Line of Demarcation. That was when the US Military Police started to take photos of us for Big Broth...uh...Uncle Sam.

I was fuming on the way back from Panmunjom. But, I couldn't stay mad for long, because our next stop was a field in the countryside where my grandmother and great-grandmother were buried. Dad's mother died just a few months earlier in the spring of 1985. After over thirty years of separation, for my father to have missed seeing her by so little time was heartbreaking. As sad was the story of his sister. She was the next oldest child after Dad. Toward the end of the war, she and first uncle were going to work in fields that the family owned. He stopped along the way to talk with a friend, but she kept going. Uncle said that they weren't sure whether it was an artillery shell or a landmine. There was just an enormous explosion and she was gone. She would have been about sixteen years old then. Dad asked them why they had gone to the fields when it was so dangerous. Uncle told him that they didn't have much choice, they either tended the fields or starved. As they told Dad the story, you could almost feel thirty years fade away. It could have happened yesterday. I suppose in Dad's mind it had.

When we arrived at the graves, the family was already there preparing a traditional memorial ceremony. The burial mounds were built into a hillside that rises above a small valley covered with rice paddies. As they prepared, everyone cried. Food was laid out before my grandmother's grave and whiskey was poured in a bowl. My father and his surviving siblings stood before the grave, then knelt and bowed to their mother three times. All were sobbing. Afterward, they packed up the food and we walked back down the hill.

We later drove about twenty kilometers to a park with a waterfall. It was a beautiful spot in the mountains. The natural setting seemed to comfort my father and his family. After a nice picnic, with lots of beer and insamsul, we walked up along the river that feeds the waterfall. Then we climbed the hillside to a Buddhist temple that had been built almost a thousand years ago. It was fascinating and peaceful. Nearby was a natural cave containing a statue of the Buddha, where monks had prayed before building the temple. For centuries, there had been a string of shrines along the valley, but this was the only one that remained. The others were bombed to the ground during the war.

We spent quite a bit of time up there with oldest uncle, youngest uncle, aunt, Chul Su, Song Hee, oldest uncle's wife and one of the Party officials. Across the valley, Korean and Chinese characters were carved into the rock cliffs. Dad said that some were DPRK slogans, but others were the names of dynastic and feudal families.

When we hiked back down, Mr. Lee was waiting for us. He and the drivers had waited patiently (I think) for us at the bottom of the mountain. He smiled and asked me in Russian if I was tired from the climb up to the temple. I laughed and said, "Nyet, Mr. Lee, ya silnuy amerikanyets." He thought that was pretty funny — either I looked exhausted or he didn't believe there was any such thing as a "strong American."

It was a beautiful family outing with people who I'd only met the day before. We had Mr. Lee take a family photo of us all. I looked like the Jolly Green giant standing there surrounded by my family. I hadn't even known that they existed before arriving in this country. We made the trip back as the sun was going down.

A while later we left older uncle's apartment to have supper at second uncle's home. Second uncle is a physician. He and his family live in a sort of suburb, though definitely not an American style suburb. When we arrived, his youngest son, wearing his red Pioneer scarf, brought me up to a portrait of Kim Il Sung and recited some sort of introduction memorized in English. I couldn't understand a word. But, my uncle seemed pleased, and his boss from the hospital nodded his approval. Uncle Doctor then took me by the arm to show me pictures of Kim and a group of medical people, my uncle included, being honored in Pyongyang. Also present at dinner were a party official and a man that I assumed to be his assistant. After we had dinner, Uncle Doctor asked me what I thought about the U.S.S. Sherman incident in 1866, and then had his oldest son ask me about hunting jobs after college in the U.S. He then showed my father presents from Kim Il Sung, which he received after being given an award by his fellow physicians: a nagahide handbag, cloth for a suit, a card, a warm coat and a medal. The makeup

Buddhist temple in the mountains outside of Kaesong.

of the dinner party created a weird dynamic. My uncle seemed like a man who had stumbled into an unexpected liability—in this case a pair of American relatives. I can't blame him too much for struggling to maintain his position, but it was still disheartening.

Afterwards we went to visit Dad's two youngest siblings. Youngest brother's home was a very nice traditional house. He and his wife, a surgeon, have three of the cutest little girls. His wife was also quite beautiful and very pleasant. We spent only a few minutes there; just long enough for their two youngest girls to each sing a Korean folk song.

Then we were off to my aunt's home. Her husband is a very nice man. Aunt's two oldest girls were rather shy and scooted off after saying hello. Kyung Hee, their third child, sat on the floor with us and stared at me the whole time we were there. I made a few faces at her and she gave me a few wide-eyed smiles. Her husband later brought in their toddler son, who slept in his arms the whole time that we were at their home. We didn't learn what a wild kid he was until the next day. We left to return to first uncle's apartment after a forty-five minute visit.

My father is losing it. They told us that we are leaving Kaesong tomorrow. I think he feels that he is being torn away from his family all over again, and he's creating a lot of confusion with his gifts. Every time he speaks with his siblings, he is half talking, half crying. I hear bitterness and desperation in his voice, and I think that they are also sensing it. I am helpless to explain it to them. He's afraid that his brothers and sister feel that he abandoned them after the war.

<u>October 13, 1985 2:00 p.m.</u>
Kaesong

After seeing a few more sites in Kaesong, we were told that we had to head back to Pyongyang. First, we visited a bridge in the older part of Kaesong where the founders of the Lee dynasty killed the last minister of the Koryo kingdom. The bridge spanned a canal and led to an old center for Confuscian scholars. The unlucky minister had been hiding there when the Lee men caught up with him. Then we drove into the mountains to the burial mounds of a Lee Dynasty monarch and his wife. It was strange how they resembled my grandmother and great-grandmother's graves, but hundreds of times larger. From there, we thought we were going to see one of Dad's old homes. But, while crossing a bridge, and apparently by chance, we met the regional Party secretary who had taken us to supper on our first night in Kaesong. He invited Dad to see his old school, which he'd attended from late elementary through high school. It was a gray day and a light drizzling rain was coming down. After seeing the school building, they said that there wasn't time to see his old home. They told us gently that we had to get back to first uncle's apartment and pack for the return train to Pyongyang.

As soon as we got back to uncle's apartment, out came the Polaroid camera to get pictures of the family, all of whom had gathered to see us off. The only one missing was one of my aunt's older daughters. Kyung Hee, aunt's littlest daughter, had by that time lost all of her shyness. She wanted me to show her the photos, to be picked up, or just to sit on my lap. She kept saying things to me in Korean. I just nodded and tickled her. I gave second uncle's oldest son my Tufts University tee shirt.

My father took two pictures of everyone. The family kept one of the pictures, the other went with us. After everyone else had been photographed, the missing cousin arrived. Dad sat her down and took her picture. When the camera flash went off, she jumped up from her chair and stood there in shock for a moment. She had arrived a bit after everyone else had been photographed and didn't expect the flash. As we went through the pictures to make sure we'd gotten everyone, all the little cousins gathered around us and yelled out the names of the people in the pictures. It was a nice feeling to be surrounded by all those cousins and my father's siblings. Second uncle, the physician, slipped away with his photos—both copies. He told my father that he looked too old in the pictures and didn't want anyone to see them. I'm not so sure that was his worry. Song Hee saw a picture that Dad had taken of me in Pyongyang and asked me for it. Just before we left, aunt also asked for the picture of her two youngest kids and me. Dad's siblings gave him two mounted pheasants, cloth made in Kaesong, sweaters, and a big box of ginseng.

They were good people and their children made me feel connected. It is strange, but after only being with them for three days, I miss them.

At 6:30 p.m. we left Kaesong. Dad's brothers, sister, and many of their spouses and children saw us off. Mr. Lee, as always, did the wise thing and made the good-byes short and relatively painless. A few tears, more than a few shed by my youngest aunt and uncle, and we rolled down the track. Chul Su chased us for awhile until the platform ran out. He'll probably be in the North Korean army before I see him next.

October 13, 1985 10:00 p.m.
Pyongyang

After breakfast back in Pyongyang, we were once again off to the various sites that visitors are shown in North Korea: the national legislature, the war museum, and the skating pavilion. We also sat through a movie about Koreans in Japan. Later, one of Mr. Lee's superiors, a man who appeared to suffer from Parkinson's disease, showed up before dinner and we talked reunification.

The legislature building was an impressive structure completed this past year. With an interior of marble, it contained a large assembly room for Kim's deputies, space for diplomatic functions, committee and subcommittee rooms, and smaller meeting rooms. All were very elaborate and physically imposing, as was the twenty or thirty foot high statue of the Premier in the assembly hall.

The museum was about what I had expected, except for the assertion by the tour guide that U.S. troops burned women and children alive by pouring gas on a house where they were kept prisoners. Who knows? The Mai Lai Massacre wasn't the first or the last. Most exhibits were based on the same set of historical facts that would be set out in an American museum. The main difference was that the North Korean interpretation stressed a different, though not completely conflicting, set of facts. The main thing that I didn't expect was the lack of reference to the participation of PRC and ROK troops. The Chinese "volunteers" were mentioned only once, and ROK participation was only acknowledged when we asked a specific question about the battle for Taejun, when an entire U.S. Army division was wiped out by the Chinese and North Koreans. More amusing than direct references to the horrors of the Korean War was how the museum staff displayed captured U.S. weapons painted black. It was very interesting, especially the descriptions and layouts of the "counteroffensive," as the North Koreans describe the initial invasion of the South.

The rest of the siteseeing went rather quickly. The skating rink was nice. They had some good young skaters, who all looked very serious. The movie wasn't one of your more action-packed flicks, but it was interesting in that the story

Bridge in Kaesong where the last minister of Koryo Kingdom was killed.

centered on pro-North Koreans living in Japan. It was subtitled and had moderately anti-West overtones. I was surprised by how favorably material wealth was portrayed. Most of the good guys (and bad guys) had cars and motorcycles, though the main protagonist rode a bicycle. It was very moralistic, above all stressing Korean morality as somehow higher and distinct from that of other cultures. At least, that is what Dad told me.

Once again the Party man with the shaky hands showed up. He seemed kind and intelligent. It is sad to think what he will have to endure as his disease progresses. For a couple of hours we talked about reunification and American troops in South Korea. I said that the North and South could learn from both the European Community and the opening up of China. He kept on saying that the partitioned peninsula was one nation, so the situation was not the same. I told him — at least I told my father, I don't know how much my father translated — that the shared culture of the two Koreas is an advantage not enjoyed by the EC. I also said that I thought a gradual (but steady) move to federal relations could work. He responded that there had been enormous difficulties during cultural exchanges, family reunification and many other failed attempts at reconciliation. He asked me how I felt about the US military presence in South Korea after our encounter with the American MP's at Panmunjom. I told him that I felt about them the way I feel about all soldiers; I don't think they're good for much of anything. He just grunted. Having to travel through Dad's filtering translation, I doubt my thoughts on the matter reached the man in their original form. On that occasion — if not throughout the trip — I think Dad did some quick revisions of my responses to our hosts' questions on politics, economics and war.

After a couple hours of this, even Mr. Lee's boss tired of the conversation, or at least he got hungry, so we went to dinner. For once there was no whiskey or beer, as there had been every time one of Mr. Lee's superiors came to eat with us. As always, the food in the hotel restaurant was excellent.

October 15, 1985 11:00 a.m.
Back in Beijing

In Pyongyang yesterday, we got up early, had a western breakfast, and were off to the Revolutionary Museum. Basically, it was a commemoration of Kim Il Sung's life until Korea's liberation from the Japanese. The story began with a mural depicting Kim's greatgrandfather leading the peasants' attack on the USS General Sherman. They told us that Kim's greatgrandfather directed the sinking of the ship (represented as a square-rigged warship) by ramming it with burning rafts. We nodded and smiled. In 1866 the Americans made the mistake of sailing up the river that passes Pyongyang and got grounded when the tide went out. The narrative then shifted to Kim's father, who we were told was a leader of the anti-Japanese underground during the early 1900s. He was said to have been captured and died in prison. I guess nothing especially exciting happened in Korea during his grandfather's lifetime.

Then began the murals of Kim himself (born in 1911 or 1912) participating in an anti-Japanese demonstration at the tender age of seven (six by western count) and yelling "Down with the Japanese imperialist aggressors. Long live Korean independence." He must have had a wonderful vocabulary as a child. Then Kim was shown crossing the mountains alone, pack on back, in the winter (lots of snow) smiling with the enthusiasm of a thirteen-year-old (twelve by western count) on his way to China to plan the liberation of Korea. The paintings also showed a fourteen-year-old (thirteen-year-old) Kim at

Andrew with Mr. Lee, Legislative Building.
Photo: Sok Nam Ko

a Chinese military school, studying the works of various socialist theorists in Chinese. From then on, we were told, Kim organized this group or that in preparation for the downfall of the Japanese imperial forces. At that point in the story, Kim was shown leading Korean resistance fighters to some unspecified battle against the Japanese. In these paintings, Kim's group took over a village, which was represented as a glorious victory. They were then depicted in the mountains, enduring incredible hardships — like Washington at Valley Forge. Ultimately, of course, they defeated the Japanese by the side of their Soviet Red Army comrades. Never was there any mention of Iwo Jima, Okinawa, Midway, Coral Sea, or the atomic bombs that flattened two Japanese cities, killing thousands of men, women and children. I would have expected them to make a point of raising the latter.

We then exited the museum building and took pictures of the huge monuments out front. They were large, especially the oversized statue of the "Great Leader Comrade Kim Il Sung." It was impressive, even if disturbingly extravagant for this poor little country.

Mr. Lee gave us a rest after lunch. We spent the time doing a bit of shopping for gifts of various sorts. We went back to the diplomatic store in the embassy district to get my father's tailor-made $80.00 suit, which is probably now his best. (At the moment my father is having communication problems with a Chinese desk clerk at the Beijing Hotel regarding a tour of the Great Wall tomorrow.)

At 5:00 p.m. yesterday we met the biggest cheese of our stay in North Korea. The Chairman of the Committee for the Reunification of Korean Families, which is a very big deal in the DPRK. He talked with my father for a while, then peppered me with the same old questions about reunification, my views on North Korea, US troops in the ROK and American foreign policy in general. Most of my answers received noncommittal grunts. He probably didn't expect any state secrets or deep insights into American society, but I think he would have preferred me to be a little more overtly sympathetic to his government's concerns. He also offered more on the DPRK's approach to reunification, citing specific proposals, most of which didn't seem very realistic to me — at least not as realistic as they should have been from a government that seems so interested in reunification. Essentially, I told him about my sympathy and affection for the Korean people (which was true) and how I saw the position of the US government in the scheme of things. They had me saying things that meant almost nothing in an attempt not to offend anyone, but at the same time protect my own integrity. I didn't mention "The Great Leader" or the "Dear Leader," which seemed to disappoint them. I had been disappointed in a similar sense many times during those nine days in North Korea.

I think they were at least partially gauging the effect of their museums, monuments, Panmunjom and pretty waitresses. The waitresses were just fine. The rest...well, in a way the rest disappointed me. I was not disappointed because of anything lacking in the people of the North; they were wonderful and the country was beautiful. But, while we traveled, I began to see how the North's expression of the Korean personality keeps its people poor and isolated. My entire life I've found it difficult to understand how their thought, emotions and culture combine to make Koreans so kind and gentle, but have also led them to be involved in some of history's most violent and tragic events—and not always as victims. The paradox isn't limited to the North: the Kwangju massacre may be worse than any single thing that the DPRK has done since the war. But Kim's Korea seems founded on that facet of the Korean personality that seeks perfection through control and discipline — even when those means have long since become ends in themselves. Everything I saw in the North, except the waitresses and my family, struck me as a part of that paradoxical desire for both order and mayhem.

That evening, we went to have a final dinner in the restaurant on the first floor of our hotel in Pyongyang. The next morning, at 6:00 a.m., we had breakfast with Mr. Lee, that forty-six-year-old father of three who looks like a thirty-year-old — the man who had to eat boiled grass as a boy because of a war that should never have happened, and who was even now far too skinny and smoked far too many cigarettes. I'm sure he manipulated our movements, even beyond the structured visits to the various show places and propaganda institutions of Pyongyang and Kaesong. He didn't even seem mildly interested in the political conversations between his various superiors and us. He was always pleasant and talkative. I wish my Russian hadn't deteriorated so far below his own, because I would have liked to ask Mr. Lee what he thought of all of this. He never resorted to rhetoric when asked a question that he could not or would not answer directly. He just gave us his subtle smile and remained silent. Of all the officials I met in the DPRK, he left the best impression. I still find it difficult to believe that a man with his charm, sophistication and obvious intelligence doesn't hold a higher position. Of course, there is still much I don't understand about that country.

By 7:00 that morning, we were on our way to the airport and said goodbye to the driver of the green Volvo, who had shuttled us around Pyongyang. And we said goodbye to Mr. Lee. Actually, he and I said "dah zvidanyeh", he in a Korean accent and I in my American. By 8:15 a.m., we were in the air for the two-hour flight back to Beijing.

—Andrew William Ko

Oct 5, 1985
Air Port Hotel
Beijing, China
9:00 a.m.

Dear Steve and Suzanne,

Andrew and I are in our hotel room waiting for a telephone call to confirm the last stretch of the trip to my birthplace. The purpose as you know is to meet whomever was lucky enough to survive so far since 1950. I am sure we will meet some other new family members (cousins) if my brothers and sisters are married and have children. However, I am very sad and disappointed that the most closely cared for and loved ones wouldn't be there to greet me and Andrew! (Then I came to my realization that this is 35 years later and many things come and go.) Such as my grandmother, mother, father and younger sister were living and well when I left home in Oct, 1950. Of course, 3 other brothers, and the youngest sister were also my dearest family members, but they being younger than me, I cannot recall or remember too well about them. I cannot even recall their faces correctly nor have their pictures. I am sure I cannot recognize their faces when I meet them. After all, it's already 35 years ago and past. They were all under 10 years old and I was only 15.

I am very thankful and fortunate that we are in an able situation to travel half way around the globe to reunite with them. Also, I had an extraordinary opportunity to come to the U.S. and become a useful person and created a new life which an ordinary Korean wouldn't have dreamt before, nor now. I cannot ever return this favor with anything in the world. However, I am hoping that what I have done in the last 35 years, and yet to do, will return a part of this favor.

Love,

Dad

Letter to Stephen and Suzanne Ko from Beijing, China, October 5, 1985.

Oct 6, 1985
Beijing, China
Capital Airport Hotel

Dear Bill and Betty,

It is 5:30 a.m. and the hotel appears to be wide awake. Sounds of footsteps, pulling of furnitures, and toilet sounds are everywhere. Motor vehicles started to running, and the restaurant down below is in full swing. There is no apparent nor customary Sunday here, as in the U.S.

We arrived here from England on Thursday, Oct 3. Since then we were negotiating visas to Korea. Finally, after several telephone calls and visits to the embassy, we received visas yesterday. At the same time, we were told that we have transportation to Pyongyang on a cargo plane, so we went to Beijing Airport with all our belongings (over 200 lbs.) and found out that they cannot take us. Therefore, we lugged our things back to the hotel. They informed me that they will call us. I think we were rushing them with our way of living – the rush, rush life of ours back in the States!

I sent my travel itinerary to the Korean embassy as soon as my travel plans were completed, 2 weeks before departure, and telegrammed a week before to request Andrew's visa. But, according to the embassy officials, they have not received anything. It appeared to me that 2 days were not quite enough for them to make arrangements to inform my family and their officials to make the necessary preparations. (Such as bring my family from Kaesong – over 100 miles of distance – arrange tours, and possibly transportation, etc.) I'm not sure that is what they are doing, but the embassy official said, "Your family has to be informed of your arrival and government officials will have to be assigned to greet you at the airport for your reunion."

Obviously, I am very anxious, trying to rush a government to attend to my private affairs.

Love
Ko

Letter to Bill and Betty Zahnleiter from Beijing,China October 6, 1985.

Oct 7, 1985
Pyongyang, Korea
Botong Gung Hotel

Dear Elaine,

It is room # 607, Botong Gung Hotel where we spent last night quite comfortably. Since we left Beijing , we were hustled and bustled past the Chinese ticket office, luggage department, security system, and arrived in the main boarding area with a minimum of difficulty because of the North Koreans' generosity and hustling effort.

We were eating room service food at 10 a.m. in our room (# 214) at the Capital Airport Hotel in Beijing [yesterday] when a Korean embassy official knocked on our door and said, "Are you ready? The plane will be leaving in 2 hours." At that time we were eating, casually dressed, and our luggages were not packed. I called the Korean Embassy, knowing today was Sunday (Oct 6, 1985). I called their embassy anyway and someone answered and said, "The man who is assigned to help you is out and will return soon to call you. Therefore you should stay in your room." It was 10:30 a.m. or earlier Beijing time.

We stopped eating and rushed to change our clothes, packed the luggage, and dragged it down to the reception desk and checked out from the hotel. A car was waiting for us to transport us to the airport with our luggages.

We were taxied out to a parked airplane (propeller driven medium cargo plane – 4 props). It was warm and I was sweating. We boarded the plane and it had about 12 seats. The rest of the seats were removed to accommodate cargo that they brought out from Korea to China and on returning. Some airforce men were on it and a female stewardess, who provided food (polish sausage, Korean pickles, a fried egg (cold), and cakes). Also,

Letters to Elaine Ko from Korea October, 1985.

she offered 7-Up like drinks ("cider"), walnuts and candies. We had interesting conversations with and airforce man and the stewardess. She said it will take 2 hours and 45 minutes to reach Pongyang, however, it only took 2 hours after take-off. The airforce man was very eager to learn about me and the reunification of Korea. His argument was that the presence of U.S. troops in S. Korea makes it very difficult to unify. I agreed, however, they (the U.S.) have their investments and they try to protect their interests (political, military, and economic, etc.). Any individual would do the same. He said, "It is the same as someone visiting a neighbor's house and not leaving when asked to get out." I am sure it is not as simple as that. I also tried to explain what President Carter tried to do when he visited S. Korea after his election. I said that in order to unify Korea, we must involve the U.S.S.R, China, Japan and the U.S. – not only both Koreas. And I gave my reasons. He pointed out that China and Russia were not in N. Korea or involved in it's self-government and independency.

As soon as we arrived at the Pyongyang airport terminal, we were met by 2 little girls who welcomed us with flowers and 2 men from the Overseas Korean Friendship Association – the vice president and a member, our guide, Mr. Lee. Our guide then lead us to the Botong Hotel.

The hotel is a beautiful and clean building, Each room has an entranceway [to an alcove] with three doors: a door to a living room (T.V., refrigerator, stereo, dish cabinets, 4 chairs, and a coffee table). Another door leads to the bedroom, with 2 nice beds and closets. The third door leads to a very nice bathroom. There is a nice terrace to observe the Botong River and see the city's buildings. I noticed much smoke rising from their factories. It is a very quiet city, wide streets, clean buildings, and a well planned city. People are fishing, rowing boats and walking around the Botong River.

[I have been thinking about how I did not have] problems of hunger nor laboring to the point when I was exhausted, or to work for long durations against my will. Perhaps I am exceptionally fortunate and lucky in some sense. But I am greatly sad and disturbed to think my own flesh and family had to suffer extraordinarily, and even lost their lives, because of a war that we had very little to do with. This event caused, since 1950, 3 family members to lose their lives, we brothers and sisters were separated without knowing each other or the other's whereabouts for 35 years. However, I am very thankful that the surviving brothers and sister will have an opportunity to reunite before all of us will die.

As I come nearer and nearer to Kaesong, I learned more and more about my family. It is too bad that we can not bring back the time and live like one family before 1950. However, it is history. There is no going back. I was told our family has grown larger and that the Ko family has greatly prospered. I know for sure that one Ko has prospered: 4 offspring – and one will be going back home with me after journeying halfway around the world.

I am sure that tomorrow will come soon enough. I am hoping that they will think of me as their brother. We are brothers and sister, nothing should come between us. I hope that we will have and opportunity to meet again and again.

Oct 8, 1985

We were met by our guide, Mr. Lee, for an early breakfast at 7:30 a.m. The dining room where we ate last night and this morning was huge and well attended by a group of Korean young ladies with the leader's button on their left side of coats. Breakfast included toast, eggs, coffee or tea, etc. This morning, we went to President Kim's birthplace (homestead) with Mr. Lee, Vice-chair of the Overseas Korean Friendship Committee and Mr. Lee our guide. It was located near an impressive mountain and the valley of the Dae Dong River. From this area, you can overlook the

City of Pyongyang and many mountains and rivers. Then we were lead to a park with 58 kinds of rides. There were only students, soldiers and some ladies, however, these would be full of people on weekends. Official work hours, we're told, are 8 hours a day except Sundays. However, some people were working on Sundays.

Noon meals were at the hotel with the Vice-chairman Mr. Lee and the guide Mr. Lee. We had many conversations and I translated some of them to Andrew. We learned a good deal about unification problems.

They appeared to know a great deal about my brothers and sister, but Mr. Lee the Vice-chairman seemed to hesitate to tell me too much. Naturally, I was very anxious. He said my brothers were all good "reds" and belonged to the Party. One brother is a hospital worker, another is in charge of some type of training, and the other is vice-chairman of a regional athletic association. At suppertime we were met by the Vice-president of the Overseas Committee as his guest in a specially reserved dining room usually used for visiting dignitaries. Again, my family problem came up, because the vice-chairman inquired to the assistant vice-chairman, who reported as follows:

My sister was killed during the war — no details. He observed that she was the closest to me in age.

One brother is in charge of a hospital treatment planning. He is a physician and second only to the civilian administrator of the hospital.

Another of my brother's is in charge of training for the entire Kaesong area. I am not sure what he was training.

My other brother is in charge of the athletic program for Kaesong. Each district has an athletic program run by the government.

My youngest sister is married and she is in charge of accounts for the equivalent of a savings bank.

They are all married and have children.

I guess that makes me an instant uncle – and cousins for Andrew. Mr. Kim was vice-chairman of the committee and an excellent historian. He asked Andrew, "If there will be a war, you will be fighting your cousins if you come to the South." Andrew said, "Not me." He seemed very satisfied with that without further comment or explanation. He talked with me about the early years of the Party and asked "Where was your hometown?" I said, "I was born in Kaesong. The Kaesong people were well known to everyone because of their commerce and stinginess." He said, " No, there are stingier people in Korea. People from Hae Ju. The people from Kaesong will open their fans halfway and fan themselves when the weather is hot. But the people from Hae Ju with open their fans all the way and shake their heads, instead of the fan." We all laughed. After the dinner party, I thanked him and said, "You are an excellent historian – as well as an excellent diplomat." He laughed again.

There was a telegraph office here in the hotel. They said they could send a message anywhere, so I sent you a "happy birthday." Hope you received it.

<u>Oct 9, 1985</u>

Again we were asked to meet our guide, Mr. Lee, at 7:30 a.m. After breakfast, we started out to visit the 175 meter tower with burning torch. It was for President Kim's 70th birthday along with many granite statues, fountains and an enormous gate opposite from the subway station. Each place we visited had English-speaking guides (all girls) who spoke with all types of accents – British, Russian, Chinese, etc.

We will leave to Kaesong by train tomorrow night, finally. I was told that we would be leaving at 12 midnight and arrive at 7:00 a.m. All arrangements were made and brothers are going to greet us at the train station and the city officials will have a welcome ceremony. We will be free to visit brothers and sister each night. Anyway, the first meeting will be at 1st brother's home. I also learned that my mother passed away in March this year. Mr. Lee wanted to know if I wanted to have a traditional ceremony. According to him, there will be preparations if I desire. He said it is quite complicated to make traditional preparations, with lots of cooking, buying fruits, drinks, etc. I suggested not to, because it will be too much problem for my brothers and sister.

I asked what would be the best gifts for their homes. Finally, he suggested the best would be a color T.V. for each. I asked what if they already have T.V.s He thinks country people have no T.V.s If they have it would be black and white. However, he doubts very much they have them. The T.V. sets that we saw were all made in Japan.

This afternoon, we went to the Museum of Korean History. They had prehistoric and modern exhibits up to 1945. We were told there is a larger museum with modern war exhibits elsewhere. I'm not sure we will get to see them tomorrow. The person in charge of the museum came to greet us and see us to the door. When we returned, we were asked if we would like to see documentary movies on the Korean War, rebuilding and flood aid to South Korea in September of 1984.

I was very sad to see and hear about such tragedy. I experienced some of that. However, I was most struck with sadness when I asked Mr. Lee, our guide, what was his most difficult experience during and after the war. He said, "hunger and cold." They were so hungry that they ate boiled grass, which made their faces swell and their sight blurry. He was 15 years old. His feet were frozen and didn't heal for many years thereafter. Children's stomachs puffed up, etc. He said when the sun was shining, they came out of shelters to warm up, but they were so hungry that they would fall asleep. Some people would fall asleep and never wake up (hypothermia).

I very seldom cry, but I found myself in tears. Not because of the war or bombing, but thinking that my brothers and sisters faced this same hardship from 1950 to 1953. I wondered if my sister died under these conditions. I cannot remember ever being that hungry during or after the war because I was unable to find food. I felt emotional pain and educational barriers in America, but I never faced starvation and physical hardship in that way.

[letter ends]

SOK KOON

April 20, 1991

I received the sad news of our brother's death on April 19. I cannot believe that unexpected news because I could not even imagine it. All of our families are filled with grief by this unbelievable fact. I cannot control my sorrow, because he passed away in a remote country far away from his home town. How could he die so soon, after once again seeing his beloved home town and country and being reunited with his brothers and sister again in his native land! I cannot suppress my sorrow.

Here, in his home town, all our families gathered and had a memorial ceremony, and expressed our condolences with burning incense. When I saw the smoke curling up silently, I thought that even the smoke of incense could not help me forget my brother. We, his siblings will change the sorrow and grief that he passed away without seeing the unification of his own country, into the strength and courage. We will work harder even for his portion that he left unfinished. My tears blur my eyes.

I will restrain the tears, pluck up my courage and do my best toward the unification of my country.

Please accept my condolences again. I wish you not to forget our country.

Sincerely yours,

—Dr. Sok Koon Ko, Kaesong
Sok's brother (4th child in the Ko family)

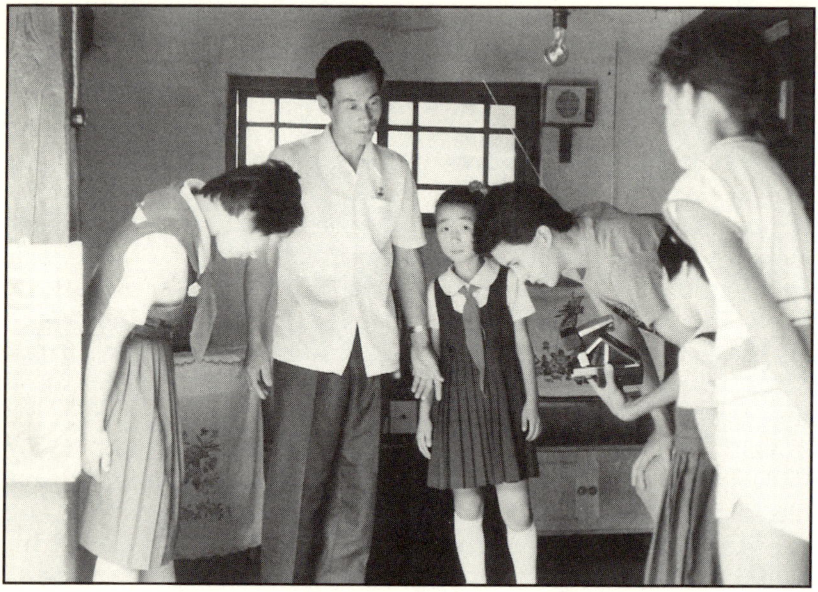

Sok Won introducing his daughters to Steve and Suzie.

SOK WON

April 25, 1991

Dear Sister-in-law and my beloved nephews and niece!

Honorable sister-in-law Elaine, beloved Andy, Timothy, Steven and Suzanne! How are you!

I had never imagined that I would have received such a sorrowful news in a month instead of my brother's letter which I had been waiting for. I was too sad and stunned to write to you immediately.

Dear Elaine, please accept my condolences. I could not believe his death. Is it really true that my brother passed away? Choking with tears, I could not believe the letters. "No, my brother did not pass away." My brother who enjoyed neither alcohol nor cigarettes, who liked playing volleyball. Is it true that he is not in this world any more?

It was only 7 years ago that I hugged with tears my eldest brother after 35 years of separation. Since he and I were separated when I was a little child, I could not even recognize his face, and recognized him only by his name. Is it true that he passed away? My heart is torn apart. I was sorry because he lived far away and now he has gone at 56 years old!

Dear Elaine, beloved nephews and niece. Should I believe this sad news!

I received the letter from cousin Chu Yul after one month since he sent it in March 18, 1991. I tried to call but I could not for some reason. I am sorry that I write so late.

We, families and relatives here, are all well and doing our best. Brother, Sok Dong teaches gymnastics, Sok Koon takes care of patients, sister Eun Ju works at a bank, and the children go to school or work.

I am very well and doing a good job managing a company. My wife is a doctor and gives patients medical treatments, and my children study very hard.

Dear Sister-in-law, Elaine and nephews and niece, How hard it was for you to lose him! I believe you could not even sleep at night. I give thanks to you from this faraway land. If I were near you, I would fly to you and hug you! Dear Elaine, Though he passed away after four operations in the hospital, he is alive in my mind as if he came into my house with his smiling face! I cannot sleep because he is still alive in my dreams. My brother is not in this world. I cannot believe it. I do not want to believe it.

I think it was not easy for my brother to leave you, beloved sons and only daughter, Suzanne. My greatest sorrow is that he could not see his children get married.

Dear Elaine, beloved nephews and niece! I cannot write anymore since my tears blur my eyes. When we meet someday, I'd like to listen to every detail about his death and all the stories you want to tell me. Good-bye.

I lovingly wish you and your children good health.

Yours truly,

—Sok Won Ko, Kaesong
Sok's brother (5th child in the Ko family)

Dr. Ko's sister Eun Ju and family, 1986.

EUN JU

April 1991

Dear sister-in-law and beloved nephews and niece,

I cannot believe the tragic and heart breaking news in the letter which I have waited for everyday. I imagine brother's last moments of his life with uncontrollable tears. Please accept my condolences.

When we brothers and sister met him after 35 years, we sincerely hoped for his health and he was sure of his health, too. How could he passed away at 56, leaving you, nephews, niece and we younger siblings?

I had received his letter in July last year and now I got this unexpected news like a thunderbolt. I cannot believe his death and I think as if he were always close to us. We, siblings had considered the eldest brother like a parent and had looked forward to seeing him again in 1991 for the third time. I feel bitter that he left this world forever. I am in despair.

Suzanne Ko, Stephen Ko, Sok Nam Ko, Eun Ju Ko in Kaesong, 1986.

Even though my brother left you unexpectedly, please live with the strong belief that you have the beloved children, and brothers and sister-in-law and keep close to my family without any change.

I hope my cousin, [Chu Yul Kim], Elaine, nephews and niece come here, to their father's home town, have the memorial ceremony together with us...celebrate the marriage, and enjoy a day with all the relatives.

Last, though it seems a little bit late to ask, I request that you place his tomb in a sunny placc and take a good care of it... I, the youngest sister, cannot forget him whom I met at 37. I miss him.

Dear sister-in-law, I guess you have had many troubles and toils. However, I cordially wish you to take a new turn. Please take a good care of your health. Good-bye.

Love,

—Eun Ju Ko, Kaesong
Sok's sister (7th child in the Ko family)

나의 죽마고우 고 고 성남

서 준 석

고인와 나는 한국의 개성에서 태어나 6살때 개성의 만월 국민학교를 같이 입학하여 6. 25와같은 격동의 시대를 같이 동고동락하며 지내온 내가 가장 아끼던 친구였다.

다시 한번 그 옛날을 회고하면 고인은 만월 국민학교 다니던 시절부터 미국의 소리 방송을 듣고 나와 함께 미국으로 건너갈 것을 의논하고 또 실행에 옮겼으며 치과의사로서의 어려운 과정을 미국에서 마치고 고등학교 친구와 결혼하여 5자녀를 두어 성장시킬 정도로 가정과 사회, 매사에 성실하고 꾸준하며 믿음직한 친구 였다.

아직 창창한 이나이에 이제는 다시 볼 수 없는 저 세상으로 갔다는 사실이 믿어지지가 않고 개성상업학교에서 고인은 축구부에서 나는 이화부에서 같이 수학하며 뛰어놀던 그 시절이 바로 어제와 같은데 6. 25동란으로 헤어지고도 먼저 미국으로 건너 간 고인이 보낸 편지를 읽으면서 어려웠던 그 당시의 역경을 이겨내던 모습을 보며 어떠한 역경도 능히 이겨내고 성공할 것이라는 확신을 가지게하였던 친구였다.

고인은 만월 국민학교 다니던 시절 바로 옆에 일본인 학생들이 다니던 심상소학교가 있었는데 당시 시퍼렇던 일제 말기하의 사회분위기에서도 굴하지않고 일본인 학생들이 뭐라고 시비를 걸면 쫓아가서 그들을 놀아 부치던 의리있고 용감하였던 친구였다.

흐르는 세월을 잡을 수가 없지만 한창 일하며 인생의 묘미를 즐길 나이에 먼저 하나님 곁에 간 그가 지금 더욱 그리워 짐은 어인 일인 지 오늘도 고인을 그리워하며 떨어지는 낙엽을 보며 눈시울을 붉힌다.

John Seo — letter in Korean, translated into English on the following page

FRIENDS

For My Dearest Friend:

Mr. Ko and I were born in Kaesong, Korea, where we attended school together until we were sixteen years old. Having endured the terrible experience of the Korean War with him, Mr. Ko was my most sincere and dear friend.

Looking back at the days when we were boys, I remember listening to radio broadcasts about the United States. We dreamed about America and planned how we would someday go there ourselves. He came to the U.S. first and, after overcoming many hardships, he married his college sweetheart, became a dentist, and raised four children. Mr. Ko was truly a persevering, reliable and persistent man. He was also a trustworthy and good friend.

Even when he was in grade school, during Japan's occupation of our homeland, Mr. Ko was not intimidated by the Japanese boys at a rival school. He was never a coward and always stood up to them. Later, at Kaesong Sang Up Hak Kyo (secondary school), Mr. Ko and I played soccer together and participated in many other extracurricular activities. Those happy times seem like yesterday, and I cannot believe that he is no longer with us.

When I think of Mr. Ko and the difficulties that we endured when we were young—the Japanese occupation, the Korean War, and challenges of life in the U.S.—I truly believe that any hardship can be overcome.

I miss him even more because he left us at an age when he should have been gathering the rewards of his hard work and enjoying life. But no one can stop the flow of time, and now my friend is with God. I do not know why I miss him so much more now that I see the leaves falling, or why I think of him and weep.

—John Seo

CHAPTER IX

RELATIVES AND FRIENDS IN AMERICA

A Mother-in-Law's Memories

Upon reviewing my diaries, I found some years when the Ko children were small that Gramp and I were in their home as many as 100–110 days a year, so we saw the family frequently. The reason we were there so often was mainly to stay with the children while Elaine and Sok were away for meetings. When the children were a little older, sometimes Gramp and I would house sit, answer the phone and tend to the dogs so that the family could vacation out of town. When Sok was gone, we served as his answering service suggesting to patients who could be called for dental care during Sok's absence.

One of Gramp's main jobs while Elaine and Sok were absent was to transport the children to and from school and other planned activities. The children learned early what they could or could not do because Sok was a strict disciplinarian. My responsibilities were to get the meals and care for the activities around the house.

Sok was an avid sportsman, so he wanted his children to participate in many sports. Consequently, each day after school the children attended practice for one or more sports. They participated in basketball, baseball, volleyball, tennis, and karate.

Sok went to many games his children played in when he could possibly get away from the office. He saw every play his children made. If he felt they could play the game better some way, he would call to them from the bleachers and/or he would go over the play on their way home. Even though I felt he was stern with his children, his precise expectations were to be admired. Sok frequently corrected his children, but never his elders. He had learned from his culture that senior citizens should never be spoken to correctively.

Gyneth Eldred Saulters — 1987.

Besides sports, each child took piano lessons. They all took up one or more other musical instruments, too, so Gramp often transported the children to their lessons.

Sok was very busy and loved his work. However, his mind was so preoccupied much of the time that he often did not listen to what folks at home told him about family plans. He would not stop to read the notes left for him and then would complain that he didn't know what was going on.

Although I felt when the children were little that Sok was too strict with them. I can see now that it has paid off when I look at them and observe their behavior now.

There are really no words to describe the warm memories, the admiration and the gratitude, too, that has come from having a son-in-law like Sok.

—Gyneth Eldred Saulters

An Ambitious Man with a Thirst for Knowledge

As a young man struggling to get acclimated to life in the United States, I viewed Ko as an ambitious individual who was making every possible effort to "get ahead." His thirst for knowledge was demonstrated day after day and year after year as he spent so much time in the pursuit of his studies. He was capable and knew he could prove his competence if given a chance. Nothing was handed to him on a silver platter; he earned all that was given to him.

In the process of acquiring his various diplomas and degrees, Ko found it necessary to earn a living in order to support his family and educational expenses. No menial jobs were beneath him. His willingness to do jobs requiring manual labor showed that he would do most anything to enhance his chances of reaching his goals.

Helen Eldred Smith.

When Ko completed his more formal studies, it was apparent that he wanted to learn all that was possible from his professional colleagues. It seemed to be his desire to become not just an ordinary dentist practicing his skills but rather to become the most skillful, competent, precise, analytical, perceptive and thorough dentist possible.

In his years of work as a dentist and/or oral surgeon he achieved his professional goals. Being a perfectionist, he showed his patients that he was conscientious, observant, kind, patient and knowledgeable. In the community and within the circles of his profession he was admired and respected.

Added to his professional life was his devotion to home and community. His interest in athletics dating back to his college days continued down through the years to his active involvement in community athletic programs. Being civic minded, he gave generously of his time and money to various civic organizations. The love of his family was expressed in his efforts to provide for the needs of each member. Besides administering to the dental needs of his patients, Ko was always very generous in providing for the needs of his wide circle of relatives and friends. Their needs received immediate attention. His generosity was greatly appreciated.

—*Helen Eldred Smith*

Creating the Dental Offices

My first recollections of Sok were when he and Elaine visited us at our camp at Lake Carmi, Vermont. It was during these visits that we became acquainted.

Then, probably in the late 60s, Ruth and I visited Elaine and Sok while they were living in Weymouth, Massachusetts. Sok was studying at Tufts University for his degree in oral surgery. Being much interested in his work, he was willing to remove my wisdom teeth which presented some problems. He performed the operation at the V.A. Hospital in Boston. Even though the operation was successful, my jaw swelled so much I looked like a chipmunk with a mouth full of peanuts. After staying overnight in Weymouth, we returned to our home in Vermont. That weekend I went into deer camp. When Sok phoned to inquire as to how I was, he learned that I had gone to camp. One thing about it, he knew that I was well enough to go hunting. Therefore, his operation must have been successful. Phoning long distance to inquire about me, let me realize what a caring doctor he was. Not many doctors would call like that!

Between July 3, 1971 and April 24, 1972 Elaine and Sok lived in Holliston, Massachusetts. While there Sok decided to set up a practice in Amsterdam, New York. He found a rental on Pine Street. It was an old house destined for urban renewal. A Mr. Fonda had a bicycle shop on one side and Sok made arrangements to rent the other side. The house wasn't in very good shape.

Sok phoned me to discuss the renovations which would be needed and we made arrangements to meet in Amsterdam to look the situation over. Much work would be needed before he could begin receiving patients. The water line, the oxygen, the nitrous-oxide and the electrical lines; all had to be installed. Lastly, the dental chairs and other heavy equipment had to be set up. Believing that with my brother-in-law Willard's help the rooms could be renovated into dental offices, Sok rented the building on January 27, 1972 and Willard and I began working on the rooms the next day. I don't quite remember how long it took us to get the job done. Not too long, I guess.

While Elaine and Sok were in Holliston I can remember visiting them. Sok was beginning to collect dental equipment which he could use in his "new" office. I remember that he had a dental chair right in the middle of their kitchen floor. In fact that is where David (our son) had his teeth taken out. In some way or other I managed to be present when some of that heavy equipment needed to be moved!

Sok used the Pine Street Office for a little over two years (from early in 1971 to October 5, 1973). During that time Elaine and Sok had moved from Holliston to 80 Locust Avenue on April 24, 1972. Immediately Sok began planning on the possibility of renovating the carriage house on the property into a set of dental offices. Again I was asked if I would be willing to tackle that project. After considerable planning with Sok, the blueprints of the dental rooms became a reality and Willard and I began working on the carriage house.

After the first couple of weekends that Willard and I were there, Sok was taken ill with appendicitus and was operated on February 18, 1973. I can remember that we went to the hospital to see him. This would date the beginning of work on the carriage house as late January or early February 1973.

The plans for the carriage house developed by making the carriage room into the waiting room and receptionist's office. The place where the horse stalls were became the operatories. The back room was converted into the recovery room and x-ray department. The carriage room had a central drain which made it necessary for us to level the floor before we could do much of anything else.

Besides this part of the project, all the things which were installed at the Pine Street Office had to be installed here: the water line, the oxygen, the nitrous-oxide and the electrical line.

We involved Mr. Finlay when the vacuum system was designed. A considerable amount of discussion was involved when we recommended an ordinary milking machine pump for the vacuum system. Sok was skeptical at first but finally accepted whatever plans I had. All through the project he was inquisitive about what was being done but never really interferred with the suggestions and decisions made. Occasionally, it seemed difficult for him to understand what we were trying to do.

We were very fortunate in most aspects of the project. Only once did I goof. We went to put the door casing on one of the doors in the x-ray room and put a screw right through a pipe. At this point our work was delayed a little because we had to cut the floor out and repair the hole. If I remember, I was somewhat upset to have created extra work for myself and those helping me.

While renovating the building, the large barn doors and the side door had to be removed. Willard decided that he could use the doors if we could just get them to his farm in Sheldon, Vermont. So with a considerable amount of effort, we made an A frame and hitched the doors to the top of my pick-up. We were heavily loaded as we traveled up the Northway in a winter storm which made us wonder if we would ever reach our destination.

The insulation throughout the building was done by a concern from Binghamton. However, we did the additional work of installing sheets of lead in all the walls of the operatories.

The usual schedule for a weekend started after my work in Lyndonville, Vermont on a Friday night. After loading my truck with tools and supplies we (sometimes my wife, Ruth, Mr. Findlay, our son, David, and Willard) would head for Amsterdam. On my way I would pick up electrical supplies in Rutland. The Gray Bar salesman would take phoned-in orders to his home and I'd be picking them up about 8:00 that evening.

Most all of the plumbing supplies came from Hulberts. Pick-up after pick-up load! Locally, most of the other supplies came from Grossman's. By the time we reached Elaine and Sok's home those Friday nights, it was time to go to bed.

For the next two mornings (Saturday and Sunday) we were up by 6:00 to begin the long days of work. Aunt Gynee always had a nice breakfast for us before we took off. We worked all day and into the evening; many times working until 10 or 11 on Saturday nights.

Then at 5:00 or 6:00 P.M. Sunday afternoon we headed for Vermont. That meant most of our traveling was done at night.

Elaine took pictures of the entire renovation project. She has an album full of pictures. It took 26 weekends to complete the project; a lot longer than I thought it would take. Folks have no idea how much work is involved in creating dental offices until they do all the work!

It appears that Elaine and Sok didn't have to do much to the carriage house since we completed the job. The entry way was changed and a little hallway to go downstairs was added. Other than that, the project is as we left it. We must have done a half-way decent job to have it last so long.

After the work on the carriage house was completed, Ruth and I made trips to Amsterdam for social functions mostly. Elaine and Sok had many years of lawn parties for their professional friends and for members of our family. Tables for the parties were needed so we used to bring over reels for this purpose. These reels came from the electric light department. They were made of wood and wire came on them. I helped with the parties by barbecuing the chicken and roasting the corn. We didn't happen to be involved in the pig roasts, but we certainly enjoyed the parties for about ten years at which the guest list included between 100 and 150 people!

Sometimes during the progress of the parties, Sok and I would get to visiting. The subjects of our conversations varied. I can remember one time when he was mentioning the fact that some doctors like to put in sutures. He felt that the extra sutures were not needed so sometimes took some sutures out. He had a deep, compassionate feeling for his patients. He felt for them when it came to money as well as to their care. It would be difficult to find a dentist who was more interested in his patients than Sok was. He was truly a professional man.

—Harland G. Titemore
Elaine's cousin

Remembering a Caring but Strong-Willed Person

The first time that I really knew Sok was when Harland and I visited Elaine and Sok in Weymouth, Massachusetts. As we got to know him better, we discovered that he had quite a sense of humor. It was expressed in ways reflecting his Korean background so sometimes it was difficult to catch.

When Harland made his many trips to Amsterdam, sometimes I went with him. We often took Jesum Crow (our pet crow) along with us, too. I enjoyed the many visits we had in their home.

One very funny thing that happened during the carriage house renovations was when Mr. Findlay ate a lot of Sok's freshly made sauerkraut. Apparently, it tasted very good and Mr. Findley ate a lot of it. That night he slept on third floor and he had need of the bathroom which is on second floor. Poor man, he was up and down those stairs all night.

During the professional and family parties I used to help prepare foods for the meals. I can remember one party in particular when it rained. It was so dark the automatic outdoor light came on. Even though the weather was horrible, folks seemed to have a good time. Sok was always busy with the preparations of the foods, particularly with whatever was being cooked outdoors.

Sok loved to experiment with cooking. He was a very good cook. I liked his cooking as long as he didn't put that hot stuff in whatever he was making. I liked those concoctions with vegetables.

Kimchi is a Korean favorite. Since it is pickled cabbage, it smells really bad. Harland reminded me of the times during the nice lawn parties when Sok brought out a big bottle of kimchi. It's a good thing we were outdoors!

Sok's hobby of photography used to fill in bits of time in the evenings. Many times his pictures and slides were of a professional nature. One set of slides illustrated an operation which he saw during his internship. The doctor cut a three-inch incision which damaged nerves where Sok would have put a one-inch incision. Sok used to sputter when doctors mutilated people when they didn't need to do so.

Because we knew that Sok was so deeply interested in his profession and studied all the time to keep his knowledge current, we trusted him. A patient felt that Sok *knew* what he was doing. Furthermore, you knew he would not do anything to hurt you. This confidence in a doctor is so important! On the other hand, if he thought he was right about anything, it was rare that anyone could change his mind. He was not easily swayed; actually he was a very strong-willed person. On a few occasions his behavior could be described as stubborn.

Along with this characteristic was the likelihood of his being stern with his children. He was determined that his children do things his way because he thought *his* way was the right way. Many of his child-rearing theories were directly from his Korean background.

In some ways, Sok was a complicated man. He was determined, strong-willed, stubborn, honest and stern especially with his children. Yet he was kind, caring and considerate with his patients. His efforts to serve his patients and his community were unending. His accomplishments were many! We have lost a very special member of our family.

—*Ruth M. Titemore*
Harland's wife

He Left the World Better Than He Found It

As to the precise time that Kay and I met Sok, we can't recall the date but, no doubt, we met at my Mom's home in St. Albans, Vermont at some family gatherings.

We never went to visit Elaine and Sok in Burlington, Weymouth or Philadelphia. It wasn't until they settled in Amsterdam that we *really* got acquainted with Sok.

We remember the many invitations to Elaine and Sok's dental and family parties. We did attend two of the pig roasts. Other parties we attended included ones with barbecued chicken served with all the fixings. It was at these parties that occasionally we would get to visiting with Sok. I can remember him telling me once about an incident during his internship. He mentioned the fact that the supervising doctor was going to make an incision somewhere on a patient's face and when he started to cut, Sok said, "Heh, you're getting too close to a nerve and you're going to paralyze the face!" The doctor's response was, "Don't worry about it!" Sok said, "How in the world could he do that?" This incident alerted me to the fact that Sok was a very observant doctor who very seriously considered the welfare of his patients and *never* intended to do anything harmful to those in his care.

One of his qualities was of being confident in decision-making regarding his patients. I can remember one incident involving my Mom. She needed some dental work done and had come to Sok for help. She *thought* she was allergic to novocaine and told Sok. He apparently thought it was all in her head and didn't really believe her. I think he *did* give her novocaine. Within the next twelve hours she did get sick. She didn't, however, immediately react to it. Now, her confidence in Sok was such that she thought she was ill from something else. She had *total* faith in him. Of course, it *could* have been something else. If Sok thought he was right about anything, he was not easily convinced otherwise. Mom never knew and there was no harm done so *if* he *did* give her novocaine, I imagine he never did it again.

Another time Sok and I were visiting about the use of acupuncture in his work. He felt total frustration over getting so much information about acupuncture while attending a special school in Korea and not being able to use the procedures here. When he returned to the States, he confronted the bureaucracy which wouldn't let him use it without a special license. He *knew* it would help people. Yet the steps which would have to be taken in order to use acupuncture were loaded with procedures he didn't approve of, so he gave up the idea eventually, saying, "With all the rules and regulations, it's not worth it!"

Regarding his search for knowledge about new procedures and new drugs he was always curious. He was continuously reading and studying about new drugs. Considering the amount of time he had left after a busy day in the office, it is amazing that he was able to stay so well-informed. Elaine says that Sok had allergies for which he was always looking for relief. So he frequently would try some drugs on himself in order to find relief from the problems with his eyes, nose and throat. Sometimes he acquired knowledge to help his patients because he had first used a medicine on himself.

Sok was always looking ahead. He purchased many items which he figured on using in the future. For example, I can remember Sok getting a package from the West Coast. I think it was from one of the outfits like U.S. Salvage. When he uncrated it, it was this huge drill press. I looked at the drill press and thought, "What in the world is he going to do with that?" Elaine told me that Sok was thinking down the road when he retired. He was going to set up a little shop and make things with his drill press and his band saw. He was buying all kinds of equipment for his dream project. He did like to work with wood but didn't dare to do it when he was practicing dentistry because of possible injury to his hands. Yet when a seemingly good deal came along, he couldn't resist the idea of purchasing equipment which might cost less now than it would later.

Besides being curious about ideas concerning his profession, he was very curious about investments. He was interested in a lot of things. Many times our conversations would lead to what would be good places to invest earnings. Like all of us, he wanted to be a wise investor. This wisdom is not always available to us but he gave many avenues of investments due consideration.

At the time Sok was getting established in Amsterdam, preparing dental offices on Pine Street and on Locust Avenue, Kay and I were living in California. Perhaps it is a good thing I was out on the West Coast! If I hadn't been, I would have been working with Harland and Willard on some of their many projects! So many thoughts come to our minds about Sok in his earlier years here in America. We saw him as an intelligent and very determined individual. He pursued his medical interest by attending Howard, Temple and Tuft Universities to become a dentist and oral surgeon. His determination to succeed gave him the strength to never give up. He put forth whatever effort it required to succeed.

While doing so, he served in the US Navy to help the country that provided him with the route to success.

Added to all this was his willingness to serve his community, particularly in Amsterdam where he served for about twenty years. Besides hosting foreign students from many lands, he worked diligently for many organizations including the Red Cross and the Cancer Society. Truly, because of his participation in so many ways, he left the world better than he found it.

—*Carroll E. Titemore*
Elaine's cousin

A Gift from Korea to the United States

Sok was strongly dedicated to his work. He was "on call" 24 hours a day. There are not many dentists who will get up from a holiday family meal like he did and go to his office to administer to a patient who has a toothache. There are not many dentists who will get up in the middle of the night to care for a patient. Most dentists and doctors will say, "I'll see you next Thursday!" He was loyal to his practice and actually enjoyed the time he was in his office. His commitment to his patients is to be remembered!

Sok had diverse interests. After his formal education at various colleges was completed, he made a conscientious effort to continue learning. He intended to have the latest information needed in caring for his patients. He was much interested and involved in sports throughout his life. He was interested in politics and liked to discuss the world problems as well as the problems close to home. He was curious about investments and frequently discussed ideas with his friends and relatives. He tried to be an informed business man. He was especially interested in bargains. Like many of us, he liked to think he had made a good deal whether it was about purchasing materials and equipment for his office or home or about items which he might use many years down the road. He was much interested in travel having gone to many places like China, Japan, North and South Korea, Russia and France. His dreams of taking more trips were shattered by his untimely death. His life time interest in photography also added to his list of interests.

With so many interests and accomplishments, we realize that Sok was a very accomplished U.S. citizen, truly a gift from Korea to the United States.

—*Kay P. Titemore*
Carroll's wife

HIS ADVICE TO ME

I want to give you some of my memories of Dr. Ko. I remember Sok as a down to earth person. One of my favorite memories of him was at Priscilla and Willard Mahoney's home in Vermont. We were all out on the porch eating and talking.

Another time I remember Sok was at the Ko home party. We played volleyball out back. Sok used to cook a pot full of vegetables and rice on the side. He also drank Coke. Because of my interest in nutrition, I remember these things.

Sok also took out my wisdom teeth. The thing I remember most was that after the surgery, they had me sleep on their bed. I was groggy from the anesthetic and was not aware of much around me. While sleeping on their bed, I bled all over their pillow. I felt really bad about it, but they said not to worry about it. Sok was very generous to others.

One time I asked Sok what his advice was to me, seeing that he was so successful. He emphasized time. He said it was necessary to get going and work hard in whatever field I wanted, because there never was enough time in life. He emphasized that I hurry because an education takes so long.

—Dean L. Titemore
Carroll and Kay's son

REMEMBERING...ESPECIALLY ROASTING THE PIG

Trying to recall specific incidents which happened over 30 years ago is extremely difficult, if not actually impossible. I met Sok for the first time at Priscilla's mother's home in St. Albans, Vermont. (The Glenn and Myrtle Titemore residence on Fairfield Street.) I can remember it was a family gathering in the winter time long before Priscilla and I were married. That dates our meeting as being long before November 1965; perhaps as early as 1961. I can also remember Sok as being very quiet. He really didn't say much. I asked Priscilla if Sok could talk. Being somewhat unsure of his English and in meeting strangers, I suspect he was playing it safe by being a good listener.

Mary Street

After this, I served in the Navy and did not see Sok again until he and Elaine were living on Mary Street in South Burlington. Pris and I remember visiting in their home after Andy was born. That would be in August 1963. I held little Andy and he cried. In fact he cried all the time we were there!

It was while Elaine and Sok were living on Mary Street that I remember they were both teaching in the South Burlington School. Sok was teaching in the Junior High. Years later, I talked with David Baril, who I now work with, and who was one of Sok's students. One time David told me about what a strict teacher Sok was. He had rather unique disciplinary procedures. One was to use a baseball bat by having the student squat down and put the bat between his legs and make it hold books. The students had a nickname for Sok. They called him "Socko!"

Sok did many nice things with his students. For example, he started a Science Club and wanted to take the kids to New York City. But the principal wouldn't let him.

Sok was very much interested in sports and organized a baseball team and a basketball team on which David played, I believe. Both teams were champions in the South Burlington area.

Weymouth

After Elaine and Sok left South Burlington, they lived in Philadelphia while Sok attended Dental School. We didn't get down to see them while they were there.

Our next memories are of Elaine and Sok when they lived in the Cape Cod house in Weymouth, Massachusetts. While there, Pris and I visited in their home at the time when Sok performed surgery on Pris by removing her wisdom teeth. (According to Aunt Gyneth's diary notes this was on February 21, 1971.) I don't remember where Sok did the job but it was in a small office.

The incident that we remember about that visit was when Sok brought home a BIG lobster that weighed around 14 pounds. I can remember when Sok was trying to get the lobster into the kettle and it didn't want to go in there at all. I said, "You'd fight, too, if anyone was trying to put you in such hot water!" Priscilla remembers that she wasn't able to have any of the lobster. After just having surgery she wasn't able to open her mouth to eat anything!

Pine Street

Time has a way of hurrying by. (According to Aunt Gyneth's diary, Sok rented a place on Pine Street in Amsterdam on January 27, 1972.) Harland was asked to change these residential rooms into a dental office. He asked me if I would be willing to go to Amsterdam to help with the job. My response was, "Where?" Harland replied, "In Amsterdam." I said, "Where in hell is that?"

I don't remember much about how we got there but we began work on January 28, 1972. I do remember that we spent five or more days diligently changing the house into a set of rooms which Sok could use for his dental offices. It was quite a job but I believe Sok moved in soon after we finished our work there; probably in early February.

Locust Avenue

Soon Elaine and Sok bought the property at 80 Locust Avenue and the family moved to Amsterdam on April 24, 1972. Sok immediately began planning for the conversion of the carriage house into dental offices. Harland was asked to complete this project with what help he could get. I know I said to Harland, "How many more of these things have we got to build?" Harland is right when he says that no one really knows how much work is involved in setting up a dentist office until he has to do it. We did it twice!

Harland traveled from Lyndonville, Vermont to Amsterdam, New York for 26 weekends beginning on February 13, 1973 (also a date taken from Aunt Gyneth's diary). I helped Harland on many weekends.

We began working during a rather warm spell in February but it was cold enough for me to wear my sweat shirt. I can remember taking out the side door where we knocked the bricks out. Harland said, "You'd better help me get this job done 'cause we're going to have some snow here pretty soon!"

On February 18, 1973, Sok was in the hospital with appendicitus. We went to see him and took a catheter. I told Harland to "break it out. It's time!" Of course, Sok knew what it was and he wanted so much to laugh but it hurt him to do so.

One incident I'll always remember is the time we moved the huge carriage house doors from Amsterdam to our farm here in Sheldon, Vermont. It must have been in late February because it was extremely cold out. We backed the truck up to the doors and pulled them on. We nailed them together like a tepee or A frame. Then we tied them on the truck. They were very, very heavy! And there was just the two of us to do the lifting! The wind was horrible that day and we traveled in a big snowstorm. It was terrible traveling on the Northway. I said to Harland, "I don't know whether we are going to make it or not!" However, we did. When we reached the farm we had to unload the doors. It was somewhat easier to get the doors off than it was to put them on. Now those carriage house doors are proudly hung on our barn as a reminder of the struggle we had to get them to Vermont.

On October 5, 1973 the carriage house dental offices were ready for Sok to move into and the Pine Street Office was relocated to Locust Avenue.

From that time on, our trips to Amsterdam were more of a social nature.

Roasting the Pig

Elaine and Sok put on many lawn parties at which time all members of our family were invited. In June 1986 when Timmy graduated from high school, a rather elaborate party was planned. Timmy and his friend, Billy Jackowski, thought it would be nice to serve roast pig at their party. Always liking to serve something new, Sok agreed to buy a pig to roast. He and Timmy went to Farmer Rick to purchase a pig and they brought it home in a bag. Sok borrowed a mechanical spit from Bob Snodgrass. Priscilla and I arrived in Amsterdam in time for me to help Sok put the pig on the spit and wrap it with chicken wire to hopefully prevent it from falling off the spit later. To dress up the situation we even put an apple in the pig's mouth. Sok and I got the fire going. By now Timmy was long gone. For awhile things seemed to be going along quite well except that the pig kept slipping off the spit.

All of a sudden it started to rain. Sok got a picnic table and a plastic cover to put over it so that we could still stay out there watching the pig while it was raining. Suddenly, the half-roasted pig slipped and the dumb thing came apart and landed in the fire. What a mess! Sok yelled for the hose as everything went flying in many directions. The table went down, the canopy went down and the retrieved hose squirted all over. By that time the pig in the fire was extremely black. Sok exclaimed, "The stupid thing! What do we do now?"

Now all this was happening at about 3 o'clock in the morning! With considerable effort and with gloves and sticks, Sok and I managed to get the blackened pig out of the fire and back in its original place on the spit and turning again. Actually, the pig meat was not damaged much. A lot of the fat was burned off, that's all. With the spit turning and roasting over the now controlled fire, I decided to go to bed. Elaine and Sok took over the guard duties. The rain stopped and Elaine told us later that this was the first time in her life that she watched the sun set and then saw it come up. When I arose in the morning, I was surprised to see Elaine and Sok still out there watching the pig. My remark was, "My God, didn't you go

Roasting the pigs.

to bed at all?" To this Sok said, "Well, I've got to take a nap because I've got a medical meeting at 8 o'clock." With this he left Elaine and me to watch the pig go round and round. By the time Sok finished his nap, the rest of the household had awakened and was getting ready to go to graduation.

By the time folks returned from graduation and it was time for the meal to be served; the pig was ready. Even though the blackened pig didn't look too appetizing, folks who tasted the meat said it was delicious. This special day certainly had a special feature—a roasted pig! I'm sure we will never forget this day!

Conversations with Sok

A very special relationship grew between Sok and me. It took a long time for me to get comfortable with him. A lot of times I just didn't understand him. When I finally got used to his ways, he was very funny. He loved to tease me and I loved to tease him. He was always kidding me about being a dumb farmer! So I called him a dumb dentist!

Besides teasing, he liked to argue. After awhile I could tell when he was really serious and was trying to start an argument. He always looked right at you when he was trying to start an argument.

The topics of our many conversations varied. Sometimes we visited about his family still living in his homeland. He was pleased that he, at last, was reunited with his brothers and sister but sad to think they were under the control of the Communists. He told them, "I don't understand why you want to be a slave here." They responded, "We don't have a choice." To this he added, "Sure you do!"

Sok didn't believe all the stories about North Korea which circulated here in America. He felt that there was a lot of propaganda printed in the newspapers or shown on TV.

When I was once asked if I ever saw Sok angry, I responded, "Not really. But I did recall a time when he was very annoyed. Priscilla and I were up at her mother's home. Sok was there with the two boys: Andy and Timmy. They did something that Sok didn't like so, for punishment, he took them upstairs to Priscilla's room which was adjacent to the attic. Now, the boys were fully dressed in little suits and it was a very hot day; probably 95 degrees in the shade. Even though there was a bed up there, Sok made the boys sit on chairs right by the attic door. I went upstairs for some reason and there they sat with the sweat running right off of them. Whatever they had done that was wrong, I'll bet they didn't do it again! Sok was a strong disciplinarian and intended that his children would do what was right.

Sok was very determined and didn't always want to give in even when he was wrong. I can remember the time when he and I were trying to find the place where Larry Titemore's wedding reception was being held. (This was in 1973.) We drove up and down the streets for an hour and a half. He kept saying, "I think it's right around the corner." I said, "Yeh, it was around the corner an hour and a half ago." We drove for what seemed like hours and never did find the place. Besides being determined and not being willing to ask for directions, I would say that he didn't travel very well.

Even though it seemed to me that traveling may not have been enjoyable to him, he liked to take pictures. Upon returning from a trip he liked to show his pictures and describe his travels. Photography was a lifetime hobby of his.

Sok was a real pusher. He was very energetic. I was always puzzled because he never seemed to want to relax very much. He sometimes seemed uneasy when he was up at our farm because he didn't have much to do. His greatest forms of relaxation were hunting and fishing and he didn't have much time for that during his visits at our house.

Sok was a very generous man, especially giving of his time. Besides serving his patients willingly many times during out-of-office hours, he worked often on weekends. He served his immediate family as well as all his relatives in so many helpful ways, especially with the dental care everyone needed.

Sok's dexterity in his dental office didn't carry over especially in the manipulation of machines. He didn't always make very wise decisions in purchasing such equipment as lawn mowers and snowblowers. Whatever he purchased he expected it to work. He had some difficulties when he tried to fix some pieces of machinery. He could not be considered a mechanical wizard!

Sok was not status-minded as far as his clothes were concerned. He'd go to the Salvation Army to get a suit or to some inexpensive department store to buy his sneakers. He always said, "It doesn't matter where your clothes come from. It's how the clothes fit you and if they are neat, clean and pressed!"

Quite often in our conversations, Sok would get to visiting about money and investments. He seemed very interested and curious about what might be good investments and did I think it was wise to invest in the stock market. Several years ago he was very cautious with where he invested, but as the years went by he seemed more willing to take chances.

Money-wise, he was never too concerned about having enough for his usual needs. His philosophy seemed to be that if he worked hard he would have enough to pay his bills. As he got older he became less serious money-wise, but more serious otherwise.

I always pictured Sok as being an old man someday, not really being satisfied with what he had done with his life; yet he had done so much. He was never satisfied with what he had done. He wanted more. How sad that he never had a chance to dream more dreams and to accomplish the many more things he wanted to do!

—Willard E. Mahoney
Elaine's cousin Priscilla's husband

Changing Professions

Willie's story is essentially mine as far as my recollections about meeting Sok and visiting in his homes on Mary's Street in Burlington and in Weymouth, Massachusetts.

During a conversation which took place between Willard and Sok while on Mary Street, they discussed Sok planning to leave teaching and going into college for medicine. Willard said, "My gosh, Sok, you're a teacher. Why in heck do you want to go back to college to be a doctor? That seems like such a waste of time!" Willard just couldn't understand why Sok would change his profession in mid-stream. As things turned out, Willard was wrong. Sok did prove himself and became a fine professional.

I have vivid memories of Sok's taking out my wisdom teeth. That was on February 21, 1971 in Weymouth just before they moved to Holliston in July of 1971. Ko was very easy on the mouth. It didn't even hurt when he gave me a shot!

Many in our family have had wisdom teeth out. Ko not only took out mine, but our daughter, Chris, had hers out just before he died. There must be a lot of wisdom lacking in our family now! Quite a few members of our family have had dental work done by Sok. There were always words of praise about his work. He took pride in doing quality work!

I can remember Willie helping Harland to convert the Pine Street apartment into dental offices *and* the Carriage House on Locust Avenue into similar offices.

On February 13, 1973 Harland and Willie started working on the carriage house in order to convert the barn into dental offices. I can remember that I had to go to our barn in Sheldon to do chores while Willard was gone for a whole week in mid-winter. There were many weekends after that when Willie went with Harland. The work was hard but Willie enjoyed it. All he talked about when he returned home was Aunt Gynee's delicious breakfasts. He looked forward to those!

Adding to Willard's story about bringing the carriage house doors to our farm, I can add that they *are* very pretty doors and have added a great deal to the appearance of our barn. However, I also remember that we had to plan our whole barn around *those* doors!

Our visits in Elaine and Sok's home have always been such happy times and we enjoyed the occasions when they came to our home. The realization that this particular exchange of visits must now be only a memory is so sad for Willie and me. Sok was a loved member of our family and we will miss him so much.

—*Priscilla T. Mahoney*
Elaine's cousin

Often Doing Things for Others

My years at Temple University are filled with fond memories of Ko. He was a major influence in my life at the dental college. I can well remember studying with him and going over exams in the sciences. He was so kind to help me with lab work. One of his contributions to dentistry was the dexterity of his hands. Not many (if any) of our classmates could match his skilled hands.

Ko was one of the students who made things tolerable in dental school. He worked hard on his own lessons; yet to the detriment of his own work he was always willing to help others.

On the lighter side, I can remember playing ping pong with him. Ko was such an excellent player; nobody could beat him.

Then, of course, there were the events related to our personal lives. I can remember baby sitting for Andy and Timmy who were little pre-schoolers at that time. Their dog, Bootsie, had to have attention sometimes, too.

There were the times when Ko would go to the Philadelphia fish market and bid on lobsters. Then I would enjoy sitting around the family table eating the delicious lobster which had been prepared. More fond memories!

On a more frightening note, Ko had a gasline piped into his basement for use in his dental lab work. With the open flame it is a wonder he didn't have a major disaster considering how explosive this gas is.

Ko was one of the most interesting people I've ever met. He had a unique personality and was a very pleasant part of my life.

—Tom Gosselin
Classmate at Temple University

Brought Cultural Diversity to Fair Haven

I read your newsletter with a mixture of sadness and, of course, memories. I do remember Ko's arrival at Fair Haven High School, and in recalling the time, I realize how very "provincial" we were. Most of us, I'm sure, had never known anyone whose roots were in Asia; cultural diversity was virtually unknown in a small Vermont town in the 50's!

Before long, however, we knew he was a very special person and quickly came to love and respect him. When I learned of Ko's death, I wanted to send a note to extend our sympathy. I hope that there will be future "newsletters" about Ko's Foundation and am happy to help insure that in which he so passionately believed will flourish.

—Evelyn and Gil Billing

Qualities Which Will Never Fade Away

The world has lost a warm and loving person who made a special difference every day; yet all those seeds of love so gently planted leave blossoms that will never fade away.

Sok had the wonderful qualities that are God-given and are the fruits of the Spirit: love, kindness, forgiveness, humbleness, goodness, self-control, joy, gentleness, faithfulness. I'm grateful for my relationship with him.

—Diane Bethea

His Integrity; His Way of Lending a Helping Hand

We have such fond memories of Sok; his integrity, his way of offering a helping hand, the respect he commanded. We were always welcome in his home. Elaine and Sok opened their home to us so many times and we cherish those memories.

—Buddy Bethea

He Reaped a Rich Harvest in the Midst of Adversity

I met Sok in early 1974 on the night his practice was incorporated and his new corporate pension was established.

Sok lived such an exceptional life. He was a very good and generous man. He reaped a rich harvest from his natural talents and the advantages that he discovered in the midst of adversity that engulfed his young life

A really warm recollection involved Sok in the context of a touch of Americana. It was while experiencing a small town baseball game where all social and economic elements of the community came together without any of the conventional constraints. It was a contest in which Sok was clearly a leader in his capacity on the team as well as being one of the superior players.

Sok seemed at his most socially comfortable self in team-oriented sports situations. This even extended to his love of hunting where he looked for a shared experience with someone else.

I was also impressed by the fact that Sok's employees perceived him as willing and eager to treat anybody who came to him in need, regardless of whether or not a patient was able to pay for his services. This was ultimate generosity.

I came to know Sok as deliberate, rational, cautious, intellectually curious, a man of integrity, honesty and fairness. It was impossible to know Sok without loving him.

The community has suffered a huge loss. Sok's many contributions to so many community services will be its own long-treasured memorial to him.

—Henry Collyer and Carol Landis-Collyer

Believed in Action

Sok Ko was one of those people who attended church on Easter, Christmas, Children's Day and maybe a family night supper. For a man who was a non-believer in the God that we Baptists acknowledge, this may seem surprising, but not so surprising for Sok, the father. He was there for two reasons: his children and, I think, his secret ambition to be a photographer. As the times changed, he became a true professional video technician. When Suzie would play a piece on the piano for Children's Day, it always began with a flash from Sok's latest 35 mm camera. And it probably began late, because being on time was not one of Sok's assets that we had the pleasure of observing.

There was one Christmas play that Sok was in plenty of time for, even with being late. The performance was "Bah Humbug" and the star role was to be played by Steve. It was scheduled to begin at 4. At 4:15, Sok went to look for our star, who was found at the ice skating rink, having forgotten the time. Steve's character had to use crutches and wear a cast. When Sok re-appeared with Steve I always wondered if perhaps it was real!

Sok was an avid supporter of the Church League Basketball Team. But more than that he supported all the kids. Long after Andrew, Tim and Steve had gone from the Armory court, you would still find Sok coming by to see how the other boys were doing. He followed our son, Matthew, through his high school years especially in sports. Even though we "disagreed" on Matthew's choice to attend the Catholic high school, Sok made sure that he was there for at least one of Matthew's games each season.

There was one game during which Matthew had jammed his finger. Sok stayed around to say hello to Matthew after the game. When he saw his finger, he told us to come over to the office in the morning and he would x-ray it. He did just that and taped it up with a tongue depresser. Then he told Matthew to make a basket for him in the next game.

I also had the experience of working with Sok on the American Cancer Society Board of Directors at the time when he was president. He made his TV debut locally during that time with some of the first local telethons put on. I learned something about Sok during this time; the fact that he did not have all the patience in the world when it came to foolishness in wasting time to make a decision. He believed in action!

One of my fondest memories of Sok was his compassion that he showed for my mother when she had cancer. Sok didn't show his concern with mushy, loving words or with hand-holding. It was in a matter-of-fact manner with little or no emotions. Yet he will never know that the time that he took one day to explain to my mother what the chemo and radiation were doing to her taste buds was information that gave a terminally ill person information that helped her to fully understand what was happening to her body. He did this for her and he was only an acquaintance!

These memories of Sok will long be remembered.

—Pat and Charles Beck

Instrumental in Bringing the First Exchange Student from the USSR

Dr. Ko was a very giving and generous person and that comes from so many people he had known.

There is a Russian proverb which sums up Dr. Ko's life: 'When everyone in town donates a thread, the naked will have a shirt.' This fact was carried out when he was instrumental in bringing the first exchange student from the U.S.S.R. to be a part of his family.

Our family will also miss the Ko's famous pig roasts.

—Evelyn Jackowski

Making a Special Video Tape

Recently my brothers and I were remembering Dr. Ko and his video skills at Deb and Bill's wedding last October. It was so thoughtful of him to have made a special video tape for their wedding. They will have it to treasure always.

Dr. Ko was such a cutie! I still laugh when I think of him taping the reception—then running in front of the camera to eat while the tape was still rolling!

—Barbara and Dick Kienleau

Touched the Lives of Thousands of People

Sok was a person who touched the lives of thousands of people. We feel honored to be among them. He was a man of greatness. He had love and compassion for others as well as his wonderful family. He will remain in our hearts and minds forever.

—Charles and Ginny Loomis

The KKK Attacks Manhattan—What a Great Time!

No, it isn't what you think. It is Dr. Ko, Dr. Kim, and Dr. Kyler on a trip to New York City. Kyler speaks no Korean, Kim speaks no English, and Ko speaks everything! We went by train from Schenectady and the conversation on the way to the city was positively exhausting. Never being able to keep his mouth shut anyway, Dr. Kyler talks to Dr. Kim constantly, which he doesn't understand. Dr. Ko hurriedly translates for Dr. Kim while trying to read the paper. He got me into this and now he was irritated that I couldn't speak Korean to Dr. Kim. Dr. Kim understood Dr. Ko's translation and, being the polite Korean gentleman, responded in kind. Much to Dr. Ko's consternation he had to translate this also so that Kyler knew what Kim was talking about. Try this for three hours! What a great time!

We finally arrived at Grand Central Station where instead of the normal taxi some young Korean picks us up in an ancient moth-eaten Chevrolet which had obviously spent most of its productive life parked on the streets of metropolis.

It soon was apparent that we were leaving all known landmarks of Manhattan. The three Koreans were all speaking at once, devouring the chance to speak Korean, with such speed as to be unintelligible even as a foreign language to the American relegated to his proper station in the back seat of this decrepit automobile. Occasionally Dr. Ko would point out, in English for my sake, that the Chinese sign over the store we were passing was his Korean family name written in Chinese. This was incalculable help to the outcast in the back seat. Has Dr. Kyler's propensity for motion sickness when riding in back seats been mentioned? Upon inquiry the destination was said to be " the South Bronx!" Yes, that area of New York where abandoned automobiles are said to be stripped at the speed usually reserved for eating by pirahna. "Sixty Minutes" had recently done a special report proving that if you visited the South Bronx you would most likely be murdered after the mugging.

We actually pulled up to a row of pleasant homes in a very quiet Bronx neighborhood and everyone trooped to an upstairs apartment. Each of us removed his shoes at the door, but when I did so, Dr. Ko instructed me to put mine back on. I refused. What was this, some ritual that the uninitiated couldn't do even if the carpet was ruined! Everyone except me seemed to know we had come to this lovely Korean home in the Bronx for breakfast. We had a wonderful meal of chicken, rice, seaweed, and tea. I loved it. Even if Dr. Ko spent most of the meal making disparaging remarks about my lack of prowess with chop sticks. I still did not know where I was, who these people were, or what I was doing there. What fun! I even tried to stand when the lady of the house came into the room we were eating in, but Dr. Ko actually grabbed my suit and pulled me down while he said in a loud voice, "Korean women wait in the other room while the men eat." What a wonderful Korean custom!

The other three men continued to talk at the speed of light. I ate. Next we were dropped off in mid-town Manhattan after another motion sickness inducing ride in that vehicle from Hell. Dr. Ko now asked me what we were going to do? When he finally speaks in a language that I can understand, it is to give me an assignment. I made a mistake then. I paid for all three bus tickets for the tour of Manhattan. I suggested this so that

Dr. Kim could see the sights while in New York City for only a short time. I violated some Korean culture law and the three of us spent the rest of the visit trying to balance out who was paying for whom, who had paid last, which gift was for what gift. In our quest to find lunch and catch the bus on time we ended up having to each have one of those cardboard pretzels sold on most New York City street corners. Welcome to American food, Dr. Kim.

The bus took us through all of the sights you would expect us to see on a quickie bus tour of Manhattan. However, I now made mistake number two! While in Chinatown Dr. Kim and Dr. Ko found an oriental medicine store with the strangest most sickening array of medicinal animal parts you could ever imagine. I agreed to tell them when the bus was ready to leave by waving through the window. I waved. I jumped up and down and waved. I jumped up and down and waved and yelled. I had to go in the store and get them and then run after the bus. The bus stopped as I panted and puffed while getting on. Dr. Kim and Dr. Ko, in animated discussion about the remarkable treasures they had found, were sauntering along while the bus waited for them to leisurely board. I was having a great time! Supper time brought us to, of course, a Korean restaurant in Manhattan that Dr. Ko had been talking about intermittently all day. As I expected by now, no one spoke English here either. Dr. Ko kindly ordered for all of us. We had mysteriously been joined by our chauffeur of earlier in the morning. To this day I don't know where he came from to join us for supper. I ate raw fish, fancy vegetables, delicious beef marinated and grilled at the table. I ate cold noodles. Please, God, I hope they were noodles. Dr. Ko finished his meal with a mixing bowl size container of cold soup with, I swear it, a boiled egg floating in the middle. He shared some of this with me. I didn't request it, but I tried it. A more intriguing time couldn't exist!

After supper the owner of the unfortunate Chevrolet disappeared and this time with Dr. Kim. I then was treated to Dr. Ko's taste in hotels, SPARTAN!!! No one spoke English here either. I did feel at home, however, since the bathroom fixtures were the same as in my great grandmother's home when I was a child. It was 7:00 P.M. and Dr. Ko got ready for bed and proceeded to get under the covers. I protested and declared we will not go to bed at 7:00 P.M. in New York City. I bought tickets for us to see a broadway musical, "Sugar Babes" with Ann Miller and Mickey Rooney. Dr. Ko showed very little interest in attending this performance, yet he enjoyed it. He must have. A man gave strict legal regulations against taking any pictures during the performance. A recorded announcement added that flash cameras and flash lights disturbed the actors. Dr. Ko began taking flash pictures, which he did by standing upright so as to get a better shot, during "The Star-Spangled Banner." He continued with the photographs throughout the show. What a great time!

Upon returning to our room in the "El Firetrappo" Dr. Ko found an actress on a T.V. show that needed her teeth fixed. I've often wondered if she has found out what a mess her mouth is in. It took him the entire program to explain to me how he could fix her teeth and jaw. I went to sleep thinking this has been one of the most interesting, funny, and exciting trips I have ever taken. It was! I am so grateful he asked me to go along that day. Why did he ask me? I'll never know, but I'll always remember this intelligent, kind, generous, and dignified gentleman. I miss him.

The Kyler home has a rice cooker which Dr. Ko presented when he bought a new one for himself. It's old and rusty now, but I still use it and think of my friend. I shall never replace it.

—Dr. Bob Kyler

Anatomically Correct

How does one select incidents to include from the memories which have become so precious about a very dear friend? It isn't easy but the following stories are representative of my memories of Sok.

One time that really stands out in my mind was about Sok's involvement in sports. He was a coach for the Elks team when our son, Kevin, was on the team. One summer day a game was being played at the Lynch Middle School. My husband came to the game right from the office. He was wearing a three-piece suit complete with vest, tie, shirt, and cowboy boots and held a cigar in his mouth. He really thought he looked very dapper!

On the other hand, Sok came to the game wearing his usual traditional baseball outfit of plaid Bermuda shorts, a shirt with horizontal stripes, brown socks that came close to his knees and, of course, his baseball hat. We all laughed at his outfit!

My husband, Johnny Laurilla, was coaching first base, Sok coached at third base and I was over on the third base line. I said to Sok, "Look at that fashionable coach you have over on first base!" Sok grunted. He just grunted. I continued, "Well, not everybody can be a fashionable oriental in Amsterdam!"

Sok replied, "We'll see about that!"

As the game progressed to about the third or fourth inning, we noticed that Laurilla started loosening his tie, took off his jacket, took off his vest and began to roll up his shirt sleeves. By the seventh inning, Laurilla was red-faced. His cigar had been thrown away. He was stomping around in his cowboy boots; hardly the dapper man who had arrived at the game earlier.

Sok, looking over his shoulder, turned around to me and said, "Fashionable oriental fine—but *I'm* the coolest oriental in town!" I certainly couldn't disagree with that!

Johnny and Sok coached the Elks Club Team on which our sons played for about two years. The records of wins won the team many trophies and honors which were given out at the Elks Club dinner parties. These, too, are fond memories.

My other fond memory of Dr. Ko was at my husband's 50th birthday party. We had decided to gather fifty of his closest friends and relatives and have a party at our favorite restaurant; the Bears Restaurant in Duanesburg. At the party we decided to take turns around the tables so that everyone would have a chance to pay a happy birthday tribute to my husband. Most guests either presented a gift, told a joke, or sang, "Happy Birthday."

Events changed when we got to Dr. Ko. He had come to the party carrying a plain brown paper bag in which he had his gift. When he presented his gift, it was a shocker simply because it really wasn't like the Dr. Ko that we knew. He presented John with an anatomically correct doll made out of a stocking. During the presentation I cannot remember his exact words but they included something about the fact that *he* worked on teeth while Johnny, being a urologist, worked on the other end so he thought this doll was an appropriate gift. Now, the doll had a beard. When you lifted up the beard, there it was; the end my doctor husband works on. Needless to say, Dr. Ko brought the house down because it simply was not what anyone expected to hear from him. The guests roared with laughter. Dr. Ko was really the hit of the party! We still have this special doll at our house and, of course, it will be even more precious as the years go by.

Another day that we really spent a lot of time with Dr. Ko was the day we took our son, Shawn, down to Temple University in Philadelphia. We had this long ride; a five-hour ride to make. Partway to our destination, Johnny decided to let Shawn drive. Even though Shawn was willing to drive, he was complaining about having an upset stomach. Being the concerned mother, I said, "Oh, Shawn, are you O.K.? Should we stop? Maybe you shouldn't drive. I hope you're not getting sick just before this interview that is scheduled at Temple!"

The Laurilla Family — Seated: Juan "Johnny", Jane. Standing, left to right: Kevin, Catherine, Sean.

Sok was grunting in the seat beside me and said, "Don't worry. It's not as bad as when he used to pitch for me. He'll get over it. Let him fly away. He's not in a bird cage, mother!"

Another story which further elaborates on Sok's philosophy of raising children comes to mind. I went to the Ko home to pick up my son, Kevin, who had been there for a considerable amount of time. Sok heard me fussing and fuming because Kevin was upstairs with Stephen and taking forever to gather his belongings to come home. Sok calmly said, "What is the matter?"

I answered, "This boy has *no* regard for time!"

Sok replied, "Is there something wrong with that?"

I continued, "You know, Sok, this is the one I lose my temper with so fast and so many times. This boy really knows how to get to me. I don't know what he is going to do in the real world!"

To this Sok gave me a little more of his philosophy. He said, "You're going to let him fly away. He'll do fine. You'll see! *But* he'll come back to the nest every once in awhile!" What a nice philosophy! I will always remember his words to wisdom, sincerely hoping that his predictions will come true.

—Jane Laurilla

Elks Club Wee-Men Major Champs — Pictured above are the members of the Elks Club team which this year captured the Wee-Men Major League baseball championship with a 16-1 record. The team won the division, playoff and city league titles. First row, left to right, Kevin Laurilla, Kevin Fabozzi, Reggie Lozado, Dan Santa Maria, Matt Spiewak and Kris DiCaterino. Second row, Co-Manager Dr. Juan Laurilla, Paul Mancini, Tony Santa Maria, Peter Guzior, Michael Santa Maria, Steve Ko, Sean Luarilla and Manager Dr. Sok Nam Ko. Missing from the picture are Billy Bartlett and Joey Tokarczyk.

Makarowsky Memories of a Very Dedicated Dentist

Joe: A very dedicated dentist. One who came away from his comfortable home at 7 p.m. to care for a patient who had a terrible toothache. Such was the case on January 31, 1991, just a couple of weeks before his hospitalization. He extracted two teeth and made me feel well again. I thought the world of him.

Just a few years ago, one of our friends had an elderly mother at home who was experiencing a toothache. He called his dentist and others, but no one would go to the home. Dr. Ko, a complete stranger to the family, went to the house and took care of the situation, and even went the next day to see if everything was going well.

Sok Nam Ko pitching.

Carm: I always remember him as being a gentleman and a hard worker. A very dedicated husband and father. I'll always remember that he cut the boys' hair real short, as did our dad. The Ko boys wanted their hair to be long, as did our boys, but as long as dad did the cutting, it remained short. I think our two families were the only ones who had short-haired boys at Tecler School.

Mike: He remembers Dr. Ko taking fishing and hunting trips with Andy and Tim and our Mark. They seemed to have had better luck with fishing than hunting. He remembers the noon hours when he was supposed to be working in the garden or mowing the lawn, but was inside eating lunch with the doctor—eating one of his famous Korean soups which had some of our zucchinis in it. We had some years when zucchini squash were so plentiful that we couldn't give them

Elks Club, 1983 City Champs and League Champs — Michael Santa Maria, Juan Laurilla, Sok Nam Ko.

away because all friends were in the same boat, except for the Ko's. Guess who took them. He learned to eat Kimchee and other spicy Korean food. From time to time, he would make soup like Dr. Ko made with chinese noodles and cabbage, with Kikkoman sauce and hot sauce. It had to be Kikkoman because that's what the doctor used!

<u>Mark:</u> His memories are about the same as Mike's because they were usually partners in crime. They were supposed to be doing yard work, but as soon as they saw the doctor going in for lunch, they quit and helped eat the food. They spent more time in Elaine's kitchen than in the yard. Mark learned to eat the Kimchee, which had an odor in itself, and he also learned to eat seaweed with rice inside, and Kikkoman, I think. I don't know which was worse, the Kimchee or seaweed. From time to time, both the boys go to Kim's Oriental Store to purchase the Kimchee. They love it. Unfortunately, the writer has not acquired a taste for either.

Both the boys remember the pig roasts, especially the first one. It was at Timmy's graduation time. I think something happened that wasn't planned. Did the pig cause a small fire? Anyway, there wasn't much left, but it was still delicious!

John: He didn't do that much with Dr. Ko because he was younger than the "bunch," but he does remember him as being very friendly. John was a great help to Joe for about three or four years doing yard work. He didn't do much eating there because he was usually with dad, and had to toe the mark. Thus, he never did acquire a taste for Dr. Ko's food.

We all thought the world of Dr. Ko and feel a real void with his passing. One thing which comes to mind as I type this. On the occasion when Joe had the extractions on the 31st, I saw his face light up with the pain gone, and I turned to Dr. Ko and gave him a kiss. I'm so happy I did that, in view of the circumstances which were to follow. I've thought of this so many times since his death.

These are just a few of our memories. There are several more packed away in our minds, but to dig them out would take a long time. We hope these few will help show what a wonderful man he was, Dr. Ko.

—Carm Makarowsky

An Example Worth Emulating

Dr. Ko was such a wonderful man and an example all young people should try to emulate. He touched so many people's lives and will be sorely missed by the whole community. He was one in a million.

—Barbara and Otto Miller

Imparting to His Children a Thirst for Knowledge

Our family became acquainted with the Kos when our daughters began kindergarten together. Suzie and my daughter, Missy, have been going to school together since then and continue to this date to be very good friends.

One story I would like to share that I thought was cute goes back to when the girls were in 7th grade. They were at the Ko residence and were doing some homework together when they came upon some kind of problem that they did not understand. Suzie decided that maybe they should ask Dr. Ko a quick question that might clear up their confusion.

The next thing they knew, they were getting out encyclopedias and other reference books. They were questioned and prodded, and forty-five minutes later, they knew the material back and forth, upside and down. As they left the room, Suzie said to Missy, "Aren't you glad we asked?"

I always chuckle when I think of that, but it's another example of Dr. Ko's enthusiasm for gaining knowledge which he tried to impart to his children. It was for this reason that when it came time in July of 1990 for Missy to go to Russia with the People to People Caravan, which Dr. Ko was chaperoning, we felt assured that her time there would not be wasted and that she would get the most from the trip as time would allow. It was a real comfort knowing she was with him."

—Carole A. Natale

Treasured Gift

When Andrew Ko was about 10, Dr. and Mrs. Ko brought him to our home. Our four daughters had a reputation for proficiency in piano and had their own small singing group. Dr. Ko was already held in high esteem in our city as both a surgeon and a humanitarian.

On that day I met Dr. Ko, the caring father. He was hopeful one of our girls could introduce Andy into the intricacies of the piano keyboard. When I explained that our two older daughters were away at college and he might not be too well served by young Sophie, who was willing, Dr. Ko clearly showed he had no ambition that his boy become a virtuoso. He just gently nudged Andy toward something he felt might enhance his son's life even ever so slightly.

Andrew accepted the challenge himself courteously each week for his lesson while a slim slip of a girl, not much taller than her pupil, gave the best of what she had.

Sophie and her slightly older sister, Connie, had been hired on the spot as frequent evening baby sitters for the three boys. Amid their instructions was the admonishment that they not pick up baby Stephen when he cried or he might "melt" — clearly no indulgence there. I marveled at the parenting skills so visibly present in these very young parents while I still struggled with my own.

The evident beauty of Dr. Ko's fatherhood, the quality of his life as he moved among us, his refusal to accept any horizons as he continued to further the cause of academia in the young of other countries thereby making his and his family's contribution to world peace—-all conferred upon me a treasured gift, the knowledge that I was once privileged to stand in the presence of true greatness.

—Alberta Thomas Riccio

Dr. Ko, the Man Who Made a Difference

Dr. Ko is one of those rare men who truly made a difference. He cared about making this world a better place for all humanity. He unselfishly gave of himself to bring people together, to improve education, to help individuals. He understood that fellowship and friendship know no boundaries and his efforts were to prove that to others.

There are not many people in this world like Dr. Ko. He will be remembered by all as a man that it has been a privilege to know. Our family feels so fortunate to have been able to know Dr. Ko as a friend, a great dad for his children, and a wonderful husband for his wife. It has also been our privilege to work with him in the past on community issues, to have him share his wealth of knowledge and his laughter with us during interesting conversations and to be guests in his home during memorable gatherings and celebrations.

—The Rumbergers: Kim, Tim, Austin, Brant and Kyle

Actions that Inspired Others

To know Sok Nam Ko was to understand a man whose life was extended beyond himself into the universe not only through words but with actions that inspired others. I'm go grateful to have known him.

—Maybelle Stewart Schere

An Educator and Believer in Our Youth

We do not remember when we first met Ko. What we do remember is that he took time to talk to Robin (our daughter) one time when we made a visit to his home. He took time to inquire about her goals and future plans and spoke about his world of dentistry. He did not know the impact he made upon a young girl who was not sure what she wanted to do after high school. She listened and took in more than he realized. She decided in tenth grade that she did not like Carmel High School and wanted an option. She chose to go to BOCES Tech Center. We discussed her choice and made a list of pros and cons. She felt she would not make it through Carmel School so I spoke to her guidance counselor. He was against her doing this because he felt she had Regents potential and college ability. However, after more discussion, it was clear that Robin wanted something different for her education and she was permitted to attend the Tech Center.

Robin took the two-year dental assistant program along with the required classes at the high school. She graduated from high school and worked as a dental assistant for four years. Eventually she realized she did not have enough education to advance. She went to college to get more education and certification as a Dental Hygienist. She talks of returning to school some day to become a teacher in her field. Whether she does that or not, the seed Ko planted will be with her always.

Ko also made an impact on Stacie (our youngest daughter) when she was around three or four years old. While on a visit to Amsterdam, Stacie had a toothache. Dr. Ko came to the rescue. At that time she fell in love with her dentist. She never feared a dentist after that and always wanted to return to Amsterdam for her dental care and to see Dr. Ko. This would have been a considerable distance to commute for dental care in that we live several miles south of Amsterdam—in Carmel, New York.

Ten years or so later, we finally made it back to Amsterdam. We enjoyed our supper and table talk greatly that day.

As an educator and believer in our youth of all ages, I commend everyone who can make an impact on a child. This is our thank you to Dr. Ko.

— Lorraine and David Smith

Learning About Hunting from Herb

I remember Dr. Ko from back in the early 80's. In about 1982, I first met him as a patient, when the dentist whom I had been going to tried to extract a tooth from the front of my mouth. After five or ten minutes of pulling and tugging, he couldn't get it out. Although I wasn't too worried about it, my dentist was. He decided he should send me to someone who was better at doing such things. So, as a result, he contacted Dr. Ko and I was sent to his office. I sat down in the dental chair where he proceeded to do the job. There was no problem at all! Dr. Ko certainly demonstrated his skill as an oral surgeon.

A short time after that we began to meet occasionally at the Amsterdam Memorial Hospital. Someone apparently told Dr. Ko that I hunted deer with a high-powered caliber pistol. He approached me and asked me about such a weapon. He wondered if he could get a pistol like mine.

I mentioned to Dr. Ko, "You know, you have to have a pistol permit for such a gun." I was surprised when he said, "Oh, I have one of those. That is no problem at all!" Apparently he had obtained a pistol permit in another state and had acquired a pistol of some kind from his father-in-law (or someone).

As we became more acquainted, I gathered some information for him. We contacted a gunsmith in Scotia, New York and Dr. Ko ordered what he wanted; basically, the same caliber pistol that I was using. He also got a scope for his pistol which is called an impoint scope. It had a red dot inside for a sighting apparatus. This would be very, very nice for hunting and shooting at anything from 50 to 150 yards away.

I can remember that Dr. Ko was very excited about his new gun and was very happy with it. Several times we went out to the Pine Tree Rifle Club in Johnstown, New York for target shooting. We started out early in the morning and would spend three or four hours practicing. Even though Dr. Ko was a very, very busy man, he managed to find some time for trying out and learning how to handle his weapon. He did very, very well with it. I was amazed at the fact that he wasn't afraid of it. He shot that gun just like it should be shot. He had a very positive attitude about anything and everything he did in hunting.

A year or two before I met Dr. Ko, I had hunted and shot a deer in back of my house in Sprakers where I usually hunted.

There was no need to travel a hundred or two hundred or three hundred miles to hunt deer. You just step out in the back yard and you may see a deer! Hearing this, Dr. Ko thought he'd like to hunt in my area.

I suggested to him that it would be nice if we chose a fall day and he could come down to look the area over. I wanted to show him where and how I hunted. I never thought much about the fact that I was asking a very busy man to take half a day off from his busy schedule. But he did find the time. There came a time in the fall of 1985 that he contacted me and made arrangements to come to Sprakers.

The day that we met at my home, my wife drove us up on the back road and left us about a mile and a half or two miles from my home. This day was a real nice fall day. The sun was shining brightly and it was just warm. The leaves were crisp under foot. It was a perfect day for such a walk and I think of it so often. We walked across the fields and down over the bank, along the canyon wall and then down into the deep Sprakers Canyon. I showed him places where we would hunt; where we would sit and wait for a deer to come along. We planned for a hunting trip which would come later.

During our walk we came upon a fence row that had three or four hickory nut trees in it. Looking down at the ground just covered with nuts, Dr. Ko said, "Look, look at all those nuts!" I said, "Yeh, they're hickory nuts. They are good to eat. They make good fudge and good brownies. They are *real* good. Do you want to pick some?"

He answered, "Why, sure!" He was very enthused about the fact we had found something that he could take home. He began picking up nuts off the ground, broke off the shucks and put them into his pockets. I decided to help him by picking up nuts, too. I had G I pants on with pockets which would hold a lot. When my pockets were filled right up full, I looked like a squirrel with cheeks full of nuts. When both of us got done, we had two pockets apiece just packed with nuts!

We finished walking the course and went home. I found a bag and Dr. Ko proceeded to empty his two pockets and at the same time I emptied the contents of my pockets into the bag. He said, "Aren't you going to keep some for yourself?"

I said, "No, there's plenty of those hickory trees up there. I can gather nuts most any time." Indeed there are a lot of hickory nut trees around here. Dr. Ko was *so* happy that he was going home with something that he had gathered while out on our trip. As I say, it was a perfect fall day and we had had such a nice walk and talk. I often think of that delightful day that we spent together.

A month or so later, when the hunting season opened up, we made arrangements for our hunting trip which we had planned so carefully. However, it was a snowy day; just the opposite of the fall day that we had on our first trip. Dr. Ko came wearing bright orange hunting clothes! I remember that *very, very* vividly! I set him up in a watch and I moved down in an area known as a runway for deer. We could both see each other. We must have stood there in our separate places for approximately two hours, waiting for something to come along. All that time it was snowing *and* snowing *and* snowing! Soon I could hardly tell where Dr. Ko was because he was all covered with snow! He hardly moved and didn't brush the snow off his waterproof clothes. After about 2 1/2 or 3 hours we moved to another spot out of the area and finally walked home.

Dr. Ko had to plan ahead for anything he wanted to do. The day of our planned hunt he had told me that he was taking one-half day off but had to be back in Amsterdam by 1:00 P.M. for office hours. He hung in there till the last minute that morning enjoying his alloted time for the hunt. You might say "to the last out of a ball game." In fact when he left my home that noon I wasn't sure that he would get to his office in time.

I associate both of those days of hunting with Dr. Ko even though they were two of the greatest contrasts in days that I have ever seen. Yet, Dr. Ko was so patient even when no deer came along. He was eager and ready for anything to happen—a real, real good sportsman! He was a man who was always looking forward. Never, *never* did I hear him complain or brag or be dissatisfied with anything during our hunting adventures. There were no complaints whatsoever whether the weather was good or bad.

I remember another time when several men came for a hunting trip. There were Dr. Ko, his boys, a gentleman from St. Mary's Hospital Pharmacy, and two other fellows. All of us had breakfast here in Sprakers and then went hunting down below us in another area. The lad from St. Mary's shot a deer! It was the first deer that he had ever shot so, of course, he was very excited. Dr. Ko and he were in the same area after the party had stretched out at different posts. Being together, Dr. Ko and the lad cleaned out the deer and lugged it to the car. Then they came and picked up the rest of the hunters. We went down to the place where the deer lay, helped get it to the car and then returned to Sprakers. Dr. Ko was *very, very* excited that day. He was certainly proud of his friend from St. Mary's; just as proud as he would have been if he had killed the deer himself. This was another nice day that we had together.

Then in the fall of 1986 I had a stroke. My hunting days were pretty much put on the back burner. I couldn't hunt much that year or since then. I've sort of had to stay at home. But I have some wonderful memories! I had such good associations with Dr. Ko. I always enjoyed being with him and the men he brought along to hunt. Even though he had little time for hunting, I was amazed how he could find the time to go up to the Rifle Club to practice shooting in order to improve his skills and then to arrange for hunting adventures.

When Dr. Ko and I met one day in August of 1989, he said, "Where did you get that wrist watch on your arm?"

I answered, "Montgomery Ward's sales catalog!" "Huh," he replied. "I flew all the way to Japan and bought one just like that but it doesn't work any more!"

I think he was referring to one of his trips to Korea at which time he bought his watch. He was ticked off because it had stopped running. I put a new battery in it for him and gave him a copy of my instruction book for the watch because he had lost his.

Besides our hunting trips and various other times together, Dr. and his wife, Elaine, along with my wife, Harriet, and I went out for dinner several times. All of these memories are so precious now. I thank the Lord for all these special times together!

—Herb and Harriet Thackrah

Cared for Others

I remember how Elaine and Sok always had a place for us at their table on holidays. No matter how busy Sok was, he found time to visit with Tommy and me.

Grandmother Thomas will be 105 years old on Thursday. When I told her about Sok she started right in telling about how he was responsible for saving her leg.

Also, I remember when I was in bed at the Ko home with an injured leg. Dr. Ko advised me to have Dr. Butler look at my leg again. It was a good thing I did as Dr. Ko suggested!

—Dorothy Thomas

Always Show Interest in Others

In the few short years that I had the pleasure and good fortune to know him, Dr. Ko impressed me as being a sincere and compassionate man.

His sudden and unexpected death came as a terrible shock to both me and my mother. She always commented how Dr. Ko never failed to ask about me during her appointments. On those occasions when I accompanied her, Dr. Ko never neglected to take out time to talk with me.

How wonderful it was that he had the opportunity to see his family in North Korea before he died!

—Fr. Joe Veneroso, M.M

Service Without Expecting Reward

There is so much that I could say about Dr. Ko. When I think of him I will remember him as someone who had high standards and stuck to them. He was a kind and compassionate doctor, serious about his work but never arrogant. He was genuinely interested in people and it showed. He got involved in so many projects helpful to the community without looking for reward. He loved to have fun and knew how to enjoy life whether it was to drop in on a baseball game at the park or to travel someplace new.

Ben and I will always be grateful for the support he gave us when Kari was an exchange student.

—Anne, Ben, Kari and Paul Wojciechowsky

Reminded of Dr. Ko

As a member of the large Ko extended family, I got to see, hear, and smell a lot that was very different for me. Anybody who has ever opened the Ko's refrigerator door knows the very different smell of kimchee blessedly brewing away. Dinner conversation was as different as the food they ate. It—the conversation—would range from bodily functions to geo-political crises, but always with humor and playful sarcasm. Even the house itself was strange to me, it could quietly absorb fifteen people. The Ko house was just big, and big was unusual for me.

My house growing up was ten people in a place that was more than just a wee bit smaller. I was accustomed to sharing my surroundings in everything I did, whenever I was doing it. My personal refuge was outside. My daily routine more or less centered around how to find some calm amidst the crowd. Life was very different at the Ko's house. I'd walk in the kitchen with Andy, sit down, eat something, talk for an hour, and not even know if anyone else was home. As much as I enjoyed the space, I was always edgy and felt very relieved when someone would appear from some door. I remember asking Andy, "Shouldn't you tell your mother that you're home?" I didn't get much of a response. It simply wasn't part of their routine, because sooner or later they knew they would run into each other. The Ko's were used to the individual space, and the family seemed to move at a very free pace. My vague expectation that something should have been happening, or that the family ought to be together in some way, made me nervous. It took a long time for me to relax in that house. I didn't have to share couch space, seek out attention of any sort, or worry about drinking the last bit of whatever there was to drink. That freedom was as foreign to me as the height of the ceilings and the concept of a separate room for each kid.

My ingrained need for chaos was eventually overcome by the peace and calm of the Ko house. The relationships I have formed with the Ko's have probably been as meaningful to my development as any in my life. Dr. Ko and Elaine have always accepted me with hugs and genuine support. That acceptance was as reliable as Dr. Ko's customary greeting, a simple and upbeat "Mr. Johnson!" Even while quietly overlooking my lack of academic ambition, they always embraced my goofy sense of humor and respected my intellect. I never felt pressured or put on the spot, which may surprise some people. I was always treated gently, as were all non-Ko children. While I was teased now and then, my shortcomings were always ascribed to the problems of youth. As I grew up around Dr. Ko, I realized that this would never completely change—I would always be young and green to him. But, I also knew that I had been completely accepted into the Ko family. In Dr Ko's vision, I was a part of his extended household and had a place in the Korean family hierarchy that he had created in this country.

It took me a long time to understand this about Dr. Ko. Even though I had been around him since I was twelve, I really didn't get to know Dr. Ko until almost seven years later. Up to that time, I thought of him mostly as Andy's father, the one who made Andy get frequent and drastic haircuts. I knew that Dr. Ko liked to fish, worked all the time, and took chickens and paintings as payment for dental services. But I didn't spend much time with him until 1982, when Andy, Jimmy Jackowski and I began our summer job painting the Ko house.

At first, painting the Ko's house seemed like a great idea, simply because I didn't have to look for other summertime work. I was also pleased with the ease and familiarity of being at the Ko's. But that summer became more meaningful to me than just a job. We tried to work hard, to do a good job and finish what seemed to be a huge project by the end of August. Our work ethic at times was rotten, and I am sure a professional could have done the job much quicker, and maybe better. But it wasn't completely our fault that the house took so long to complete. As we plugged away at it, Dr. Ko found us odd tasks, like digging holes, cutting trees and mowing the lawn.

We also had what I remember as really wonderful lunchtime conversations in the Ko kitchen. Dr. Ko could make soup out of anything. While he cooked, he talked. We discussed a lot of socio-political-economic issues. Republican vs. Democrats, that kind of stuff. The back and forth was not always high-minded, but for me it was always fun. He seemed to enjoy it as well, always pushing the argument further, testing us, belittling us when he'd been backed into a corner, and cracking jokes throughout. He seemed especially interested in figuring out how Jimmy's Polish or my Irish heritage had affected our obviously flawed or underdeveloped thought process. He was always funny and sarcastic and caring at the same time. He would only offer small glimpses of himself—that was Dr. Ko's personality—but what came out of his mouth was always interesting. I had never before spent time talking with an adult in that way. I now understand what a special gift it was to have spent that time with him.

Looking back now and seeing the kind of philosophical optimism Dr. and Mrs. Ko have had concerning the community, education and children, I see where that summer and my other experiences with the Ko's come together. For me, those conversations were much like the commitment they made to supporting foreign exchange students who have lived with them over the years. Housing the foreign students and eating lunch with paint-covered teenagers were both chances for Dr. Ko to relate closely with others, and part of his need to learn from them and to share with them what he had learned. I came to know Dr. Ko better once I understood his fundamental belief that exposure to diverse cultures, thoughts and opinions enable us to understand our world and in turn contribute to its development.

I know that Dr. Ko understood that such opportunities to share culture and ideas are only temporary experiences unless they happen within the context of honest, caring and committed relationships. I know the relationships I have made with the Ko's will always endure and continue to grow. The summer of house painting and lunch-time debates with Dr. Ko cemented my relationship with him and his family. For me, growing with people who care was the meaning of that entire summer, and that bond has been the undercurrent of my experiences with the Ko's ever since.

The challenge and humor and love that the Dr. and all the Ko's have shared with me—for a long time now—were the starting points for me. Even today working with very young children, I can feel the effect of my relationship with Dr. Ko and his family on my growth as an individual. Sometimes, when I talk with the children, I can hear myself being silly, challenging and hopefully caring. Though it is in my own words and as my own person, I find myself often pleasantly reminded of my times with Dr. and Mrs. Ko.

—David Johnson

Once again the city of Amsterdam has been dealt a tragic loss. This time it isn't the loss of another store in the mall or the loss of more city services; it is the loss of a wonderful humanitarian and consumate professional person.

However, it was his love of life and people that made him so very special. My son, who is mentally retarded, was but one of the many people he took under his wing and to whom he so unselfishly gave of his time and his wisdom.

He had promised my son that we would come to his graduation party. Although he got called in to the hospital to perform emergency surgery for two hours, he still would drive the 15 miles to the graduation party.

He was always giving of himself for others in the community and he did it because that's the special kind of man he was.

To his wonderful wife and family I send my family's condolences. It is with a heavy heart that I say goodbye to a man who I respected and cared for a great deal. Goodbye Dr. Ko and I know that God will bless you always.

JOHN H. NICHOLS, Amsterdam

Letter in *The Amsterdam Recorder*, March 19, 1991.

APPENDIX A

CURRICULUM VITAE

November 5, 1934

Born in Kaesong, Korea to Jin Myeong and Sahm Oak Ko; oldest of seven children

Japanese occupy Korea from 1905 to 1945

United States and Soviet Union partition Korea at the 38th Parallel, Kaesong in southern zone under American control, 1945

June 25, 1950

The Korean War begins; North Korean forces occupy Kaesong on the first day of the war

Ko's father, Jin Myeong, taken by North Korean soldiers and not seen again

Kaesong the site of a number of major battles throughout the war

Separated from his family, Ko later meets George Harrington

October 1952

Arrives in Castleton, VT; lives in the home of George and Betty Harrington (later Betty Zahnleiter) until 1958

July 27, 1953

Korean War Armistice; fighting ends, but Korea remains divided

Kaesong and Ko's family now under North Korean control

July 17, 1956	Granted United States permanent resident status by private bill passed in Congress
June, 1958	Graduates from Castleton Teachers College
August 14, 1960	Marries Elaine Hogaboom
November, 1962	Becomes a Citizen of the United States
August 21, 1963	Andrew William Ko born, Burlington, VT
March 18, 1965	Timothy Allen Ko born, Philadelphia, PA
June 14, 1968	Graduates from Temple Dental School
Dec. 12, 1970	Stephen Olin Ko born, Weymouth, MA
December, 1971	Establishes oral surgery practice, Amsterdam, NY
April, 1972	Family moves to house at 80 Locust Avenue, Amsterdam, NY
April, 1975	Returns to South Korea after more than 20 years in the United States
June 9, 1975	Suzanne Elaine Ko born, Amsterdam, NY
Oct. 10, 1985	First trip to North Korea with Andrew; reunited with surviving brothers and sister in North Korea
August, 1986	Second trip to North Korea with Elaine, Stephen and Suzanne (Timothy in South Korea)
October, 1987	Reunited with the family of Chu Yul Kim, his only Korean relatives living in the United States
March 16, 1991	Ko dies and is buried in Castleton, VT on April 20th

Education:

Mahn Weol Public School, Kaesong, Korea, 1940-46

Kaesong Commercial Middle-High School, Kaesong, Korea, 1946-50

Fair Haven High School, Fair Haven, VT, 1952-54

Columbia University, New York City, NY, American English, 1957

Castleton State Teachers College, Castleton, VT, B.S. in Education, 1958

National Science Foundation Grant for Physics, Howard University, Washington, DC, 1960

National Science Foundation Grant for Biological Science, University of Vermont, Burlington, VT, 1961

University of Vermont, Burlington, VT, B.A. in Liberal Arts, Major Zoology, Minor Chemistry, 1962

Temple University School of Dentistry, Philadelphia, PA, 1964-68, D.D.S., 1968

Tufts University School of Dental Medicine, Boston, MA, School of Oral Surgery, 1968-69

Veterans Administration Hospital, Boston, MA
Internship in Oral Surgery, 1968-69
Residency in Oral Surgery, 1969-71

Kyung Hee University Medical Center, and Seoul National University Medical School, Seoul, Korea, Acupuncture, 1975

Military Service:

United States Army and Army Reserves
Enlisted, Corp of Engineers, December 16, 1957
Active Duty, Fort Dix, NJ, 1958-1959

Honorable Discharge, U.S. Army Reserves, SP5 E-5, December 22, 1963

United States Navy Reserves, 1965-90
Honorable Discharge, May 31, 1990

Rank:

Ensign, August 6, 1965
Lieutenant Junior Grade, December 14, 1965
Lieutenant, December 1, 1967
Lieutenant Commander, July 1, 1972

Assignments:

U.S. Naval Reserve Dental Corp, Dental Company 4-8, Temple University School of Dentistry, Philadelphia, PA, 1965-1968

U.S. Naval Academy, Medical-Dental Indoctrination, Annapolis, MD, July 8-29, 1966

Dental Clerkship – Naval Air Station, Willow Grove, PA, July 5 through October 3, 1967

Dental Company 1-2, Tufts University School of Dental Medicine, Boston, MA, 1969-71

Chelsea Naval Hospital, Chelsea, MA, June 15 to June 28, 1969

U.S. Naval Air Station, South Weymouth, MA, April 23 to May 7, 1970

U.S. Naval Air Station, South Weymouth, MA, May 17-28, 1971

Navy Reserve Support Unit 3-84, Scotia, NY, Dental Officer, 1973-1975

Naval Regiment Medical Center, Albany, NY, 1976

U.S. Naval Hospital, Newport, RI, September 13-21, 1976

Professional Life:

Teacher, South Burlington Junior and Senior High Schools, South Burlington, VT

General Science, Math and Biology 1959-1963

Lecturer and Clinical Instructor in Oral Surgery, Tufts University School of Dental Medicine, Boston, MA, 1969-71

Private Oral Surgery Practice, Framingham and Marlborough, MA, 1971

Hospital Affiliations:

Framingham Hospital, Framingham, MA
Marlborough Hospital, Marlborough, MA
Leonard Morris Hospital, Natick, MA

Private Oral Surgery Practice, Pine Street and 80 Locust Avenue, Amsterdam, NY, 1972-91

Hospital Affiliations:

Amsterdam Memorial Hospital, Amsterdam, NY
Saint Mary's Hospital, Amsterdam, NY
Nathan Littauer Hospital, Gloversville, NY
Johnstown Hospital, Johnstown, NY

Professional and Civic Associations:

Dental Associations:

American Dental Association Fulton, Hamilton and Montgomery County Dental Societies

Fourth District Dental Society

New York Society of Oral Surgeons

American Dental Society of Anesthesiology

American Gold Foil Society, Temple University School of Dentistry

Delta Sigma Delta fraternity, Temple University School of Dentistry, President

Staff Member at Amsterdam Memorial, Saint Mary's and Nathan Littauer Hospitals

Civic Associations:

American Cancer Society, Montgomery County Chapter

President
Public Education Program Chairman
Instructor, Smoking Cessation Program

Leukemia Society of America, Upstate Division

YMCA of Amsterdam, Board of Directors, President 1984-85

Amsterdam Rotary Club, District 7190, 1986

Chairman, Polio Plus Committee, 1987
District Youth Exchange Committee and Co-Chair, 1988

Rotary exchange student host family beginning in 1978

People to People, Delegation Leader to the Soviet Union, 1988 and 1989

Youth basketball and baseball coach

Waterfront director and swimming instructor, New York and Vermont summer camps

American Red Cross, First Aid Instructor

Other Honors:

Citizenship Award, Alpha Lambda Society, Castleton State Teachers College

Jim Hannan Memorial Service Award, Montgomery County Chapter Cancer Society

Public Education Award, Cancer Society New York Division, 1980

Amsterdam Rotarian of the Year, 1988

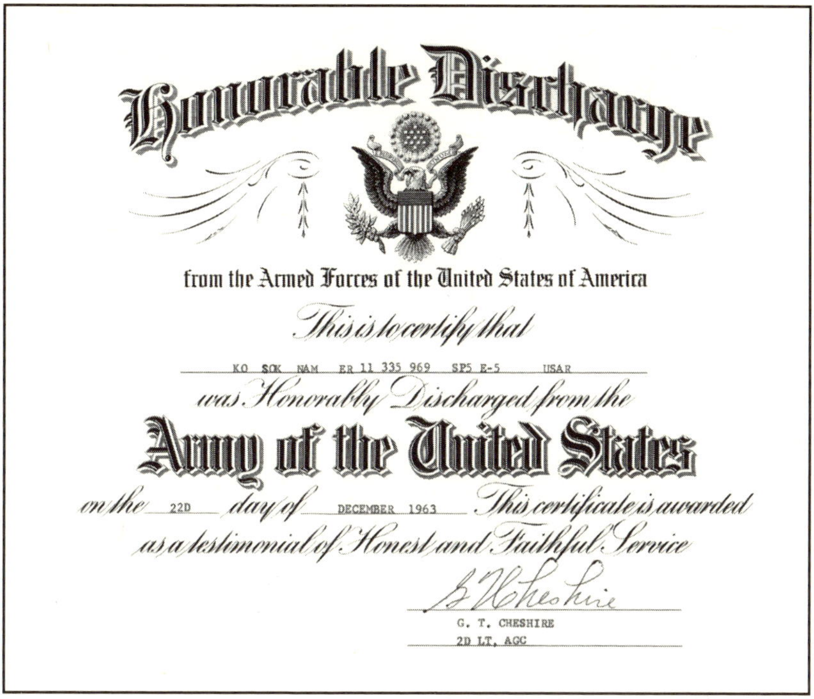

Honorable Discharge

from the Armed Forces of the United States of America

This is to certify that

KO SOK NAM ER 11 335 969 SP5 E-5 USAR

was Honorably Discharged from the

Army of the United States

on the 22D day of DECEMBER 1963 This certificate is awarded as a testimonial of Honest and Faithful Service

G. T. CHESHIRE
2D LT, AGC

Army Honorable Discharge Certificate.

Army Photo.

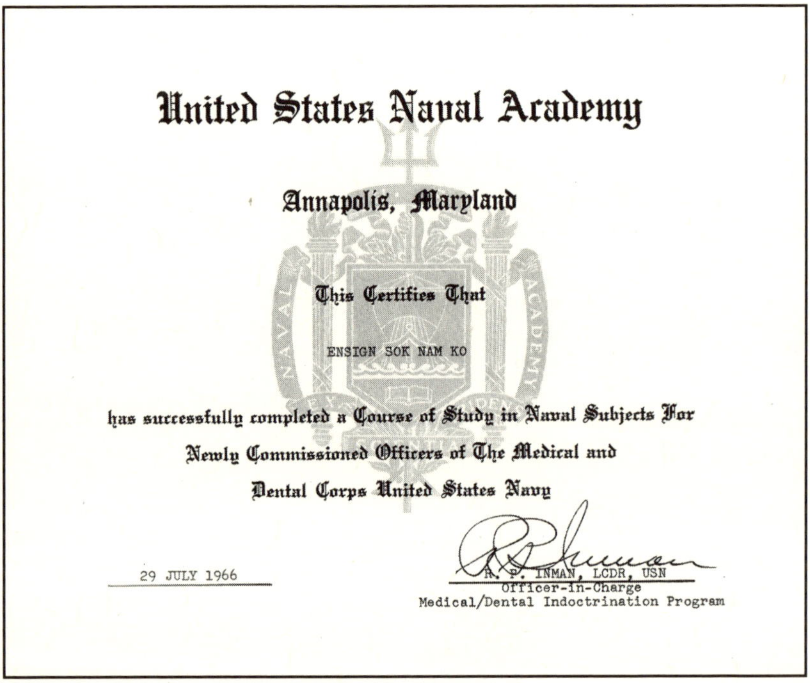
United States Naval Academy

Annapolis, Maryland

This Certifies That

ENSIGN SOK NAM KO

has successfully completed a Course of Study in Naval Subjects For Newly Commissioned Officers of The Medical and Dental Corps United States Navy

29 JULY 1966

R. P. INMAN, LCDR, USN
Officer-in-Charge
Medical/Dental Indoctrination Program

United State Naval Academy Certificate.

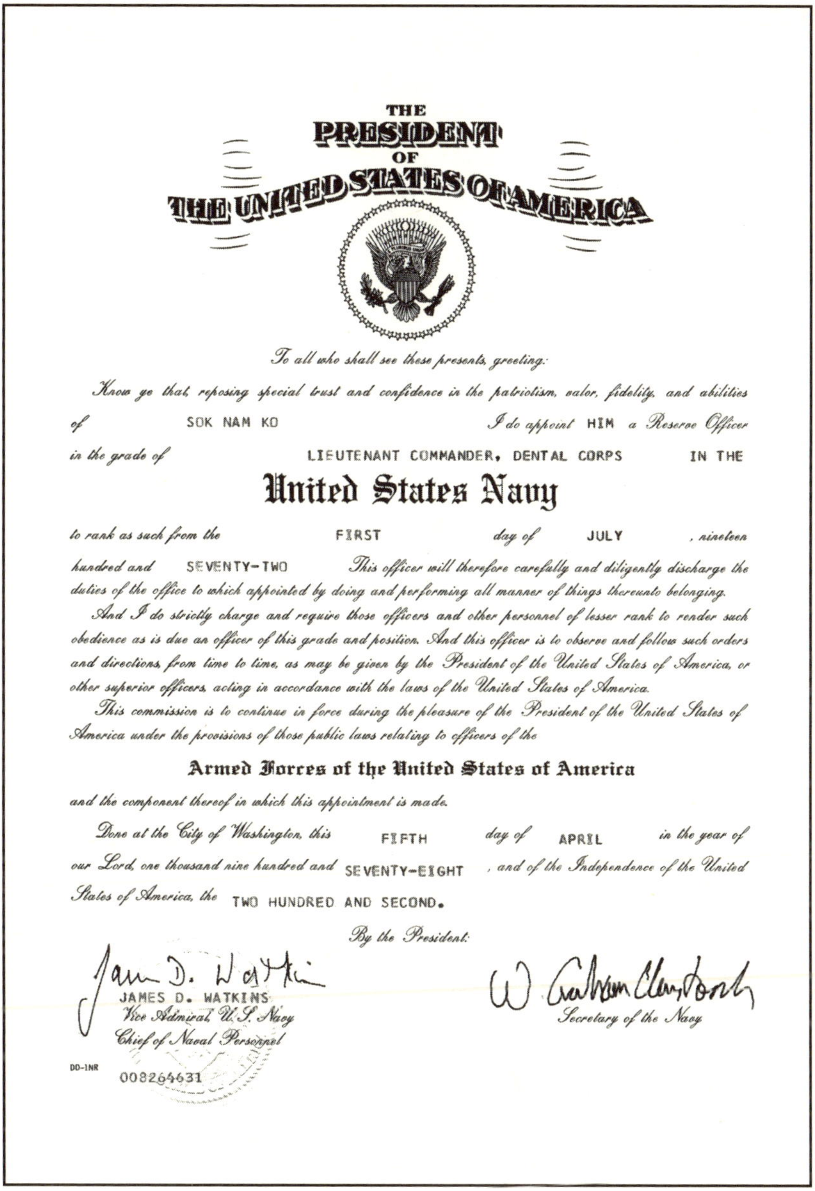

THE
PRESIDENT
OF
THE UNITED STATES OF AMERICA

To all who shall see these presents, greeting:

Know ye that, reposing special trust and confidence in the patriotism, valor, fidelity, and abilities of SOK NAM KO *I do appoint* HIM *a Reserve Officer in the grade of* LIEUTENANT COMMANDER, DENTAL CORPS IN THE

United States Navy

to rank as such from the FIRST *day of* JULY *, nineteen hundred and* SEVENTY-TWO *This officer will therefore carefully and diligently discharge the duties of the office to which appointed by doing and performing all manner of things thereunto belonging.*

And I do strictly charge and require those officers and other personnel of lesser rank to render such obedience as is due an officer of this grade and position. And this officer is to observe and follow such orders and directions, from time to time, as may be given by the President of the United States of America, or other superior officers, acting in accordance with the laws of the United States of America.

This commission is to continue in force during the pleasure of the President of the United States of America under the provisions of those public laws relating to officers of the

Armed Forces of the United States of America

and the component thereof in which this appointment is made.

Done at the City of Washington, this FIFTH *day of* APRIL *in the year of our Lord, one thousand nine hundred and* SEVENTY-EIGHT *, and of the Independence of the United States of America, the* TWO HUNDRED AND SECOND.

By the President:

JAMES D. WATKINS
Vice Admiral, U.S. Navy
Chief of Naval Personnel

Secretary of the Navy

DD-1NR

008264631

United States Navy Promotion Papers.

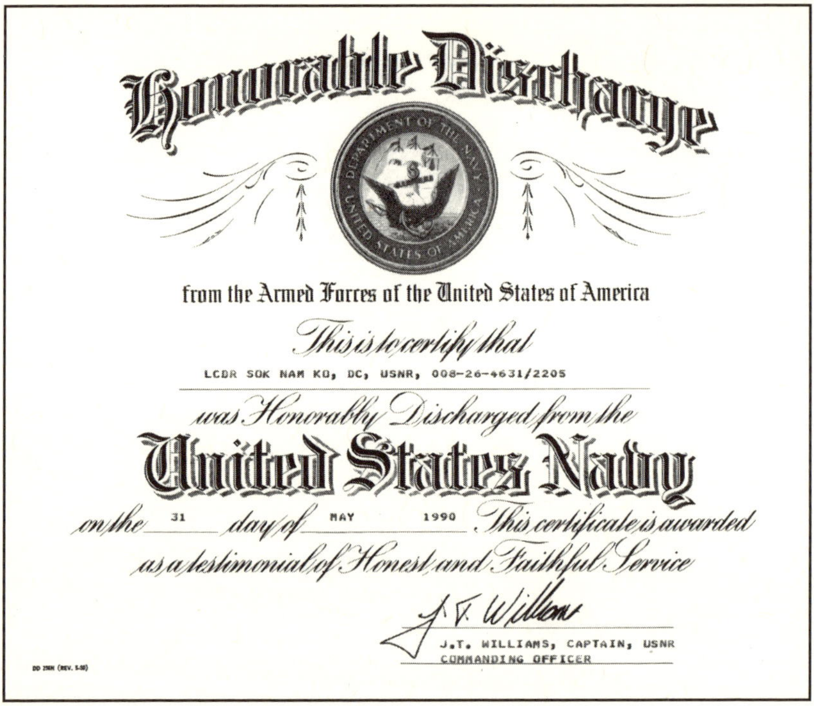

Honorable Discharge

from the Armed Forces of the United States of America

This is to certify that

LCDR SOK NAM KO, DC, USNR, 008-26-4631/2205

was Honorably Discharged from the

United States Navy

on the 31 day of MAY 1990 This certificate is awarded as a testimonial of Honest and Faithful Service

J.T. WILLIAMS, CAPTAIN, USNR
COMMANDING OFFICER

United States Navy Honorable Discharge Papers.

Sok Nam Ko, Lieutentant Commander, Dental Corps.

APPENDIX B

IN MEMORIAM

MARCH 16, 1991

The family of
Dr. Sok Nam Ko lovingly thanks family and friends for the beautiful cards, food, messages, flowers, spiritual bouquets and comfort given during these difficult weeks.
Dr. Ko's family invites you to attend the Committal Service on April 20, 1991 at 10:30 a.m., in Hillside Cemetery, Castleton, Vermont.
The family especially thanks all those who have donated to the "Sok Nam Ko Exchange Student Foundation" in his memory;
Elaine, Andy, Tim, Steve and Susie

Amsterdam Recorder, April 17, 1991.

Come Help Us Celebrate the Life of
Sok Nam Ko

Born: November 5, 1934
Died: March 16, 1991

We loved him, and his loss has revealed how precious our family and all of our friends are to us. We have also come to understand that our time together in this world is brief.

We hope that you can spend Saturday, April 20, 1991 with us in Amsterdam, New York. We'll be taking Sok to Castleton, Vermont on Saturday morning and return to Amsterdam to spend some time together.

It made Dad happy to visit with old friends and to get to know people whom his wife and children have come to care about. We'd like to continue that tradition. Life sometimes carries us along without a thought of the passing of time, but we hope that you can be with us on April 20th. We'd love to see you and for you to meet other people who are important to our family. It would also make it easier for us to say goodbye to our husband and father.

Place: Ko Home
80 Locust Avenue
Amsterdam, New York 12010

Arrive: Friday, April 19, 1991 (arrive any time)

Committal Service: April 20, 1991 at 10:30 a.m.
Hillside Cemetery
Castleton, Vermont

Get Together: At Ko's in Amsterdam,
April 20, 1991 at 3:00 p.m.

RSVP: Elaine and Suzie in Amsterdam 518-843-4811

Information:	Andy in New York City	212-529-3387	
	Tim in Albany	518-465-7783	or
	Steve in Portland, Oregon	503-777-0292	

Transportation:
Train (Amsterdam Amtrak Station by NYC Grand Central Station), Plane (Albany County Airport), and Automobile (New York State Thruway, Exit 27). Give us a call for help getting to the house. We've also enclosed instructions on how to get to Castleton.

Biography:
Before Sok's death, Elaine's aunt, Helen Smith, had begun to work with him on an autobiography. Completing the work has become very important to us. If you knew Sok, please think back on the times that you spent with him for (1) things that he told you about himself, (2) things that he said and (3) experiences that you had with him. Please don't limit yourself to only happy or flattering memories. Sok was like other people in that at times he was funny, sad, angry, confusing, enlightening, frustrating, as well as a joy to be with. It would help us greatly if you could find the time to write down as much as you remember about Sok's life and stories that he told you. If there are particular memories or stories that you would like to share with others in April, please send them to Helen Smith at 3877 Highland Road, Cortland, NY 13045 by April 10th.

HOPE TO SEE YOU IN APRIL

Invitation to memorial service, April 20, 1991.

THE SOK NAM KO EDUCATIONAL EXCHANGE FOUNDATION

was formed following Dr. Ko's death by his family and friends. Contributions may be given in his name to: Atty. Douglas E. Landon
25 Evelyn Avenue
Amsterdam, New York 12010

A BIOGRAPHY OF SOK NAM KO

Before Sok's death, Elaine's aunt, Dr. Helen Smith had begun to work with him on an autobiography. Completing the work has become very important to us.

If you knew Sok (KO), please think back on the times that you spent with him for (1) things that he told you about himself, (2) things that he said and (3) experiences that you had with him. Please don't limit yourself to only happy or flattering memories.

Sok was like other people in that he was at times funny, sad, angry, confusing, enlightening, frustrating, as well as a joy to be with.

It would help us greatly if you could find the time to write down as much as you remember about Sok's life and stories that he told you.

Please send these memories and stories to:

Dr. Helen Smith
3877 Highland Road
Cortland
New York 13045

Dr. SOK NAM KO

1934-1991

SERVICE ABOVE SELF*

IT'S OKAY

It's okay to be afraid
of things we don't understand
It's okay to feel anxious
when things aren't working our way.

It's okay to feel lonely...
even when you're with other people
It's okay to feel unfulfilled
because you know something is missing
(even if you're not sure what it is).

It's okay to think and worry and cry.

It's okay to do
whatever you have to do, but
just remember too...
that eventually you're going to
adjust to the changes life brings your way
and you'll realize that
It's okay to love again and laugh again,
and it's okay to get to the point where
the life you live
is full, and satisfying and good to you...
and it will be that way
because you made it that way.

* Motto of Rotary International
Verse given to all exchange students.

COME HELP US CELEBRATE THE LIFE OF

SOK NAM KO
Born: November 5, 1934
Died: March 16, 1991

Readings from the Bible	
Poetry	Rev. Olof C. Johnson
Remembering Sok Nam Ko	
Thoughts, Remarks	Relatives and Friends
Prayer and Benediction	Rev. Alfred Kahler
Korean Farewell	
Flag Presentation	

****

The Ko Family invites you to join them in celebration of our husband and father's life at 3:00 P.M. today 80 Locust Avenue, Amsterdam, New York.

Sok Nam Ko Memorial Ceremony: Program.

MEMORIAL SERVICE, HILLSIDE CEMETARY, CASTLETON, VERMONT

Elaine Ko:

"You probably have many thoughts and memories you'd like to share with us. I know I have a lot of memories. I will share them with you in Castleton and in Amsterdam. (I forget where I am, whether in Castleton or Amsterdam.) I want you to share things; memories that you perhaps have.

I also invite you and our family invites you back to Amsterdam. We'd love to have you all come back and spend some time with us there. Thank you again for coming. You've come from all over the world. We really appreciate it."

George Harrington:

"Those who sit close to the front can jump up and take the stage.

I have been associated with Dr. Sok Nam Ko for 39 years. I'm 39 years old and my name is George Harrington. (Fighting tears) I wasn't going to do this but here we go!

I was very impressed as I looked around at this great gathering. I see friends from Amsterdam. I see dear friends from Castleton, from Korea, from Finland, from Russia. I think to myself, what is the common thread that brings us all to this little town in Vermont? That common thread was the strength of the personality of the man whom we used to call Ko, who most of you call Sok. I still have trouble with that. But we all knew who he was. We all knew that this man had courage, had strength, determination and unselfishness. And although he is gone, his gift will continue to give, as we remember in our hearts, during those tough times when we think we can't make it. Here was a guy who made it in spite of tough times. Keep that in your heart and keep him alive in your heart, I pray. Thank you."

Kathy Deal (Representing the Office Staff):

"Dr. Ko was our employer, boss and more...

The word friend is defined as:

A person attached to another by respect and love.

A person who is kind to another.

A person who aids another with support and guidance.

Dr. Ko was this and more to each of us.
We have truly lost a friend."

Sister Margaret (Head Nurse in the Operating Room at St. Mary's):

"I can't help but recall the many times he demonstrated his commitment to our staff, the Sisters of St. Joseph and the patients under his care, Dr. Ko was a true professional in every sense of the word. He was global in caring for patients—not selective—and was always available regardless of time of day, day of the week, on call or not on call.

Robert Louis Stevenson once said that a man is a success who has lived well, has filled his niche and accomplished his task, who leaves the world better than he found it, who never lacks appreciation of earth's beauty or failed to express it, who looks for the best in others and gave the best he had.

All of this was accomplished by Dr.Ko in a space of time too short for those of us gathered here today. May the good Lord of all sustain his family and his friends in these difficult times and grant him eternal rest."

Andy Johnson:

"I'm Andy Johnson who grew up in Castleton with Ko. He helped me play baseball. There are a lot of things that I learned from Ko. There was one time, I was still living in Castleton. I had a necktie that was too long. I asked him if he would look at it. He did and he cut it in half. When I put it back together it was the length I wanted. My confidence in myself was influenced by his confidence in me. I always knew he had confidence in me and that I could take care of whatever came. That means a lot these days when things are real tough. Confidence in myself is something Ko gave me."

Mrs. Pat Galea:

"I am the mother of Dr Jon Galea, a young man who could not decide what he wanted to do before Dr. Ko befriended him. Jon spent all one summer in Dr. Ko's office and with him at St. Mary's Hospital. After that summer he knew he wanted to be a dentist, and hoped to be like Dr. Ko. He sends his love to Elaine and the children."

Lissa Kim: (Uncle Kim's daughter spoke in behalf of her father and the family):

"My father and Dr. Ko grew up together in Korea. They were separated during the war. When my father came here, he tried to look for Dr. Ko. Eventually he got a letter from North Korea in 1987. They wrote in Korean "Amsterdam." My father didn't know what they meant. He knew Amsterdam in the Netherlands. As soon as he got the letter he called New York information. They looked up Amsterdam. In about 15 minutes he got in touch with Dr. Ko.

My father doesn't have any other relatives here besides us. Seeing Uncle Sok, whom he hadn't seem for 35 years, made him so happy. I just want to say thank you for keeping him until we found him."

Prayer and Benediction, Rev. Kahler:

"Let us pray. Lord God — As we are gathered here at the site of the final resting place of the earthly remains of our friend, father and husband, Sok, we also commit his soul into your keeping. The writer of the book of Ecclesiastes says that there is a season and a time for everything, even life and death. It is a mystery as to how longevity is decided. I guess longevity is not the question but what has been accomplished in the life of the individual as it has been lived. Sok's life has been full of accomplishments. The writer of the book of Revelation says that even in death their works do follow them. The effect of the life of Sok will long be remembered by many—the exchange students and their families, the community and most of all his family. His life changed many other lives and he will be long remembered and we thank you for that. You, O God our Creator, send people along our paths to create change and I thank you for allowing us to have Sok to help create change.

Lord, as we give thanks for and commit Sok into your keeping, our hearts and minds go to those who remain, his family and friends. Give each one strength to carry forth in their own ways of service. Bless the family and friends, the extended family. As the sorrow of separation creeps in, give solace. As the tears of grief are shed, let them heal. May the understanding of your presence undergird each one who remains.

Now, Lord, bless and keep each one as we depart. May God's presence sustain us, keep us and give each one peace. Amen."

Flag Presentation, David Betz:

"As Sok Nam Ko served his country in time of need, we present this flag.

On behalf of Elaine, I want to thank everyone for attending this morning. We know many came from far away and had to take time out of your busy lives. We deeply appreciate it. Thank you. Please depart."

Guests visited with family members and each other as preparations were made for the burial by Sok's Korean relatives and friends. The urn holding his ashes was placed in a container, which was then sealed and lowered into the ground. Sok's family friends then placed flowers with him inside the grave.

Beyond the cemetery, the church bell in the village was tolling. Relatives and friends filled the grave with dirt, creating a small Korean burial mound. Reverend Johnson, who married Sok and Elaine, dropped his book just before giving the words of committal. He asked God for strength, comfort in our hearts, and victory of life over death. Many more flowers were placed on the grave.

Korean relatives and friends, Elaine and Sok's children continued with the traditional Korean ceremony. Wine was poured from a bottle into a cup. Participants knelt three times on the ground and bowed their heads toward the grave. Each then stood up, accepted the cup and drank some of the wine—slowly pouring what remained on the grave.

Family pictures were taken while other guests chatted quietly before leaving the cemetery.

RUTLAND DAILY HERALD - APRIL 17, 1991

Obituaries

Dr. Sok Nam Ko

AMSTERDAM, N.Y. — A graveside service for Dr. Sok Nam Ko, a former resident of Castleton, Vt., who died March 16 at Albany Medical Center, will be held Saturday at 10:30 a.m. at Hillside Cemetery in Castleton. The Rev. Olof Johnson, former pastor of the Castleton Federated Church, and the Rev. Alfred Kahler will officiate.

Arrangements are under the direction of Mallory Funeral Home, 4 South Park Place, Fair Haven.

APRIL 20, 1991

Dr. Sok Nam Ko Rites

CASTLETON — A committal service for Dr. Sok Nam Ko, who died March 16 at the Albany Medical Center, Albany, N.Y., was held at 10:30 a.m. Saturday at the Hillside Cemetery in Castleton.

The Rev. Olof Johnson, a longtime friend of Dr. Ko and former pastor of the Castleton Federated Church, read Scripture and poems. George W. Harrington led family and friends in thoughts and remarks remembering Dr. Ko. The Rev. Alfred Kahler of Amsterdam, N.Y., read prayers and gave the benediction. The flag was presented to Dr. Ko's widow by David Betz. A traditional Korean farewell and prayer service were conducted. The Rev. Johnson then offered the committal prayer. Arrangements were by the Mallory Funeral Home, Fair Haven.

Letters to the Editor

Rutland Daily Herald ▪ Friday Morning, April 19, 1991

Remembered in Castleton

Dr. Sok Nam Ko of Amsterdam, N.Y., who died March 16 at age 56 at the Albany Medical Center, is remembered in the Castleton area as the young teenager from Korea who came to Castleton to live with the Harrington family in 1952.

He attended Fair Haven High School and graduated from Castleton State College in 1958 with a bachelor of science degree in education.

It was while at Castleton State that he received national attention as the result of a basketball game in Canada. When he returned with his team to the border he was detained when his papers were questioned. This led to deportation proceedings. After two trips to Washington with Attorney Harrington and through the efforts of then U.S. Rep. Winston Prouty Ko achieved permanent residency status. This was accomplished through an Act of Congress. Ko later became a citizen in 1962 in Rutland.

Following graduation from Castleton he taught in South Burlington Junior High School and attended the University of Vermont. In 1963 he graduated with a bachelor of arts degree in zoology ...

Dr. Ko was always interested in the medical profession: He enrolled at Temple University and graduated with a doctor of dental science degree. In 1969 he graduated from Tufts University Graduate School of dental surgery.

The Ko family has been host to many students from foreign countries through the Rotary Exchange. Also Dr. Ko was active in the People-to-People Ambassador program. He recently led a group from Amsterdam High School to the Soviet Union. At the time of his death there were three foreign visitors living with the Ko family. One of them the first Russian student in the Rotary program.

Ko has been active in school and civic organizations, serving as chairman or president. He was never too busy to help others.

Ko made several trips to South Korea in search of his family and finally in 1985 he was reunited with his brothers and sister in North Korea. It was a bittersweet reunion. His mother had died just months before this reunion...

Ko made his mark in Castleton and leaves many friends in the Rutland area.

BETTY H. ZAHNLEITER
Castleton
DOROTHY W. KNAPP
Poultney
GEORGE W. HARRINGTON
Poughkeepsie, N.Y.

'he Burlington (Vt.) Free Press,. March 20, 1991

DR. SOK NAM KO

AMSTERDAM, N.Y. — Dr. Sok Nam Ko, 56, died March 16, 1991, in Albany Medical Center after a brief illness. Dr. Ko was born Nov. 5, 1934, in Kaesong, Korea, where he attended Mon Wal Public School from 1940 to 1946, and Kaesong Public Middle School from 1946 to 1950. He was the son of Gyn Myung and Sam Ok (Kim) Ko.

He came to the United States in 1952, to live with the Harringtons of Castleton, Vt. Graduating from the Temple University School of Dentistry in 1968, Dr. Ko received his graduate degree in oral surgery from Tufts University School of Dental Medicine in 1971.

As an active member of Rotary International Youth Exchange Program, Dr. Ko was host to foreign students from Argentina, Finland, Germany, Sweden, Japan, Mexico, Australia, and other nations. He also arranged the program's first student exchange with the Soviet Union.

Aug. 14, 1960, he was married to Elaine Hogaboom, originally of Enosburg Falls, Vt. Other members of his family include three sons, Andrew W. Ko of New York City, Timothy A. Ko of Albany, N.Y., and Stephen O. Ko of Portland, Ore.; one daughter, Suzanne E. Ko of Amsterdam; one sister, Don Ju Ko of Kaesong, Korea; and four brothers, Sok Dong Ko, Sok Kon Ko and Sok Won Ko, all of Kaesong, and Chu Yol Kim of Glenburnie, Md.

Dr. Ko will be buried April 20, 1991, in Castleton. In lieu of flowers, contributions may be made in his memory to the Sok Nam Ko Educational Exchange Foundation, care of Douglas Landon, 25 Evelyn Ave., Amsterdam, N.Y. 12010.

The Boston Globe
March 20, 1991

Dr. Sok Nam Ko, 56

Dentist, former Mass. teacher

Dr. Sok Nam Ko of Amsterdam, N.Y., a dental surgeon there since 1972, died Saturday at Albany Medical Center in New York. He was 56.

The Korean-born Dr. Ko graduated from Castleton State College in Vermont in 1958 and Temple University dental school in 1968. He taught mathematics and biology at Burlington (Vt.) High School from 1959 to 1963.

Dr. Ko studied oral surgery at Tufts Dental School in 1968-69 and practiced in Framingham and Marlborough in 1971-72.

He was a former president of the Montgomery County (N.Y.) chapter of the American Cancer Society and of the Amsterdam YMCA. He was a host of exchange students from the Soviet Union since 1979.

Dr. Ko leaves his wife, Elaine (Hogaboom); three sons, Andrew W. of New York City, Timothy of Albany and Stephen of Portland, Ore.; a daughter, Suzanne E. of Amsterdam; three brothers, Sok Dong, Sok Koon and Sok Won, all of Kaesong, Korea; and a sister, Oon Ju of Kaesong.

No service is planned.

Amsterdam Recorder
March 17, 1991

Obituaries

Sok Nam Ko

Dr. Sok Nam Ko, 56, of 80 Locust Ave., Amsterdam, died Saturday morning at Albany Medical Center after a short illness.

Dr. Ko was born Nov. 5, 1934, in Kaesong, Korea, the son of Gyn Myung and Sam Ok (Kim) Ko.

KO

He attended the Mon Wal Public School in Kaesong from 1940 to 1946 and the Kaesong Public Middle School from 1946 to 1950.

Dr. Ko served as an interpreter during the Korean War with the 8th Armored, 17th Field Artillery Battalion, U.S. Army.

He came to Castleton, Vt., in 1952 at the invitation of attorney George Harrington and his wife. From 1952 to 1954, he attended Fair Haven High School, Fair Haven, Vt. He graduated from Castleton State College, Castleton, Vt., in 1958 with a bachelor of science degree in education.

Dr. Ko served in the U.S. Army from 1957 to 1963. While attending Temple University School of Denistry, he joined the U.S. Navy Reserve Dental Corp. in 1965. He held the rank of lieutenant commander in the U.S. Navy Reserves at the time of his death.

After leaving the Army, he taught math, science and biology at South Burlington Junior and Senior High School, Burlington, Vt., from 1959 to 1963.

Dr. Ko graduated in 1963 from the University of Vermont, Burlington, Vt., with a bachelor of arts degree in zoology, from Temple University School of Denistry, Philadelphia, Pa., in 1968 with a doctorate of dental science degree, and from Tufts University School of Dental Medicine, Graduate School of Oral Surgery, Boston, in 1969.

Dr. Ko served an internship in oral surgery from 1968 to 1969 and a residence in oral surgery from 1969 to 1971 at the Boston Veterans Administration Hospital, Boston. He served as a clinical instructor in oral surgery at Tufts University School of Dental Medicine, Boston, from 1969 to 1971.

He operated a private practice in oral surgery in Framingham, Mass., and Marlborough, Mass., from 1971 to 1972.

Dr. Ko operated a private practice in oral surgery at 80 Locust Ave., Amsterdam, from 1972 until the time of his death. He was affiliated with Amsterdam Memorial Hospital, St. Mary's Hospital in Amsterdam, and Nathan Littauer Hospital in Gloversville.

He was a member of the American Heart Association, the American Dental Association, the Fulton, Hamilton and Montgomery Counties Dental Society; the Fourth District Dental Society, the New York State Society of Oral Surgeons, the American Dental Society of Anesthesiology, the New York State Society of Dental Anesthesiology, the American Gold Foil Society, the Delta Sigma Delta Fraternity, the Alpha Lambda Society, the Mohawk Valley Leukemia Society, the Amsterdam Rotary Club and the Montgomery County Chapter of the American Cancer Society, where he also served as a past president.

Dr. Ko served as a past president of the Delta Sigma Delta Fraternity at Temple University, as president of the Montgomery County Chapter of the American Cancer Society, where he received the first Jim Hannan Memorial Service Award; a president of the YMCA, co-chairman of the District 719 Rotary Exchange Program, chairman of the Rotary's Polio Plus Committee, a host of exchange students over the last 12 years and a leader of the People to People Ambassadors program to the USSR in 1989 and 1990.

Through the Rotary Exchange Program, Dr. Ko was instrumental in bringing the first exchange student from the U.S.S.R. to live in the United States with the Ko family of Amsterdam.

Dr. Ko was listed in Who's Who in the East and the Dictionary of International Biography.

He was active in men's volleyball and served on a team that captured the league championship in 1977 and division championship in 1979.

On Aug. 14, 1960, he married Elaine Hogaboom, who survives.

Other survivors include three sons: Andrew W. Ko of New York City, Timothy Ko of Albany, and Stephen Ko of Portland, Ore.; one daughter, Suzanne E. Ko of Amsterdam; three brothers: Sok Dong Ko, Sok Koon Ko and Sok Won Ko, all of Kaesong, Korea; a sister, Oon Ju Ko, of Kaesong, Korea; several nieces and nephews, one cousin, one aunt.

It is the request of the family that there be no calling hours or funeral service.

Interment will take place in the spring in Castleton Cemetery, Castleton, Vt.

In lieu of flowers, contributions may be made in his memory to the Sok Nam Ko Educational Exchange Foundation, care of Douglas E. Landon, 25 Evelyn Ave., Amsterdam.

Arrangements are by the Betz Funeral Home Inc., 171 Guy Park Ave., Amsterdam.

Obituaries

Sok Name Ko, Surgeon

Dr. Sok Name Ko, 56, of 80 Locust Ave., Amsterdam, an oral surgeon who was a North Korean refugee, died Saturday at Albany Medical Center Hospital of complications during cancer surgery.

He was born Nov. 5, 1934 in Kaesong, Korea, and fled from North Korea at 16, leaving behind his entire family. He was employed doing odd jobs and as an interpreter at a U.S. Army base when he befriended George Harrington, a captain in the 8th Armored Division, 17th Field Artillery. Harrington brought Ko home with him in 1952 to Castleton, Vt. There he lived with the Harrington family and attended Fair Haven High School.

Dr. Ko was active in sports at his high school.

He graduated from Castleton State College in 1958 with a bachelor of science degree in education and taught junior high and high school.

He served in the Army from 1957 to 1963 and joined the U.S. Navy Reserve Dental Corps in 1965, where he held the rank of lieutenant commander.

He graduated from the University of Vermont in 1963 with a bachelor of arts degree in zoology and from Temple University School of Dentistry in 1968 with a doctorate of dental science degree and from the Tufts University School of Medicine's graduate school of oral surgery in 1969.

He moved to Amsterdam in 1972, opening an office on Locust Avenue. He was also affiliated with Amsterdam Memorial Hospital, St. Mary's Hospital in Amsterdam, and Littauer Hospital in Gloversville.

Dr. Ko was active in exchange programs. He hosted 12 Rotary exchange students in the last 12 years. He also organized a trip for Amsterdam High School students to visit the Soviet Union and helped set up several recriprocal visits. At the time of his death, he had three foreign visitors staying with him.

He was a member and past president of Delta Sigma Nu Fraternity at Temple, the Amsterdam YMCA, and the Montgomery County Chapter of the American Cancer Society, where he won the first Jim Hannan Memorial Service Award. He was also co-chairman of the District 719 Rotary Exchange Program.

He was a member of the Fulton and Montgomery Counties Dental Society, Fourth District Dental Society, New York State Society of Oral Surgeons, American and New York State Dental Societies of Anesthesiology, American Gold Foil Society, Alpha Lambda Society, Mohawk Valley Leukemia Society and Amsterdam Rotary Club.

He married Elaine Hoagaboom. She survives.

Additonal survivors include three sons, Andrew W. Ko of New York City, Timothy Ko of Albany and Stephen Ko of Portland, Ore.; one daughter, Suzanne Ko of Amsterdam; four brothers, Sok Dong Ko, Sok Koon Ko and Sok Won Ko, all of Kaesong, and Chu Y. Kim of Glen Burnie, Md.; several nieces and nephews, one cousin and one aunt.

Schnectady Gazette
March 20, 1991

Dr. Sok Nam Ko, 56, Amsterdam oral surgeon

AMSTERDAM — Dr. Sok Nam Ko, a North Korean refugee who became an oral surgeon and was active in community affairs in Amsterdam, died Saturday at Albany Medical Center Hospital from complications after cancer surgery. He was 56.

Friends, relatives and family gathered at the Ko home at 80 Locust Ave. yesterday to mourn his loss and share stories of how he touched their lives.

"He was a real American hero," said George Harrington. Harrington was something of an adoptive little brother to Ko in the years after Harrington's father, George, brought Ko back home from Korea to Castleton, Vt., after the Korean War. When Harrington's father died, Ko became a father figure to him, he said.

"He pushed you to a potential you may not have believed you had," Harrington said. "He gave strength to people. He just wanted to toughen you up, because he knew that to make it in life, you had to be a survivor."

Harrington said that attitude began with Ko himself. As a 16-year-old, he fled North Korea, leaving behind his entire family, with whom he wouldn't be reunited until more than three decades later, only days after his mother's death.

Ko was working at a U.S. Army base doing odd jobs and acting as an interpreter when he was met and befriended by Harrington, a captain in the 8th Armored Division, 17th Field Artillery. In 1952, Ko came to Castleton and lived with the Harrington family and attended Fair Haven High School.

One of his first challenges was to win over the people of Castleton, which then numbered 2,000 inhabitants, few of whom had ever set eyes on a Korean. He did that by joining every sports team he could, and excelling at them. "He was able to capture their hearts," Harrington said.

Dr. Ko was born Nov. 5, 1934, in Kaesong, Korea.

He graduated from Castleton State College in 1958 with a bachelor of science degree in education, and taught junior high and high school, but he always planned to enter the medical profession, said Ko's American "mom," the former Betty Harrington, now Betty Zahnleiter.

"Teaching was just a stepping-stone," she said. "He had a plan all the way through, and he never lost sight of what he wanted to do."

Dr. Ko served in the U.S. Army from 1957 to 1963 and joined the U.S. Navy Reserve Dental Corp. in 1965 where he held the rank of lieutenant commander.

Dr. Ko went on to graduate from the University of Vermont in 1963 with a bachelor of arts degree in zoology, from Temple University School of Dentistry in 1968 with a doctorate of dental science degree, and from the Tufts University School of Dental Medicine's graduate school of oral surgery in 1969.

He moved to Amsterdam in 1972 and opened an office on Locust Avenue. Dr. Ko was affiliated with Amsterdam Memorial Hospital, St. Mary's Hospital in Amsterdam and Nathan Littaur Hospital in Gloversville.

Over the past 12 years, his family took in a dozen Rotary Exchange students from Sweden, Finland, Japan, Mexico and other countries.

He was also active in the People-to-People Ambassadors program, in which he helped lead a group of Amsterdam high schoolers to the Soviet Union, and helped set up several reciprocal visits.

His interest in the student exchanges was symbolic of his continuing interest in education, said his wife, Elaine. At the time of his death, he had three foreign visitors staying at his home.

Ko was a member and past president of Delta Sigma Nu Fraternity at Temple, of the Amsterdam YMCA; and the Montgomery County Chapter of the American Cancer Society, where he won the first Jim Hannan Memorial Service Award. He was also co-chairman of the District 719 Rotary Exchange Program.

He was also a member of the Fulton and Montgomery Counties Dental Society, the Fourth District Dental Society, the New York State Society of Oral Surgeons, the American and New York State Dental Societies of Anesthesiology, the American Gold Foil Society, the Alpha Lambda Society, the Mohawk Valley Leukemia Society and the Amsterdam Rotary Club.

In addition to his wife, the former Elaine Hoagaboom, survivors include three sons, Andrew W. Ko of New York City, Timothy Ko of Albany and Stephen Ko of Portland, Ore.; a daughter, Suzanne Ko of Amsterdam; four brothers, Sok Dong Ko, Sok Koon Ko and Sok Won Ko of Kaesong, Korea, Chu Y. Kim of Glen Burnie, Md.; a sister, Oon Ju Ko, also of Kaesong; and several nieces and nephews a cousin and an aunt.

Memorial contributions may be made to the Sok Nam Ko Educational Exchange Foundation, care of Douglas E. Landon, 25 Evelyn St., Amsterdam.

Arrangements are by the Betz Funeral Home, 171 Guy Park Ave., Amsterdam.

The New York Times
March 20, 1991

KO—Dr. Sok Nam, Oral Surgeon, 56, of Amsterdam, NY died on March 16, 1991 at Albany Medical Center after a brief illness. Dr. Ko was born on November 5, 1934 in Kaesong, Korea, where he attended the Mon Wal Public School from 1940 to 1946 and the Kaesong Public Middle School from 1946 to 1950. He was the son of Gyn Myung and Sam Ok (Kim) Ko. He came to the United States in 1952 to live with the Harringtons of Castleton, VT. Graduating from the Temple University School of Dentistry in 1968, Dr. Ko received his graduate degree in Oral Surgery from the Tufts University School of Dental Medicine in 1971. As an active member of the Rotary International Youth Exchange Program, Dr. Ko was host to foreign students from Argentina, Finland, Germany, Sweden, Japan, Mexico, Australia, and other nations. He also arranged the Program's first student exchange with the Soviet Union. On August 14, 1960, he was married to Elaine Hogaboom, originally of Enosburg Falls, VT. Other members of his family include: three sons, Andrew W. Ko of New York City, Timothy A. Ko of Albany, and Stephen O. Ko of Portland, OR; one daughter, Suzanne E. Ko of Amsterdam; one sister, Oon Ju Ko of Kaesong, Korea; and four brothers, Sok Dong Ko, Sok Koon Ko and Sok Won Ko, all of Kaesong, and Chu Yol Kim of Glenburnie, MD. Dr. Ko will be buried on April 20, 1991 at Castleton, VT. In lieu of flowers, contributions can be made in his memory to the Sok Nam Ko Educational Exchange Foundation, C/O Douglas Landon, Esq., 25 Evelyn Ave, Amsterdam, New York 12010.

Memorial in Kaesong, Korea

Sok Dong, brother; Eun Ju, sister; Sok Koon, brother

The Ko family at Sok's memorial, Kaesong, Korea

IN MEMORIAM

Dr. Sok N. Ko

Not so very long ago, a gentleman passed through my door. He wanted to say hello to the Dean who was his teacher many years ago. I am the Secretary and Assistant to the Dean, but when I greeted the visitor who stood in front of me, my thoughts drifted back to when I was the Secretary to the Chairman, Department of Physiology and the man he came to see today chaired the department. When I told Dr. Ko I remembered him and why, a smile came to his face. Dean Tansy greeted and also recognized Dr. Ko. They chatted briefly. As I said goodbye to Dr. Ko and told him how proud he and his family should be, I could see that indeed he was.

Rosann Souders
Secretary and Assistant to the Dean
Temple Dental School Magazine

Tree Memorials

Two trees have been planted in Israel
in memory of
Dr. Sok Nam Ko
by Dr. Gary and Renee Greenberg
and
by Dr. Harry and Kay Lebman
Planted by
Mrs. Catherine Lebman
49 Fairmont Avenue
Amsterdam, New York 12010

The Lofty Oaks Association

The Betz Funeral Home, Inc. of Amsterdam has arranged to have a young tree planted in memory of Sok Nam Ko. This memorial tree will be planted on New York's public lands.

This living memorial to Sok Nam Ko is part of a large endeavor, in cooperation with the State of New York's Conservation and Reforestation Programs, to restore the landscape and our environment with the eternal beauty of living trees. The individual tree is meant to provide a broad reaching legacy to all the people of New York; it will grow as an important part of its natural surroundings without personal inscription. It is hoped that the planting of this tree will bring peace and comfort to the many who pass its way in years to come.

The planting of this living memorial is an example of the sincerity and caring of the Betz staff.

Bruce B. Hadlock, President
Lofty Oaks Association

Special Tribute

By Sue Hemingway

DR. SOK NAM KO

In addition to being named as a member of the "Who's Who" in the East, and serving on the Medical-Dental Staff at St. Mary's Hospital and Memorial Hospital in Amsterdam, New York, Dr. Sok Nam Ko has earned recognition, along with respect and of course appreciation, from the Montgomery County Unit.

Their nomination of him for Special Tribute Volunteer stems from his 10 years service helping the ACS. Those who've worked with him on various committees cite Dr. Ko for his work "far and above other professional medical men in serving our community."

He has served as president, public education chairman, legacy chairman for the ACS and board member of the Mohawk Valley Leukemia Society. As a maxillofacial surgeon, Dr. Ko gives free oral cancer exams at health fairs, senior citizens organizations, and he has conducted many Stop-Smoking clinics.

What more deserving words of praise could be written on his behalf than the words sent with his nomination for this honor? That is to say, "Dr. Ko *never* turns down any duties he is asked to perform for the ACS . . . He gives unselfishly of his time to further the causes of the American Cancer Society."

RICKY PAULL GOLDIN

WOODY and JIM from FLY-92

YASMINE BLEETH

Telethon dedicated to Dr. Ko

The Montgomery County Unit of the American Cancer Society's 1992 Celebrity Cancer Telethon will be held Sunday at the Amsterdam High School and broadcast live from 10 a.m. to 7 p.m. on Gateway Cablevision Channel 8. This year's telethon will be in memory of Dr. Sok N. Ko who died in 1991.

The celebrities appearing will include Ricky Paull Golden, "Dean Frame" of *Another World* and Yasmine Bleeth, "Lee Ann Demerest" of *One Life to Live.* Several celebrity guests who will be on hand are Woody and Jim from FLY-92 Wake-Up Service; Cap Capello, popular musical entertainer from the Tri-Cities area; and Don Diehl of Ideal Enterprizes Entertainment Management Company, an associate member of the National Academy of Recording Arts and Sciences (The Grammy awards and Song Writers Guild of America).

Rob Camacho of *Mainstreet Highlites* and Lou Stellato, formerly of FLY-92 will be the hosts throughout the day.

Telethon organizer, Lorraine DiMezza of Lordi Productions has scheduled many entertainment acts, which include Louie Velez presenting his famous Sammy Davis Jr. tribute and Stacie Herschel from Catskill. Dancers include Eleanor's School of Dance, the Love Shack Dancers, Guys and Dolls, Marge Tynan's School of Dance, Melissa Sgambelluri and Jennifer Schotts.

Singers include Pat Walsh, Amy Walbroehl, Rachelle Cotugno, Valerie Beekman, Janet Pagano, Wendy Adamkowski and Orin Griffin and singer-songwriter Bob Hazelton.

Also appearing will be Old 55 Band, Metro Stars and H.L.R. Praise Ensemble and an demonstration in self defense from the Amsterdam Judo and Health Club.

Recovering cancer patient Jeff Rocas will also be on hand for a discussion. There will be a presentation by the Breast Cancer Detection Awareness Task Force.

Local VIPs will be available throughout the day to take phone calls.

Executive director Shannon Knapik invites the public to join all the celebrities and volunteers at the Amsterdam High School to help raise money for cancer. All pledges may be sent to the Montgomery County Unit of the American Cancer Society at 67 Division St., Amsterdam, N.Y. 12010.

Recorder photo: Tom Nevich

Golfing for a cause

The 1992 American Cancer Society Golf Classic will be held in memory of Dr. Sok Ko on June 4 at Antlers Country Club. Organizers of the event include, left to right, committee members Dr. Thomas Milko, Dr. Vincent Filanova, Carmen Paone and honorary chairpersons Paul Parillo and Elaine Ko. Missing from the photo are committee members Margot Freedman, Douglas Landon, Melinda McGuiness and Steven Singer. The committee has a goal of raising $10,000 this year. Cost for the mixed scramble tournament is $80 per player, which includes carts, greens fees and dinner. A total of 144 golfers will tee off at 12:30 p.m. in three divisions, with the winning team advancing to the state American Cancer Society tournament at the Nevele Country Club in the Catskill Mountains. To sign up call the Amsterdam Cancer Society office at 842-5580.

APPENDIX C

THE FOUNDATION

The Sok Nam Ko Educational Exchange Foundation

The Ko Foundation was formed soon after the death of Dr. Sok Nam Ko, reflecting his interest in the Rotary Exchange Program and the People to People Exchange Program, both of which he was very involved with.

His family has hosted students and individuals from both organizations for more than twenty years.

Dr. Ko was a former educator and before that an immigrant. He knew the value to young people of better understanding the world they live in. However, many students can not afford this opportunity and hence the foundation was formed to help committed students attain their goals to study and learn about another culture. This help may be given to current or outgoing high school students.

The founding board consists of five members: Douglas Landon, Thomas Dwyer, Laurel Ilagan, Timothy Ko, and Elaine Ko.

The income from Dr. Ko's book, *The Way Back Home*, will be donated to the Sok Nam Ko Educational Exchange Foundation.

– Helen Eldred Smith

Ko student foundation started

AMSTERDAM – A foundation has been established in honor of the late Dr. Sok Nam Ko to help students participate in the Rotary Exchange Program.

Mrs. Elaine Ko explained the Dr. Sok Nam Ko Exchange Student Foundation will help offset the cost for students who study abroad and offer financial help for foreign students who come to this country to study.

The foundation received about $3,000 at a fund-raiser Friday night at the Raindancer restaurant.

Mrs. Ko said her family decided to start the foundation because of her husband's interest and involvement in the student exchange programs. She noted the Ko family has hosted 12 exchange students over the years.

The Ko family is now hosting Herwig Pape of Germany, who is attending Amsterdam High School; and Tanya Larina, a teacher from the Soviet Union who is teaching Russian in Amsterdam schools and at Fulton-Montgomery Community College.

Area residents interested in donating to the Ko Foundation should contact Attorney Douglas Landon on East Main Street.

The Schenectady Gazette *April 15, 1991*

Remembering Sok Nam Ko:
A book and an educational foundation

Elaine (Hogaboom) Ko '60 calls her late husband, Sok Nam Ko '58, "a pioneer" at Castleton. It is likely he was the first foreigner, certainly the first Korean or Asian, to attend Castleton. In his graduating class of 38 students, only one — from New York City — listed a home address that was not in Vermont. By then "Ko," as he was called by classmates, was a Vermonter himself. When asked by a reporter if he would like to go home to Korea, he said, "This is my home. I have no other."

At the time of his death in 1991, Dr. Ko was working on an autobiography with the help of Elaine's aunt, Helen Smith, a retired professor at SUNY College at Cortland. That book is now being expanded to include the recollections of family, associates, and friends.

Dr. Ko's family and friends also established the Sok Nam Ko Educational Exchange Foundation in his memory. The foundation helps high school students from the Greater Amsterdam, New York, area to spend time in other countries and brings students from abroad to Amsterdam.

Ko was born in Korodong, Kaesong, a city that is now in North Korea. He saw his family for the last time as the Communists swept south and he went with the retreating Americans as an interpreter. He was befriended by Captain George Harrington, a lawyer from Castleton, who brought Ko here as a student, first at Fair Haven High School, then at Castleton.

From the beginning he showed great ability in science and mathematics. At Castleton he ran cross country, played basketball and baseball, and was active in many clubs. But his residency status was unclear. On a basketball team trip to Canada, he was nearly deported. Special legislation, ushered through Congress by U.S. Senator Winston Prouty of Vermont, allowed Ko to remain in the U.S.

After graduation he taught junior high school and earned a degree in zoology at UVM. Later at Temple University School of Dentistry, he was named outstanding clinician of 1967-68. He also attended Tufts University School of Dental Medicine. He practiced oral surgery in Amsterdam for 19 years.

The Ko family hosted more than a dozen exchange students, including the first Soviet Rotary exchange student to the U.S. He was also a participant in the People to People Friendship Caravan on a visit to Russia.

"Dr. Ko believed strongly in the value of cultural exchange on a person-to-person level," Elaine said. "During his life, he was committed to supporting young people in this endeavor."

SOK NAM KO
EDUCATIONAL FOUNDATION

SCHOLARSHIP LUNCHEON

Friday, October 23, 1992
Raindancer Steak Parlour

STATEMENT OF PURPOSE

The Sok Nam Ko Educational Exchange Foundation was established March 16, 1991, and is dedicated to the memory of Dr. Sok Nam Ko.

Its purpose is to carry on the efforts of Dr. Ko with respect to broadening educational and cultural experiences of high school age students.

The Foundation will provide funding to enable and assist students who want to widen their horizons and perspectives by spending time in countries other than their own, but who are financially unable to cover the entire costs of their visits.

Through the Foundation, students from the Greater Amsterdam, New York area will be afforded the opportunity to learn first-hand the cultures, lifestyles and languages of societies in other nations. Likewise, interested students from abroad will be brought to the Amsterdam area to study and observe the way of life here.

Dr. Ko had a deep interest in, and commitment to, educational exchange. The Foundation honors that commitment and will attempt to continue his objective. A nonprofit entity, the Foundation is administered by five directors, Elaine H. Ko, Timothy A. Ko, Douglas E. Landon, Laurel M. Ilagan, and Thomas J. Dwyer.

PROGRAM

WELCOME, Tom Dwyer

Introductions

LUNCHEON

EXCHANGE STUDENT PANEL

Peter Iversen, *from Denmark to US*

Suzanne Ko, *from US to Denmark*

Lynn Marie Luffman, *from US to Argentina*

Amy Quandt, *from US to Germany*

Steffan Vollstadt, *from Germany to US*

Program—Scholarship Luncheon

Fred Quist introducing Elaine Ko, Timothy and Suzanne Ko.

Friends of Ko Educational Foundation Luncheon Oct. 23, 1992.

April 14, 1991

Fund-raiser helps Dr. Ko Foundation

By JOSEPH L. AMADIO
Recorder News Staff

A foundation recently established in the memory of an Amsterdam oral surgeon will allow students to participate in the Rotary Exchange Program.

The Dr. Sok Nam Ko Exchange Student Foundation, established by Dr. Ko's family, will help defray the cost for local students who want to study abroad. It will also provide financial aid to foreign students who want to come to the United States, according to Dr. Ko's wife, Elaine Ko.

Dr. Ko operated a private oral surgery practice for 19 years in Amsterdam. He died March 16.

About $3,000 was raised Friday night at a fund-raiser held at the Raindancer Restaurant on Route 30, Mrs. Ko said. The Ko family decided to establish the foundation because of her husband's long-term involvement with the Rotary Exchange and People to People programs. The Ko family has hosted 12 exchange students over the years, Ko said.

"The reason for establishing the foundation was because a great deal of his work was with students," Ko said. "He was a former schoolteacher and he coached basketball and baseball — Dr. Ko always put everything back into the community."

Anyone wishing to donate to the foundation should contact Amsterdam attorney Douglas Landon, Ko said.

Dr. Ko also helped bring the first Soviet Rotary exchange student to the U.S., she said. That student, 17-year-old Edourd Shpikalov, is currently attending Amsterdam High School.

The Ko family is also playing host to 17-year-old Herwig Pape of Germany, who is attending AHS, and Tanya Larina, a Soviet teacher, who is teaching Russian to students in the Greater Amsterdam School District and at Fulton-Montgomery Community College.